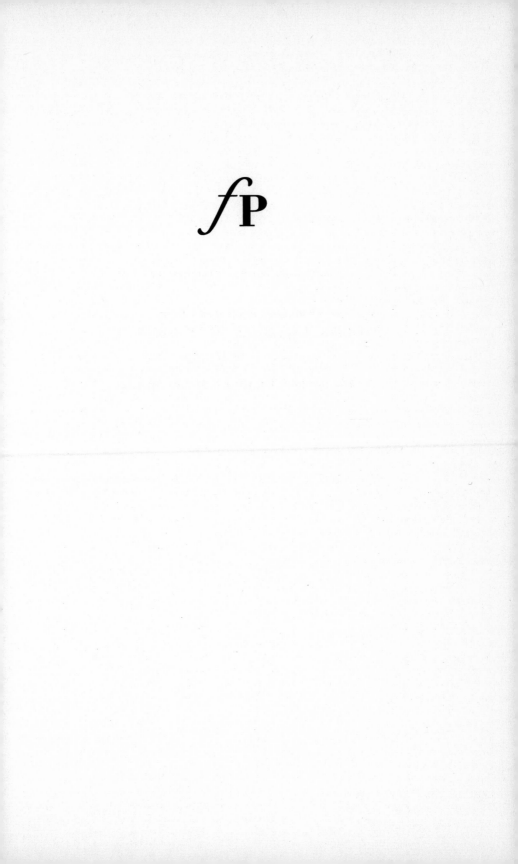

Also by Mark Oppenheimer

Knocking on Heaven's Door:
American Religion in the Age of Counterculture

Thirteen and a Day:
The Bar and Bat Mitzvah Across America

WISENHEIMER

A Childhood Subject to Debate

Mark Oppenheimer

FREE PRESS
New York   London   Toronto   Sydney

FREE PRESS
A Division of Simon & Schuster, Inc.
1230 Avenue of the Americas
New York, NY 10020

First Free Press hardcover edition April 2010

FREE PRESS and colophon are trademarks of Simon & Schuster, Inc.

For information about special discounts for bulk purchases,
please contact Simon & Schuster Special Sales at 1-866-506-1949
or business@simonandschuster.com.

The Simon & Schuster Speakers Bureau can bring authors to your live event.
For more information or to book an event contact the Simon & Schuster Speakers Bureau
at 1-866-248-3049 or visit our website at www.simonspeakers.com.

Certain names and identifying characteristics have been changed.

Excerpt from the *Springfield Republican* © The Republican Company.
All rights reserved. Reprinted with permission.

Manufactured in the United States of America

1 3 5 7 9 10 8 6 4 2

Library of Congress Cataloging-in-Publication Data
Oppenheimer, Mark.
Wisenheimer: a childhood subject to debate / Mark Oppenheimer.—
1st Free Press hardcover ed.
      p. cm.
1. Oppenheimer, Mark, 1974—Childhood and youth.   2. Oppenheimer, Mark,
1974—Language.   3. Oppenheimer, Mark, 1974—Knowledge and learning.
4. Debates and debating.   5. Springfield (Mass.)—Biography.   I. Title.
CT275.O565A3   2010
      974.4'26—dc22   2009041160
                 [B]

ISBN 978-1-4391-2864-0
ISBN 978-1-4391-4698-9 (ebook)

For Curt Robison

WISENHEIMER (wis·en·heim·er): *n.* a wiseacre or smart aleck. Also, **weisenheimer.** [WISE¹ + *-enheimer* (abstracted from names of German origin, such as *Oppenheimer*)]

—The Random House College Dictionary, Revised Edition

WISENHEIMER

INTRODUCTION

When people hear that I was a high school debater, they usually just nod, trying to be kind; if they are less tactful, they scrunch their faces up into a look that means something like "But debaters are such *losers*." An ex-girlfriend of mine—someone with whom I had traveled the world, someone who had brought me home to meet her parents—told me after we'd been dating for a year that she had almost refused to go out with me because she'd heard that I'd once been a debater. She was not the only one for whom my past was a liability. Here's the cruel irony: the better a debater you are, the bigger a loser you're assumed to be. A third-string member of the debate team, one who goes to just a couple of tournaments a year, might be a normal, likable guy. But a champion debater, a debate team captain, with a wall of gold-spray-painted trophies at home, is most definitely to be avoided.

I can't pretend there isn't something to the stereotype. It's pretty much true that if juvenile delinquents are boys with too much time on their hands, debaters are those with too many words. High school debate and oratory draw heavily from the ranks of the annoying: the walking dictionary, the wordsharp, the talker, the gasser, the jiver, the bloviator, the wisenheimer.

You know this boy (he's usually a boy). You went to high school with him, and even if the two of you never talked—even if you

1

turned the other way when you saw him approaching by the lockers—you still know him, because you saw him on television or in the movies. He's Alex P. Keaton, the necktie-wearing young Republican on the 1980s sitcom *Family Ties*. He's at least three characters played by Matthew Broderick and two played by Jason Bateman and one by Val Kilmer. He's the boy with more brains than brawn. The boy who makes wisecracks from the sidelines of football games he'll never play in.

In the movies, and in real life, this boy turns to debate because it's the one place where he can be rewarded for talking. His teacher may get exasperated by his compulsive hand-raising, his parents may tell him to stop arguing and just accept "Because I said so!" and his friends may roll their eyes when he launches into yet another disquisition on drug legalization, the designated-hitter rule, or Apple versus IBM. But on the debate team, his facility with words and his fund of knowledge are unquestionably good. He may be useless at sports, but by debating he can win glory for his school. He may not have a wide circle of friends, but on the debate circuit he'll meet peers from around the state, the country, even the world.

Sometimes, especially in the movies, debaters are even inspirational. In *The Great Debaters*, Denzel Washington coaches a team of debaters from an all-black college, and they are a credit to their race. In *Thumbsucker*, a 2005 movie based on a novel by Walter Kirn, the protagonist overcomes his thumb-sucking habit (with the help of Ritalin) to become a debate champion. In *Rocket Science*, from 2007, a boy with a debilitating stutter joins the debate team to get a girl; he can't defeat his stutter or win the girl, but his futile attempts are nonetheless a kind of triumph.

But in the popular imagination debaters are more like Denis Cooverman, the profusely sweating protagonist of Larry Doyle's 2007 comedic novel, *I Love You, Beth Cooper*. The night after he gives the valedictorian's speech at the Buffalo Grove High School commencement, Denis discovers that being good at interscholastic oratory doesn't help when trying to score with a girl in a car: "Denis spoke nine languages, three of them real, had countless debate trophies (16), had won the Optimist's Club Oratorical Contest with a speech the judges had called the most pessimistic they had ever heard. Was there no romantic line, no conversation starter, no charming anecdote, no bon mot, no riddle or limerick he could pull out of his ass right now?"

I'll admit it: my younger self was part Denis Cooverman. I was also part Hollywood movie debate hero, part Alex P. Keaton, even part Kirk Cameron in the atrocious 1989 debate movie *Listen to Me*. I was all the stereotypes: girl-shy nerd, policy wonk, glib wiseass, credit to his school.

But I was also something more than that: I was a boy who loved language. For me, debate was not just about winning trophies or getting into college. It was about finding the other boys and girls who cared about words. Becoming a debater was like finding my tribe. Once I had been lost, but now I was found. I was like a gambler seeing the lights of Las Vegas rise up before me in the desert. I was the adolescent *Star Trek* fan, ridiculed at school, finding love at a sci-fi convention. I was a Jew in the land of Israel. A rock climber in Yosemite. A gay boy at musical theater camp.

And debate wasn't just about camaraderie. No movie has ever captured the artistic ecstasy I found at those tournaments. One's speech in a round of debate is, if everything is working just right, an eight-minute aria, with pauses for breath, with high notes and easy notes, with glimpses beyond the footlights to see if the audience is listening and to see if they love you. The aria has its distinct sections: approaching the lectern, pausing, rifling through sheaves of paper lightly jotted upon, greeting the audience—"Worthy opponents, honored colleagues, distinguished guests"—beginning, going off script and making eye contact, seeing that they're with you, listening, listening some more, returning to the script, saying something you didn't even know was funny, hearing them laugh, knowing that now they're yours, pausing, clicking through the arguments, hearing your points land with a satisfying thud, hearing their mur-

murs of assent, casually adjusting the knot of your tie, improvising, seeing eyebrows arched knowingly and affirmingly, returning to the text, decelerating, perorating, offering thanks, stepping down.

All debaters love winning, but I also loved debating itself. I loved the aria of the speech and the ballet of the room, the debaters' rising and sitting, gesturing and gesticulating. People don't believe me when I tell them this, but I never got upset when I lost—only when I stumbled over words or dropped an argument, or when a lame joke I never should have attempted fell flat. Speaking was an art; I'd always felt that way, since before I'd had the words to say so. As a kindergartner, I would ask adults about the differences between *who* and *whom* or *further* and *farther*. I listened closely to syntax, wondering why one boy would call another "a big fat idiot" instead of "a fat big idiot." I could hear my heart beat when an orator paused dramatically, for effect. My parents hated Ronald Reagan, but I loved listening to him speak. He might not put language to the most agreeable ends (or so the adults told me), but he took language seriously, and I noticed. As a nine-year-old watching a black-and-white broadcast of Martin Luther King Jr.'s "I Have a Dream" speech, I started sobbing. In 1984, when I was ten, I rooted for John Kerry to win the open Senate seat from Massachusetts, because he gave better speeches than Ray Shamie, his Republican opponent.

For many years, I carried a kind of secret shame about the love I felt for oratory. Next to my friends' passions, mine seemed so trifling. In high school, college, and graduate school, I had friends who played classical cello, or ran the mile in just over four minutes, or could quote from memory Petrarch's sonnets for Laura. As a hack actor in high school, I would watch from the wings as my more gifted classmates made real art onstage; during our run of *Guys and Dolls* in eleventh grade, I listened every night as Adam Donshik sang "More I Cannot Wish You," and I thought that I would trade anything for a voice like his. Singing was beautiful and glamorous; public speaking was not. It was 1991, the elder George Bush was president, and his speeches were less memorable than Dana Carvey's lampoons of them. Who, I wondered, gave speeches anymore—the real kind, the kind that people applauded without realizing they had jumped to their feet?

Well, I tried to, about every other Sunday when school was in session. Competitive speaking was the most vital thing in my life, in that era before wife, children, dog, mortgage. I never debate now, and I hardly ever give speeches. When I do it's to talk about some book I've written; my spoken words are entirely in service to my written words, and there are no trophies anywhere (I donated them all to my high school, where they sit in a cardboard box in Mr. Robison's office, waiting for the trophy case that the school promised the team years ago). There are no extant videotapes of what I did, no YouTube clips, nothing that could ever show up on Hulu. But there are memories, lots of them, of speeches given on wintry days in cold classrooms in brick buildings in small New England towns. And of traveling the world, meeting teenagers from other lands, getting drunk, almost getting laid.

In debate I also made friends I haven't seen since but whom I truly miss. I would love to ask them why they started debating. For some it may have been a chance to get away from their boarding schools on weekends; others, I'm sure, were interested mainly in their college applications. But many of them were like me: Words were my thing. Talking was what I did. I had no choice. Debate was my first experience of the power of art, and it turned what otherwise would have been a bearable, often lonely, largely forgettable adolescence into a thrilling time.

I

When I was a small child, Walter and Rebekah Kirschner, my mother's parents, were my favorite people in the world. They were kind and generous and interested in what their young grandson thought about things. Visiting them in Philadelphia at their big house on Carpenter Lane—my grandfather was a retired carpenter, and he lived on Carpenter Lane, a bit of serendipity that I found marvelous—I would go to bed late, usually after my grandfather and I had watched an 11 P.M. rerun of *Benny Hill* on the snowy UHF channel, and rise early. Coming downstairs in the morning, I would find my grandmother in her housecoat, leaning forward in her seat at the kitchen table, her big, thyroidal eyes scanning the morning newspaper from behind large plastic frames. Approaching from behind, I would hug her around the neck; without looking up from her crossword puzzle or word jumble, she would say, "Good morning, lover." (That old-fashioned, noncarnal sense of the word has all but been lost, but my grandmother refused to abandon it.) The kitchen smelled of coffee, soft-boiled egg, and toast; my grandfather was somewhere on the grounds doing his gardening or, if we were in the fallow months, working with wood in his garage or basement.

More than the smells—of the seedlings my grandfather was planting, of sawdust, of coffee in the kitchen, of yesterday's perfume still lingering about my grandmother's neck—I remember the sounds of Carpenter Lane. Classical music was always on the hi-fi, as my grandfather called it. The dial was set to public radio, which in those days mostly played music (my grandparents were part of that small, now forgotten column of people who mourned as news and talk shows slowly pushed aside their music on NPR). When he heard a piece that displeased him, something too modern or atonal, my grandfather would switch off the radio and put on a vinyl record of Eugene Ormandy conducting the Philadelphia Orchestra. For decades my grandparents went faithfully to the Academy of Music to hear those concerts, even after Ormandy gave way to Riccardo Muti as conductor. Toward the end of his life, my grandfather began to acquire compact discs, but he never played them, and it's the warm sound of vinyl, with its intermittent pops and scratches, that I remember.

The sounds of their home, the aural landscape, comprised not just music but words, carefully chosen. My grandparents spoke a kind of English that one hears less and less today. They rarely raised their voices, they spoke slowly, they spoke with care. My grandfather had been raised speaking Yiddish, and my grandmother had grown up with a mix of German and accented English, but when they spoke English it was with the General American accent, the Ohio or Nebraska sound that television newscasters are trained to use. A practiced ear could hear a slight trace of Philadelphia in the way my grandfather said "merry"—it sounded like the name "Murray"—but in general he spoke like a college graduate from Anywhere.

My grandfather was one of eight children, my grandmother one of ten, and all their siblings had good grammar and literate vocabularies, but my grandparents had higher standards than that. My grandparents were old socialists to the core, believers in rule by the masses, but that did not mean they believed in speaking like the masses. One might say that they were Leninists, insofar as they believed that there had to be an educated vanguard to lead the people to revolution. Perhaps. But it would be more accurate to say that in addition to being socialists, they were snobs.

It's not an unusual combination, or even an unexpected one, leftism and snobbery. When my grandfather graduated from high school in 1929, he found that many of the people he met who shared his interest in books and the arts, especially among fellow Jews, were members of the Communist Party. Communists read, and they talked about ideas, and they had theories about the place of art in the world. They read Dreiser and Dos Passos and Steinbeck, then argued about which ones had good politics and which ones' politics were damnable. To these Communists, culture mattered. For my grandparents, then, being a Communist was a way of being learned, and it was also a way of being unusual, being more than just another working-class Jew.

But there was also an ethical dimension to my grandparents' snobbery. When so many people don't have the schools they deserve, when there is so much illiteracy in the world, what kind of ungrateful person would refuse the lessons of a good education? If you're fortunate enough to have good teachers, or to have been exposed to books, it's incumbent upon you, they believed, to use what you've been given. And only the worst kind of ingrate would put on uneducated airs, as a pose—that was like spitting on your schoolteachers' hard work. If my grandfather had ever met a folk-singing wannabe who affected a hobo's background, a troubadour of the ersatz–Woody Guthrie school, he would have been bemused.

That's not to say that my grandparents spoke the Queen's English. In one of those perverse twists of snobbery, they also looked down on people whose affectations ran in the other direction, too fancy. My grandmother always said that she didn't like the way that her friend Adele Margolis said "foyer." "It's not *foy-ay*," my grandmother would insist aloud, after a visit with Adele. "We're not in France."

My grandmother, in particular, had an explicit belief in language as the backbone of a civil society. She wrote letters. She called people on the telephone to ask how they were doing. She made social calls on her neighbors. She believed in social intercourse, and for that one needed language, preferably well spoken and adhering to certain agreed-upon rules. One morning I came downstairs to find her at the kitchen table in her housecoat, not working on a crossword puzzle or a word jumble but writing a letter.

"Who are you writing to, Grandma?" I asked.

"*Whom*," she said, a little disappointed that by age ten I had not yet mastered the object pronoun. Her tone was kind, however, and I knew not to take it personally. She only corrected her children and grandchildren, the people she felt closest to. "I am writing to Vincent Fumo, my state senator. It's about our license plate."

"What's wrong with your license plate?" I asked. "Did it fall off?"

"Not my license plate. Everyone's. The motto on it reads YOU'VE GOT A FRIEND IN PENNSYLVANIA. But that's not correct. It should be YOU HAVE A FRIEND IN PENNSYLVANIA. The *got* is unnecessary. I'm writing to him to say that they should change it."

That was morning activity in my grandparents' house. Whenever I wonder where I get my love for language, my close attention to it, my deep investment in it, I think about my grandmother bent over a piece of stationery, demanding that her state senator change the Pennsylvania license plate. I wasn't the first wisenheimer in my family.

I'm not even the second.

My mother also has very particular views about language. Like her mother, she would never say *foy-ay*. In fact, whenever anyone on television does say *foy-ay*, she says, "My mother always hated it when Adele Margolis talked like that." I've never met Adele Margolis, but I can never hear any French pronunciation come from the lips of an American—*foy-ay*, *oh-mahzh* (homage), *ahn-deeve* (endive)—without thinking about my grandmother's occasionally snooty frenemy. My mother also has a particular objection to non-Jews using Yiddish words, to the point that she once got annoyed with a Gentile friend who printed an invitation to her "40th-birthday shindig," until I pointed out to my mother that *shindig* was not a Yiddish word. "Well it sounds like one!" she said. (Of course, my mother is right to take exception to the locution of another friend of hers, a WASP from

Greenwich, Connecticut, who talks about her husband's "chutz-
pah," with the accent on the second syllable.) My mother is sensitive
about the pronunciation of her name, Joanne, which she pronounces
with a somewhat broad *a*—not quite Jo-*ahn*, but getting there—and
won't allow to be pronounced with the accent on the first syllable or
with any nasal action on the second. And she can't abide the word
girlfriend when used with a nonromantic connotation. If my younger
sister wanted to give my mother a coronary, she might try saying,
"Me and a couple girlfriends are going to get a manicure." I once
asked my mother where she got that prejudice against *girlfriend*, and
she said that her mother had frowned upon the word. "I used it once,
and she said to me, 'We don't talk like that.'"

Who did talk like that? The residents of South Philadelphia,
for one thing. My grandparents didn't approve of *American Band-
stand*, which adolescent girls all over Philadelphia watched on TV
every afternoon, broadcast live from a studio on Market Street. "If
my father saw me watching it, he would say, 'Now why don't you
turn that off,'" my mother once told me. "The primary thing was, it
was TV. But he also didn't approve of those girls, with their teased
hair and their pencil skirts. And he thought they must cut class at
the end of the day to get to the studio on time. Why weren't they
home studying? That's what afternoons were for, or for French club
or Spanish club. My mother didn't approve of the way they talked.
When they did the roll call, the girls would get up and say, 'Annette,
South Philly.' My mother would say, 'We don't talk like that. It's
South *Philadelphia*.'"

In my earliest years, then, the importance of language was all
around me. It was there implicitly, in the careful way my elders
spoke, and it was there explicitly, in their pronouncements and har-
rumphs of disapproval. Yes, this was snobbery. My parents did try to
keep the snobbery within the family. We were taught from a young
age not to correct other people's speech, so that we wouldn't be per-
ceived by friends or neighbors as elitists. And doesn't every family
have its snobbery? The happiest, most close-knit families are close-

knit because they have a culture of the family, a sense of the particular traits they share. Some families are musical, others are good at tennis, or especially pious, or perhaps just unusually numerous (I could write a whole other book about being the eldest of four children). For our part, we talked a certain way.

When I think about my grandmother, who died when I was fifteen, or about my grandfather, who died recently at age ninety-five, I think about their language. I can hear my grandfather talking about his friend Joe Ehrenreich, always carefully pronounced "Ehren-reich*hh*," with the German fricative against the back of the throat. I can hear his overly correct pronunciation of the great Philadelphia river, the Schuylkill, which most Philadelphians call the Skookil—no first *l*, the whole word pronounced quickly—but which he languorously, luxuriously called the School-kill: "I love to see the houseboats lit up at night on the banks of the School-kill," he said. I miss hearing him talk that way. Nobody else makes the river sound so beautiful. Except, now that I think of it, my mother.

II

If you asked my two brothers and my sister about language in our family, I don't think that they would have the strong sense I have that people talked differently at 90 Bronson Terrace, Springfield, Massachusetts. I probably have the greatest attachment to language as a total vocation, comprising writing and speaking. My brother Daniel, two years younger than I am, speaks more haltingly, and as a young child he was shy in the way of many boys with talkative older brothers. Still, he is now a professional writer. And my brother Jonathan, six years younger than Daniel, is a very gifted rapper; he would probably be famous if Eminem hadn't taken our culture's designated spot for Famous White Rapper. (We could have tried carving out a spot for him as Famous Jewish Rapper, but all three Beastie Boys got there first.) Jonathan, by the way, was a French major in college, and our sister Rachel, who was born when I was fourteen, nearly majored in Italian.

What my siblings might say is that we Oppenheimers do language because we can't do anything else. That was certainly true of me. I wasn't musical, wasn't mathematical, couldn't draw. I didn't have an extraordinary IQ. But more than any of my siblings, even more than my parents and grandparents, I was articulate.

My mother's family heritage found its ultimate expression in me:

I had the nature to go with the nurture. I knew very big words and knew how to use them. More than that, I had mastered the entire conversational affect of a much older person. By the time I was six years old, I deployed adult clichés—*dive right in, hit the road, take one for the team*—with no self-consciousness. When talking with me, people would forget my age. I remember Mr. Nowak, my fifth-grade social studies teacher, telling me what he'd done over the weekend (I was the kind of child who asked his teachers if they'd had a good weekend): "It was great," he told me. "Tommy and I played golf yesterday." It took me a moment to realize that "Tommy" was Mr. Rice, my English teacher.

Compared with the other students in the gifted classes, I was nothing remarkable. Yet the average adult, if introduced to two smart nine-year-olds, a girl who can do geometry and a boy who uses words like *dissembled* and *eviscerated*, finds the boy more astonishing. At that age, speaking well is a better party trick. But my gift, verbiage, presented a unique problem: you can have the words, but without the wisdom they don't count for much. There are nine-year-olds who can do postcollegiate mathematics, and nine-year-olds whose music virtuosity does not betray their age, but there has never been the nine-year-old who wrote accomplished adult poetry or a moving novel. If your gift is for words, you can write stuff that's good *given your age*, but not stuff that's good, period.

I felt this constraint, keenly. I even think that, if asked, I could have described what I was feeling: that someday I could be a fine wordsmith, but for the time being I just had all these words and no place to take them. So I did what millions of boys before me—and girls, too, but not as frequently as boys—had done. I began to think of myself, around fourth grade, as a master of words. I became a wiseass.

Or maybe I was a *smart aleck*, or even a *wisenheimer*. I like those terms better, not just because they are less crude but because they suggest a real person—some prepubescent named Aleck who always corrected his teachers' grammar in junior high and always had the best cracks about other kids' moms. (Can't you picture this little

Aleck Wisenheimer? In my mind he's Jewish, probably has glasses, and after insulting you runs out of the room before you can throw a punch. He's like Eddie Haskell but without the gift for amusing his friends' mothers.) Note the linguistic tropism, too, how the good connotations of *smart* and *wise* are subverted: a smart aleck is a smart guy gone bad, a boy whose smartness is being used stupidly, while a wisenheimer actually lacks wisdom. He might not be cruel, he might not mean any harm, but a wisenheimer is a smart guy you wish had a little less smarts.

From the time I learned my first words, my parents were worried. For one thing, I never stopped talking. Some children never stop moving, other children never go to sleep, but I never stopped talking. All young children go through their inquisitive stages—"Why is the water blue, Mommy?" . . . "But *why* does it reflect the sky?"— but mine was extreme. What my parents remember about me as a two-year-old accords perfectly with my own faint memories of that age: the unquenchable desire to say more, to be understood better, and, above all, to have conversations with adults. I found children my age maddeningly slow. I'd ask them a question, and they didn't know what I meant, or they would take forever to answer. Grown-ups, by contrast, talked smoothly, without hesitation, and their conversations went on and on.

I'd try to engage my mother in adult conversation, and she tried to be patient. But my brother was born when I was just twenty-one months old, and when I was two my father got a new job. He was home more than most fathers; we had left New York City for Spring-field in 1976 so he could teach at a small law school that had just opened, and being a law professor is a good, family-friendly occu-pation. But some days my mother would pick up the phone at two, after Daniel had gone down for a nap and she was hoping for a brief rest. "Tim, you have to come home," she would say. "He won't stop talking . . . Mark, that's who—he just won't stop talking . . . *Please*, I need a break."

I wasn't being rude, or raising my voice, or using bad words—I wasn't doing any of the things I'd been told not to do with my words. I had just been talking, that's all. But my mother was almost crying.

It wasn't just how much I talked, but what I said. All children ask inappropriate questions, but mine came more often and at a younger age. I remember one morning when I was three years old. Sue Garvey, a round-faced woman, was watching over me and some other children at Mudpie, the child-care cooperative through which my parents had met most of their new Springfield friends.

"Sue, I have a question," I said.

"Yes, Mark, what is it?"

I was sitting on the floor and Sue was in a chair. I remember looking up from her feet to her face; she was hunching forward, to be closer to me.

"Why are you so fat?"

She uncurled her body and sat upright. All of a sudden, her face was far away from mine.

"It's because I have a health problem called lupus," she said. "I take drugs that make me gain weight."

"Oh."

"But Mark?"

"Yes?"

"It doesn't make people feel good when you ask about their weight."

"It doesn't?"

"No, Mark, it doesn't."

"Oh."

How do you convey to a child that his natural curiosity needs to be tempered? Or, more difficult, how do you tell him that not everyone will think that his use of language—which is so impressive to Mommy and Daddy and Grandpop and Grandmom—is such a good thing? One day I was an infant being praised for saying my first words, and barely a few months later my parents were trying to figure out how to dial me back. I asked our next-door neighbor in Springfield if she dyed her hair. I wandered around a women's clothing boutique in Pittsburgh, one owned by a childhood friend of my father's, approaching customers and guessing their ages. I wasn't good for business.

It was especially hard for my parents to convince me there were boundaries to how I could talk, because they surrounded themselves with people who thought that talking and arguing were really good things. Their friends in Springfield were the other parents who sent their children to Mudpie, which was housed in the auditorium of an Episcopal church on Oakland Street. Mudpie had been founded, shortly before my parents' arrival in Springfield, to provide a nonracist, nonsexist, egalitarian environment in which like-minded people could supervise each other's children. These were political people, the Mudpie parents. They included a Spanish-American couple whose anticlerical families had left Spain after the rise of Franco; an Amherst College graduate who had become a mailman in the 1970s because he and the other members of his secretive, radical underground movement decided to enter working-class professions and organize the workers from within; Julius and Ethel Rosenberg's younger son, Robert, and his wife; and several of my father's most politically left-wing colleagues at Western New England College School of Law.

Mudpie was the site of my earliest vivid memories. At Mudpie, I once accidentally locked myself in the bathroom and had to wait for firemen to come and break in the door; they told me to stand at the far back of the small room as they chopped at the hinges. During one lunch at Mudpie, I saw a sick boy, I forget who, spew vomit so liquefied that it spread slowly down the long, plastic folding lunch table. I'll always remember my dread as the vomit kept spreading, every second coming closer; in the nick of time I gathered my lunch into my arms and pulled my chair back from the table. It was at Mudpie that I met Adam and Derek, my oldest friends.

Aside from specific moments and scenes, the most enduring residue of my two Mudpie years was a very keen sense that language was powerful, and a little dangerous. The parents who staffed the place were all politically correct before the term became popular. So attention to language was in Mudpie's genetic code; it was in that big auditorium that I heard these other adults, people who weren't my parents, correct my language: "It's not *mailman*, Mark," I was told. "Say *letter carrier*—it's not sexist." "It's not *fireman* . . ." "When you talk about going to the doctor, you don't have to say *he*—the doctor might be a woman . . ." Yes, they could be extreme in their sensitivities, but there remains something quite admirable in their sense of the possibility of language. These were men and women whose lives had been changed by the right book at the right time: *The Communist Manifesto*, *The Feminine Mystique*, *The Autobiography of Malcolm X*, *Death at an Early Age*. Language could change the world. It mattered.

These were also parents who took children seriously; their political ideology encouraged them to level hierarchies, and, in principle anyway, the distinction between parent and child was cast as an artifact of bourgeois society. This belief could lead to some unfortunate silliness—I was unnerved by a peer of mine who called her father by his first name; its lack of intimacy seemed sad. But, I learned as I got older, it also meant that children were included in their parents' conversations. The spring that I was nine, I went with my parents to a Memorial Day cookout at the house of an old Mudpie family. In the back yard, Bruce Miller, a law professor whose daughters had arrived at Mudpie after I'd graduated, explained to me a Supreme Court case I had heard about on the radio: "It's strict scrutiny, not heightened scrutiny," he said, then proceeded to tell me about the difference, in language a fourth-grader could understand.

My parents had another friend, Hank, who was far less amiable in conversation. Hank was a steel-plated leftist, a total creature of the Movement: whatever humanity he had distinct from his political beliefs was stored safely in an interior lockbox. He seemed to think that smiling or appearing to have a good time was evidence of bourgeois sympathies. In most social circles, this monomaniacal and decidedly dour purity would be repellent—he wouldn't be much fun on the golf course or around the poker table—but to people who shared his politics Hank actually held a certain charm. They were impressed by his commitment. He had the courage to refuse joy—what could be more hard-core than that?

About once a year, starting when I was about nine and ending when I was old enough to stay home and skip gatherings of my parents' friends, I'd end up in an argument with Hank. The subject was usually something I'd read about in my father's copies of the *Nation*, like affirmative action or the closed union shop. The argument would be at a cookout, or a Thanksgiving dinner, and it would get pretty heated before one of my parents intervened.

"Hank, what are you working on these days?" I asked him at one gathering. I'm sure I was imitating my dad, whose easy conversational style—"these days," "what've you been up to?" "how'd that work out?" etc.—always made everyone feel they had news to share.

"I'm doing a lot of work around the election," Hank said, sitting on a picnic table bench with his back to the table. It was 1984, and all of my parents' friends were committed to Ronald Reagan's defeat.

"You're working for Mondale?" I asked.

Hank just smiled.

"Why do you like Mondale so much?"

Hank uncrossed his legs and took a sip from his can of beer. He was Jewish but had a distinctly nonethnic look, like a character from a Rockwell painting—or, as he'd have it, from a social-realist propaganda poster. He looked like the prole everyman he wanted to be. Just one of the masses. "Well, it's not that I like Mondale so much," he said. "He's fine. Best we can hope for. Reagan is really quite the fascist. He's putting people on the bread lines, breaking unions, throwing blacks out of jobs."

That didn't sound right to me. My parents didn't like Reagan at all, and I'd heard them grouse at length about everything that was wrong with him, but I hadn't heard this. "He's throwing blacks out of jobs?" I asked.

Hank took another sip of beer, then smiled benevolently. He was about to explain to me the way things were.

"Well, you end affirmative action, you appoint people to your Justice Department who don't enforce the laws . . . people get the idea. The message goes out. And then the racists who want to fire people, they know that they can. He doesn't have to do to every black man what he did to the air traffic controllers. He doesn't have to send the pink slips himself. He just has to take away government protections, then let nature take its course."

"So by ending affirmative action, he's firing black people?"

"That's the way it works."

"But couldn't you just see ending affirmative action as guaranteeing the rights of white people who want jobs?"

"That's the way the power structure wants you to see it, of course."

"Who's the power structure?"

"The forces acting upon you. The superstructure. They want you to see things that way. They make sure that you do."

This was a new concept, being told that my ideas were given to me by the power structure, and I did not like it. My ideas were mine—I had come to them through my own thinking! I had read op-ed columns in the *Springfield Daily News*, and, when I went by a *USA Today* newspaper box, if I had thirty-five cents in my pocket I would buy a copy and always read the editorials. On Sunday nights I watched *60 Minutes* with my parents. I was not your average ten-year-old, and I wanted Hank to know that.

"So who is the superstructure?" I asked, cocking an eyebrow to show my skepticism. "I don't see them. Nobody's telling me what to think. I read the newspapers."

Hank looked away and into the distance. I could tell that he was annoyed; he had tried to explain things patiently, and I didn't seem to be getting it.

"It's the forces of capitalism," he said. "Our news media are owned by people with *interests*. They don't want people to unionize. They don't want you to ask tough questions. The newspapers aren't going to report about every demonstration or outbreak of dissent. That's part of the superstructure."

"You mean they're censoring our news?"

"Of course. There's a lot of dissent you don't hear about. Demonstrations, wildcat strikes, sit-ins."

I thought about this, and it occurred to me that there was a flaw in his argument.

"But if the newspapers don't report about dissent," I asked, "how do *you* know about it?"

Now Hank cocked an eyebrow at me, then drained the rest of his beer. He was getting *really* annoyed.

"I have other ways," he said, in a voice so quiet it seemed he was trying extra hard to stay calm.

"You have *other ways*? Like, special ways? That aren't available to the rest of us?"

"Yes."

"What are they?"

"Networks. Coalitions. People who keep me in touch."

"Do you think if the newspapers knew about your networks and coalitions, they might write about them?"

"No."

"But wouldn't it be news?"

"Yes. But not their kind of news."

"What's their kind of news?"

"Crimes. They like writing about police busting black people. Not about unionized people."

"But police have unions, don't they?"

At this point, Hank stood straight up and his eyes got very wide. I'd never seen him make a sudden movement before; he was usually so slow and deliberate. I got a little scared.

"Look, *Mark*," he said, opening and closing his fists, as if to stretch his fingers, "I'm sure you don't see it now, but there's a lot of the world you'll see when you get out there and work. When you work, you'll see how things work. It makes sense you wouldn't understand it now, but you will. You will, *okay?*" He spoke slowly, but more loudly than was his manner.

I didn't know what to say next, but then I heard, from over my right shoulder, my father's voice.

"Hank, cool it," he said. "He's only ten."

And Hank looked at my father, gave him a thin, tight-lipped smile, turned right with an almost military precision, and walked away.

"Are you okay, babe?" my dad said. *Babe* was his most tender diminutive, used when something tapped his deep fund of compassion.

"Yeah, fine." I was shaking a little, from fear but also from exhilaration. Hank had gotten pretty scary at the end—but I had a lurking suspicion that I had just won an argument.

Years later, I asked my mother about my fights with Hank. I wasn't sure she would remember, but she did.

"Daddy and I never knew when to intervene," she said. "Hank didn't have any sense that you were just a kid. You'd keep arguing with him, and instead of him saying, 'Well, I guess there are a lot of ways of looking at it,' and just letting it go at that, he would keep arguing back at you. Because that's what he did when he was in a political debate with someone his own age. He wasn't used to getting it from a kid. His kids didn't argue with him that way. None of the other kids did. They just listened and accepted what he had to say. He wasn't used to it. Dad and I were used to it, because we lived with you."

And she remembered, too, the time that my father had asked Hank to lay off. As I heard her recall the incident—just as I remembered it, with the same language about my age: "You were only ten!"—an emotion came back to me, strong as the moment I first felt it: *I was angry at my father for interceding.* I was sure that I could take care of myself (hadn't I just proved it by bringing Hank to grief?), and I was humiliated that my father thought I needed rescuing. His intervention allowed Hank to walk away the victor, as if he had been pulled off me in a bar brawl. After assuring my father I was okay, I had turned on him: "What did you do that for? I didn't need you! We were just talking!" Having repaid my father's kindness with ingratitude, I had stomped off, leaving him alone at the picnic table.

I didn't necessarily like my parents' friends and acquaintances, but they kept me interested. In 1983, my parents and Adam's parents sent us to Timberlake, a boys' Quaker camp that—in homage, I suppose, to the original, seventeenth-century Friends, some of whom were nudists—was clothing-optional. Most of the nudism was just skinny-dipping at the waterfront, but some boys and counselors went naked for other activities. One night, some bunkmates and I sneaked away after lights-out and found the staff down at the meadow, square-dancing with staff from the girls' camp across the lake, all of them nude. My parents came to visit on Parents' Day, and I'll never forget my mother's reaction to what she saw at the waterfront: "Quakers are very white, aren't they?"

When the summer ended, I told my parents that I would not be returning to Timberlake. "They're *crazy*" was my verdict. So the next summer, prevailed upon by another couple from their circle of friends, and bearing in mind their promise that they would consider only camps with traditional attitudes toward clothing, they sent me to Camp Kinderland, an old Jewish-socialist camp in the Berkshires where the bunks were named after dead leftist heroes—I lived in Eugene Debs, which was right next to Joe Hill and not far from Woody Guthrie.

At Kinderland, my peers and counselors were still crazy, but in a more accessible way: instead of being nudist Quakers, they were garden-variety humorless socialists. Now *these* were people I knew. They were just like my parents' worst friends, except they were my age! Naderites with training wheels. I spent that summer in pleasurably heated arguments with politically minded bunkmates who had never questioned any of the premises on which they'd been raised. I'd ask questions like "But don't you think a fetus *might* feel pain?" and "But what harm could there be in having a missile-defense shield, just in case?"

In truth, I agreed with the Kinderlanders more often than I let on.
I just liked goading them. The Kinderland kids were different from
the Mudpie kids and their parents. They were more clannish and
more smug. Many of them were from families who only left Brooklyn or the Upper West Side of Manhattan for these few weeks in
the summer. I met so many kids from Park Slope that it seemed as
if the whole neighborhood had migrated to Tolland, Massachusetts, for the month of July. Back home, they attended lefty schools,
shopped at lefty food co-ops, and had only lefty friends. People who
questioned their assumptions were deemed weird, deviant, and sinis-
ter. I later learned that the camp had nearly come apart in the 1970s
because of internal divisions between Stalinists and anti-Stalinists. *In
the 1970s.* That didn't surprise me.

By contrast, my parents' friends, most of them anyway, took life
less seriously. There was more whimsy. In fact, now that I am a dad in
my mid-thirties, I wouldn't mind traveling thirty years back in time
to hang out with my parents and their friends. They liked to dance,
for one thing, and not just to guitars and folk songs. The Mudpie
community got together several times a year for the "Friday Night
Live" parties, where Joel Meginsky's band played oldies, with a heavy
dose of soul. (They did a great "Hand Jive.") Some of them were life-
style liberals, too, such as Owen Lynch, who later moved to Oregon
and became a chiropractor. He once rolled a joint while I was sitting on his lap in my parents' kitchen. "What's that?" I asked. "It's a
cigarette," he said, through his magnificently nimbuslike beard. To
which I replied, "It doesn't look like my dad's cigarettes. Or smell
like them." He smiled, and puffed on.

Owen was nothing like my parents, who are very straight people.
I have never known my parents to smoke dope. The freakiest my
father ever got was growing his curly hair to a rather high altitude
in the late '70s. Given their rather mainstream tastes and appear-
ances, it was their commitment to ideas that gave them common
ground with the other Mudpie folks. They were feminist, prolabor
peaceniks. They saw them themselves as oppositional, even if you

wouldn't have known it by looking at them. When I was growing up, my father and I had a running argument about whether he was "radical." He would say something like "Well, when your politics are left or radical, like mine . . ." and I would say, "You're not a radical!"—which always got him upset. He'd explain that he was a radical, that he thought society needed revolutionary change, not just reform.

I knew that my dad enjoyed those little arguments, just as I did. Unlike the Park Slopers at Camp Kinderland, who were made uncomfortable by any sign of dissent (the camp director, a mother in her thirties, ridiculed me for wearing a Ralph Lauren Polo shirt with the horse insignia), my parents' community of adults thought, for the most part, that it was great if their children wanted to argue politics with them. So when I'd concede that my dad was a radical—even though he didn't seem particularly radical, lying on the sofa in his tattered bathrobe, reading the *New York Review of Books* or the latest John le Carré thriller—when I'd say, "Okay, okay, so you're a radical!" and walk away, I suspected that my argumentative ways made him at least a little proud.

III

From the beginning, I had a hard time with teachers, and they had a hard time with me. In kindergarten at Sumner Avenue School, I asked Mrs. Sessions what her first name was; she told me—it was Jean—but she wasn't happy about it. In first grade, I had Mrs. Silvestri, whom I liked better, but in the middle of winter, with the whole class watching, she slipped on a patch of ice; she stood up, and she looked fine, but she had broken her back, and after that day we never saw her again, and a string of indifferent substitutes finished out the year. I spent the remaining months at Sumner Avenue leaving class, with the substitutes' permission, to go upstairs to the library. There I would stretch my ten-minute passes into twenty or thirty minutes, reading books from the shelves and trying not to return until class was almost over.

For second grade, my parents enrolled me in Pioneer Valley Montessori School, a small, well-meaning place on Parker Street, five miles from where we lived. It was the kind of progressive school that would have stocked some of the more adventuresome young adult authors, such as Judy Blume or Robert Cormier, if books had been part of the curriculum. But, like teachers at a lot of supposedly student-centered schools, the teachers at "PVMS" were deeply suspicious of students who just wanted to talk or read. For these teachers, good elementary schooling was about physicality, movement, using one's hands and feet. Reading was for later. At PVMS, the math and science curricula were splendidly thought through, filled with the individualized attention, and the touching and feeling and hands-on learning, that public schools did not offer. But our reading was limited to excerpts from the *Junior Great Books* anthologies, short volumes comprising redacted selections from Beatrix Potter and Aesop and the like. I read through the entire *Junior Great Books I* and *Junior Great Books II* volumes in the first few months of third grade (I don't remember what qualified as language instruction in second grade), and for the last year and a half of my Montessori education I was encouraged to take what I could from the lone bookshelf that constituted the school's library; nobody paid much attention.

It wasn't just that the school's theoretical matrix encouraged this neglect of verbal kids, but also that the teachers had no interest in teaching language arts. They had not become Montessori pedagogues because they enjoyed grammar or penmanship. The features that made the school special—the metal pie segments used to teach fractions, the trips into the woods behind the school to learn the taxonomies of shrubs and trees—were related to math and science instruction. That's what put the "hands" in "hands-on." Sitting in a corner and reading, which would have made the unstructured, open classroom blissful for me, was not exactly the kind of learning-by-doing that got these teachers up in the morning.

The math and science kids thrived; one of them, the redoubtable Eli Brandt, used the school's freedom to start simple algebra when he was eight. He's now a Google software engineer. My gifts, however, seemed to be held against me. The school sold itself as a place where students could be individuals, but my endless quarreling, my hunger to challenge my teachers, wasn't seen as a good urge that needed proper channeling; rather, it was treated as a rebellion against the harmony that the school was supposed to embody. It was one thing for Eli to sprawl on the floor, chewing on his pencil as he did math problems well beyond his years—that was the glory of a Montessori education. But a student who approached the teacher and asked why there weren't desks and a blackboard, as there had been at his old school, and wondered why we called teachers by their first names here, and was curious what *Montessori* meant anyway, was just a troublemaker. At a school so proud of its progressive ways, I struck the teachers as somehow reactionary.

My first year, when I was seven and in second grade, went well enough. It wasn't as boring as first grade in public school had been, and Gail, the head teacher in the grades 1–3 classroom, had a sort of exasperated patience for me. But the next year, when the school added a fourth grade and I was moved into a 3–4 classroom, Lisa, a new teacher presiding over her first classroom, couldn't stand me. She was young and she looked it, with big glasses and a short, dark, boy's haircut. And she was noticeably immature, with some very odd ideas. The first week of school, she asked all ten of us in the third and fourth grades to sit in a circle on the floor, then passed out short, fat white candles. She lit her own candle with a match and said, "These candles represent our unity as a classroom. I'll light Craig's candle, and then Craig will light the candle of the person to his left, and we'll go around until all the candles are lit." Which we did: ten children, ages eight through ten, most of us holding fire for the first time. When all the candles were lit, Lisa said that this would be our class tradition, a way to make our sharing time sacred, and we would do it throughout the year.

That night, I told my parents that the new teacher was some sort of crazy person bringing religion into the school. My father called to complain, and fire/sharing time was never held again.

Lisa never forgave me for ratting her out. We moved immediately into mutual antagonism, and for all of third and fourth grades I had the peculiar experience of being despised by my teacher, who drew on the deep well of loathing that most teachers have only for miscreants. At eight years old, I somehow had her number, even though I didn't want it. Every young child wants his teacher to like him, but for our two years together every comment I made, every question I asked, drove Lisa to distraction, like a high frequency only she could hear.

At first I antagonized her unintentionally, but after a certain point, when it was obvious that Lisa would never like me, I decided—though I could not have articulated this decision at the time—that it was self-esteem suicide to keep trying for her approval. In a class of only ten students spread over two grades, I couldn't slouch down in a desk in the back row (even if we'd had desks, or rows), so my response was to defy Lisa by championing myself. I began to write my name as "Mark the Great" in the upper right corners of my papers. Knowing that she found me uppity, I got even uppitier, redoubling my use of large words and further complicating my syntax. I was trying to remind myself that I was worthy, and I was also fighting back.

The tension between us became a *thing*, like a family feud or a gang rivalry. Everyone just knew that we hated each other. Worse still, my classmates were at an age when they followed the teacher's lead, rather than rebelling against it—so being on the outs with the teacher, which could have made me cool in high school, made an uncool kid even less cool in third and fourth grades. The one friend I had at the beginning of third grade, Hawkeye Thompson, a shaggy-haired blond kid whose parents were liberal lawyers like my dad, dropped me by the end of the year, choosing to hang out instead with Marcus Jackson, who among other virtues got MTV at his house. The other boy I wanted to be friends with, Josh Greenberg, turned on me, too, joining Hawkeye and Marcus in an alliance. In fourth grade, the only person who wanted to be my friend was Katie Risley, a fun, smart, impossibly kind girl who one time invited me over to her house to play board games; I reciprocated once but, feeling weird about having a girl for a friend, found an excuse to turn down her next invitation. (More than ten years later, the week after graduating from college, I came downstairs to breakfast at my parents' house and my mother handed me Katie's obituary in the *Union-News*. She had been killed in a boating accident, her neck snapped. I went to her funeral and afterward told her father that there had been a year of my life when the only person who was nice to me at school was Katie.)

It's hard to know whose cruelty took license from whose. My classmates were encouraged in their meanness by Lisa's example, but I also think that their distaste for me made Lisa feel justified in her own. After all, she figured, if my classmates didn't like me, they must have their reasons. Whatever her reasons, Lisa abandoned moral stewardship of that classroom. When for a math activity we all had to take surveys of our classmates, turn the most popular answers into percentages, and then make pie graphs, Lisa didn't stop one student from taking a survey of "best friends." When two out of ten students responded that Hawkeye was their best friend, he got the biggest pie slice, 20 percent; the whole survey was mounted on a wall, where it was easy to see whom nobody had claimed as a best friend.

Incredibly, that was not the most dysfunctional classroom survey of the year. That honor would go to a survey taken by Lisa, who one day, after I said something she took as rude—something that, admittedly, may have been rude—decided to put me in my place. Her eyes narrowing, she leaned toward me and said in a low voice, "You think you're so great, Mark? You think you're so great? Let's *see* who thinks you're great." And then she stood up from the table where we were seated, looked around at the students scattered across the carpeted room, working on their projects—science experiments, maps being drawn, long unspooled paper for history timelines, piles of beads representing the multiplication of numbers—and called for their attention. "Hey everybody," she said loudly, "could I have your attention? I have a question. Who here thinks Mark Oppenheimer is great? Who here *likes* Mark?"

My classmates looked at her with a kind of wise disbelief, as if, though too young to know exactly why their teacher's behavior was wrong, they felt a certainty beyond their years that it was.

Nobody said anything. Lisa looked at me and arched her eyebrows, as if to say, *"See?"*

* * *

By the end of fourth grade, I was angry. I had no friends in school. My teacher hated me. And my parents were still ambivalent about my verbal ability. They were proud of me—like most parents, they wanted their child to be smart, and in addition to being well spoken I was a very advanced reader. But they were worried that I was using words to be cruel, and that my facility with words somehow made it all too easy to be cruel. At the time, I often quarreled with my brother Daniel, and our fights had begun to follow a predictable pattern: he would do something that annoyed me (ask me to let him watch a different TV show, take the last English muffin, sneeze too much), I would insult him, usually deriding him as unintelligent ("You're such an idiot, Dan . . . You don't know anything . . . What was that? . . . Stop stuttering!"), and then he would lunge at me, yanking my hair out and scratching at my eyes. Our fights were the typical older/younger brother fights, except that we both failed to perform as nature intended: intimidated and shell-shocked by my abuse, Dan's verbal ability in my presence regressed to that of someone even younger than he was, and in the face of his fearless fists I cowered as no self-respecting older brother should. Humiliated, I intensified my efforts to degrade Dan with insults: "You don't even know how to spell your name!" . . . "Mom and Dad love me more."

One time, after I had said something that enraged him, Dan chased after me, trying to pull my hair, and I ran into the upstairs bedroom with the TV in it; I must have been about ten years old, at most, because Jonathan was still quite young. My parents were lying on the double bed, watching some program, and as Dan followed me into the room I expected them to look up and tell us to both cut it out. "Cool it, guys," my dad would usually say. But this time they looked right through us as Dan chased me in circles. "He's trying to kill me!" I screamed. Nothing, no response. I jumped up on the bed with them, and they craned their necks to keep watching TV. Dan jumped up, too, and grabbed a clump of my hair. "Make him stop!" I yelled, pleading. They did nothing. I don't remember how it ended— I probably escaped and ran into the bathroom, then held the door

31

shut until Dan gave up trying to force his way in—but when it was over I had a realization: they had planned this. My parents had evidently decided that I needed to be taught a lesson and that only having to defend myself against Dan's wrath would persuade me to stop belittling him. I don't know if their plan worked as efficiently as they hoped, but soon Dan and I stopped fighting. We then ignored each other for ten years, until he joined me at Yale, a freshman when I was a junior, and we soon became good friends.

So it was hard for my parents to take unalloyed pride in my abilities, because they saw how I used words to batter my brother. What's more, while my parents didn't think much of Lisa, they were spending good money, at a time when my father was in the first, unprofitable years of a private law practice, to keep me in a school where I couldn't make peace with my teacher. When, they surely wondered, would I learn to just tone it down a bit?

That sense of exasperation helps explain one of the few great parenting mistakes they made during my childhood. It happened when I was nine years old, as the end of fourth grade was drawing near. At school I'd been fighting with Lisa constantly, but at home I had been stoic about the situation; maybe because I was ashamed, or because I knew that I wasn't entirely innocent, I rarely gave my parents enough details about the ongoing battle for them to form a fine-grained impression of what I was up against. As far as they were concerned, I just didn't like my teacher—a common enough experience, one that a young boy could be expected to negotiate for a year or two. But after one particularly difficult week, I complained so bitterly about Lisa that my parents made an appointment to talk with Gail, the director, Lisa's boss. The following week, I came home from school one afternoon to find that my parents had met with Gail during my father's lunch hour. I hadn't known they'd been at school that day, but I was heartened to hear that they had. "So, what happened?" I asked hopefully. Had they told Gail that she had to fire Lisa? Had Lisa been at the meeting, lamely defending herself? Was I free?

"It sounds as if there are problems," my dad said. "Gail knew that. It's obviously not *just* you."

"What do you mean?" I knew it wasn't "just me"—it wasn't even mostly me. It was Lisa being her insane, malevolent self.

My father exhaled, doing his expanded-cheek thing and letting the air out slowly. I didn't understand—was he annoyed with *me*?

I was sitting on the radiator in our dining hall. It was still cold, maybe late February or March, and I felt the heat through my threadbare corduroys. For once, I did not know what to say.

My mother finally spoke. "Gail had spoken with Lisa—Lisa wasn't there—and she knew there were problems. It sounds as if you provoke her sometimes, and she may not always handle it as well as she ought to."

I still did not know what to say. My mother's formulation wasn't just off course, it was on a different planet, and I had no idea how to bring her back to Earth.

"I think you'll both be happy when the school year's over," she said.

My parents were standing close to each other, the picture of unity. They agreed in their assessment, both sympathetic but certain that I had to share some of the blame for this pedagogical relationship gone wrong. It was because they were a little bit right—just a little bit, but that was more than enough—that I couldn't fight them on the Lisa question. They wanted to believe that this was a moral wash, that I'd done bad things and she'd done bad things and we should all try to be mature. They had to believe this, because if it was partly a question of my moral failing, then it was less a question of their parenting—and, after all, they had no idea how to parent a precocious child. (Nobody does.) If I'd been twenty years older, I would have suggested that maybe there's no such thing as culpability shared equally by an adult and a nine-year-old; but of course that's one thing a nine-year-old can never say. Especially a nine-year-old like me, who thought that sounding like a grown-up made me a grown-up.

Instead of arguing back that Lisa was the bad one, not me, I just
started crying. I sat cross legged on the radiator and buried my head
in my hands and sobbed. At first, I wasn't sure what was wrong; as
was often the case with me, I didn't know what I was thinking until
I spoke it.

"Don't you understand?" I said, in a pleading voice. "Don't you
understand what it's like to be me?"

My father came over and put his hand on my shoulder, but I shook
it off. I couldn't look at them, so I kept my eyes down and tried to
tell them what I meant.

"Don't you know how different I feel? Marcus and Hawkeye and
Josh aren't my friends anymore, and I don't know why. I think it's
because I'm too smart, but I don't even know. Sometimes I try not to
talk the way I do, and I think it will make things better, like maybe if
I try to sound less smart and use smaller words they'll want to be my
friends, but they don't. *Nothing* I do matters. *Nothing* seems to work."

My parents weren't expecting this, and neither was I. I was hurting in places I hadn't known.

After a long pause, during which I kept my eyes cast downward,
my father stepped close to me again, although this time he didn't try
to touch me. "We do understand," he said. "We do."

"No, you *don't*." This came out angrier than I had intended, but I
meant it. They didn't understand, because if they had—if they'd had
any sense of the depth of my loneliness at school, its all-encompass-
ing, smothering clutch, which held me from the moment the school
bus deposited me in the morning until the second its doors closed
behind me at night—they would have gotten me out of there. "You
don't understand what it's like to be me. You think that I just have
trouble communicating with my teacher, that we get each other's
goat sometimes, or that she can be a difficult person but that I fail to
rise above it and be the bigger person." My mother was always telling
me and Daniel to rise above things, be the bigger person, "kill them
with kindness." "But that's not it. I don't know how to be friends
with people who don't understand what I'm saying. I don't know

34

which words that I use will make people laugh or roll their eyes. I try to be better, to get along with people better, to be their friends, but sometimes it doesn't work, and *you don't understand*."

I finally looked up and wiped away my tears; my parents were huddled together, as if seeking shelter in a storm. I was sure one of them would say something kind now, something to make it all better. My mother started to speak, then stopped before the first word came out, then found her voice and started again.

"What are you *talking* about, sweetie? Your father and I were both good students. We were both always in the top classes at school, and friends with the other top kids. We know what it's like to be smart."

There was a defensive quality in my mother's voice, as if I, by saying that my parents didn't understand what I was going through, had called her stupid. Or maybe she was coping with the challenge of parenting me by telling herself that it wasn't an unusual challenge after all, no more difficult than what her parents or in-laws had faced. Either way, it seemed a matter of her own self-preservation to tell me that I wasn't so special, that I didn't have as much to complain about as I thought. I needed sympathy, and in its place she offered me pity for how deluded I was to think that I had real troubles, and how that delusion was holding me back. What my mother seemed to be saying was that only by renovating my outlook on the world, or my personality, or my spoken vocabulary, could I find happiness at school. But even if I had had a preternatural self-knowledge of what kept me from having more friends or being more beloved by my teacher—and what unpopular child doesn't wish he knew how to be popular?—the changes required would have been a kind of self-annihilation. Maybe I could have used simpler words, pretended to love Matchbox cars, and worn corduroys less and blue jeans more. Maybe there was a recipe, but looking back I'm glad I didn't know what it was.

Now that I am a father, and I can begin to fathom how helpless I'll feel if one of my daughters is ever that unhappy, I know that there was some attempt at compassion in what my parents said and didn't say. They didn't get it right, but at the time they thought that putting it back on me at least allowed for hope, as if there were some remedy to be tried. To their ears, it sounded a lot better than the truth, which would have gone something like this: "Yeah, life sucks, kids are mean, your teacher hasn't been very nice to you, but life will get better. It will take years, maybe four or five years, which is more time than you can wrap your small head around. But you'll get there, and you'll be happier then."

As elementary school wore on, as I turned eight, nine, then ten, I began to feel that I was fighting to have any friends at all. Derek and Adam, my old Mudpie friends, had dispersed to other schools, and I saw less of them. Sometimes, after school, I would still cut through my backyard to the other side of the block, where Adam lived, and find him on his sofa drinking a Coke and watching television. About once a month, when the weather was nice, Derek and I played one-on-one stickball with a tennis ball behind Sumner Avenue School: he would pitch me the ball, I'd hit it, and he'd run back to field my pop-up. I had never been close with my brother Daniel, and it seemed harder than ever to try; he preferred to stay inside with his friend Jason and play Super Sunday football on the Apple IIe computer. So I rode my bicycle around the streets of Springfield. This was before children wore helmets, and I got a thrill riding down the steep hill at the entrance to Forest Park by the highway.

Otherwise, there was not much fun. Places were always closing, including the two most fun places at the asterisk-shaped intersection of Dickinson Street, Sumner Avenue, and Belmont Avenue, known as the X: both the X Bowling Lanes and Cinema X are now gone. (In their place are a twenty-four-hour Walgreen's and a wide parking lot.) There were always closings, but from my whole childhood I remember only two good openings: the ice cream shop called B-Kool, on Dickinson, and next door to B-Kool a baseball card emporium called Bob's Hobbies and Collectibles, whose owner, Bob, dyed his hair a wilted orange as he got older and I became a teenager.

It was boring to be alone. I was ill equipped to talk to most boys and girls my age; new people were turned off by the way I talked. And my social isolation was increased by frequently switching schools. Springfield had one set of schools for kindergarten through fourth grade, another for just fifth and sixth, then junior highs for seventh through ninth, and then high schools. What would have been three schools before my teenage years became four when my parents switched me to the Montessori school. As a result, whenever I did forge a fragile, nascent friendship—just when some potential playmate had gotten used to my attempts at high-minded political discussions, or when I had learned to back off and stop trying—I was off to a new school, where I was once again trapped behind the barriers I always seemed to build.

Sometimes fellow students were the least of my problems. I could be rough on teachers, especially those who misused or mispronounced words. In fifth grade, I had a teacher who corrected the word *specifically* on a paper of mine, crossing it out and writing "pacifically." After class, I brought the paper to her to inquire about it, and she gently told me that there was no such word as *specifically*. But there *is*, I protested: "As in 'I told you *specifically* not to use that word.'" My teacher, whom I had liked so far, just a week into the school year, laughed. "No, sweetie, that word is *pacifically*, like 'I told you *pacifically* not to use that word.'" I did not know what to say next. Later that afternoon I told my parents what had happened. "Well, it's good that you let it drop," my mother said.

My parents had managed to teach me some simple, easily remembered rules: don't correct people, let other people have a chance to talk. But while I could obey the rules, I still saw nothing wrong with my desire to use my advanced vocabulary, my baroque constructions, even deliberately complicated phrasings. And I was always an outsider, so through all the turmoil of school in those years—the shifting cliques that I never learned to negotiate, the teachers who were baffled by me, the teachers who were cruel to me—it also became a matter of ego survival to valorize my skill, to decide there was something good about it.

Fortunately this was a time in America, the mid-1980s, when the wiseass-cum-elitist was enjoying a cultural moment. Television characters like Alex P. Keaton on *Family Ties*, Alan Pinkard on *Head of the Class*, and Matthew Burton, the character played by Jason Bateman on *It's Your Move*, as well as the great Ferris Bueller in the movie *Ferris Bueller's Day Off* and Chris Knight, the Val Kilmer character in *Real Genius*—these teenage boys were all onscreen inventions of the years 1984 to 1986. In some ways, they were very different characters. Matthew, for example, was an amoral con artist, and his pranks made him seem far darker than the populist hero Ferris. Alex was very political, and very conservative, and had they ever met he would have abhorred Ferris's anarchic fight-the-power message. What they all had in common was that they made clever sexy. Their appeal, to fellow boys and, when they got lucky, to girls, was the antithesis of the Fonz's leather-jacket allure, and it had nothing in common with the strong and silent James Dean majesty. It wasn't way-out or groovy or hippie, and it wasn't radical (at least it didn't look radical—Ferris seemed subversive, but he was basically just a truant). It was wholesome and American, but it was way more glib than a parent might deem proper.

Ferris, Alex, Alan, and Matthew inspired me to take pride in my big words, and they gave me permission to discount my parents' warning that sometimes I came across as rude or intimidating. After all, their parents thought *them* rude, and sometimes their peers resented them, but in the end they were heroes. I wanted to master their tricks. It was one thing to be a wiseass, but how would I leave my mark? What bits of my cleverness would become school legend?

I honestly didn't have the guts to come up with ingenious acts of truancy like Ferris's, and the one week of fifth grade that I copied Alex by carrying a briefcase to school I never got over the embarrassment—I just wasn't committed enough to the persona to make it work. What did seem within my grasp was the kind of glib effrontery that a genius like Chris Knight practiced toward his elders— that's what I must have thought I was imitating when, shortly after I abandoned the briefcase, I decided to pick a fight with the Food Bag lady. She didn't do anything to deserve it, and no matter how cool I convinced myself I was, nothing can excuse the way I treated her.

Food Bag was the small convenience store by the Citgo gasoline station on Dickinson Street. It sat on a raised, gray-washed concrete platform a few feet above the blacktop where the cars gassed up, and to get to the front door you had to climb two steps. On the landing that encircled the small store like a tightly fitted, oblong doughnut flush with the bottom of the glass door, Derek and I would sit and dangle our feet, drinking red slushy beverages, looking at cars coming in and out of the parking lot, watching the drivers exit and head inside, brushing past us on their way to pay. "Give me ten on two," they'd bark, dropping a ten-spot on the counter and heading out before the glass door had begun to swing shut. This was before the pumps took credit cards. The drivers would be in and out before you had time to take a bite of a Twizzler or unstick a Gobstopper from your upper molars.

The incident happened when I was about ten, an age when my afternoons were still monotonous. I'm now at an age when the idea of an afternoon with nothing to do sounds wonderful and free, but when life is just a succession of such afternoons it's bleak and boring. So I tried to make some fun at the Food Bag. Not by vandalizing the place, which would have been hard since it was open around the clock. Not by stealing, either. I found fun in being rude to the pinched, sad woman who worked there about sixty hours a week. I never learned her name, but she spent entire days there, from six in the morning, before the school bus came, until late, after dinner, when in the spring, if it was still light, I might be allowed to walk there to buy Chipwiches for my parents and brothers. She was always either behind the counter or outside on a smoke break. She'd stand on the gray-washed landing, one foot propping the door open, crossing her arms to stay warm and bending down to take drags on her cigarette. In the other hand, the noncigarette hand, she'd clutch the soft pack, encased in its loud, crinkly plastic wrap. When there were just a few cigarettes left she'd squeeze the pack, as if for comfort. Her face was tired—she looked like a forty-year-old who looked fifty—and her brown hair was styled in a tight, curly perm. No matter what time of year, she didn't put on an overcoat for her cigarette break, just wore the thin brown smock with a FOOD BAG patch on the breast. There was no time for a coat: most shifts she was on her own in the Food Bag, and the smoke break could last only until a customer came by to put ten on two for gasoline.

She wasn't very friendly, this overworked, chain-smoking, tightly permed woman who, to judge from the phone calls she sometimes had to take while ringing up a sale, had a boyfriend or an ex who made her life tougher than she would have wished. She got annoyed if you took too long counting out change, which as broke ten-year-olds we often did. She never smiled. She was especially stingy with etiquette when ringing up her youngest customers—I was well aware that my father got perfunctory smiles when he paid for gas, but my candy purchases were treated as annoyances, not worthy of even a "thank you." That was my justification, as I recall: if she was going to be rude to me, I was going to be rude to her.

Also, I thought maybe Derek would be impressed. He was taller and a year older, and a much better athlete, but he was shyer with adults. This was a chance to press my one skill.

"Do you take credit cards?" I asked one hot spring day, when I was trying to buy a soda.

"No," the Food Bag lady said. "Come on, let's go. We only take cash, you know that."

But I had seen my father pay for his gasoline with a credit card. It was just *like* her not to treat me like an adult.

"That's *age discrimination*," I said. "You're not allowed to do that. If you take credit cards from adults, you have to take them from me."

"Come on kids, do you have money?" Derek was standing next to me, saying nothing. "There's a line behind you," she said, looking down and tapping her long fingernails on the counter. They looked like Lee Press-On Nails, which were advertised on Channel 20 practically every hour.

"There's no line behind me," I said, looking around. "Where? Where's the line behind me? You're just making that up. I want to buy this soda with my Master Charge, and you have to let me, or else it's age discrimination, and I could bring my father in here. He's a lawyer. Or I could talk to the manager—is the manager here?"

"There's no manager. I'm the manager. You have to pay with cash."

"I only have my credit card, and you have to take it. *By law.*"

She was beginning to get nervous. Or maybe that look was fatigue, or worry about what awaited her at home after she got off, or maybe just that it was time for her smoke break and she had to clear all the customers out before she could leave the store. But she finally cracked:

"Okay, lemme see your credit card."

Which of course I didn't have. I no more had a credit card than I had a driver's license or my own bank account or pubic hair.

"*Pffff.*" I made this noise as I scowled and looked away, as if to say, "*Whatever.* I'm too good to give you a credit card anyway!" I walked past Derek, grabbing his arm on the way out. "Come on, let's go," I said.

As soon as we got outside to the gas station's blacktop, he started shaking his head. "Oh my *God*, you were so rude to her! What were you *doing?*" He did not seem impressed, and he clearly sensed that I'd taken leave of my best judgment. He knew that you didn't just mouth off to the Food Bag lady for no reason. Even if we didn't get caught, it was still wrong. Why had I thought he would approve?

But I had my justifications. "She's so mean! She's so polite to parents, but she acts like kids are going to steal or something."

Derek exhaled, still shaking his head and looking down, his eyes shaded by the brim of his Phillies baseball cap.

"I mean, *right?*" I said, a little desperately. "I don't care what she thinks about us. Do you care?"

Derek didn't say anything. Inside himself now, he just shook his head and smiled, as if he hoped I knew what I was doing.

"Why?" I asked. "Do you think it was wrong of me?"

"No, it's just . . . I don't know what you get out of it. Why were you being so rude to her? She didn't really do anything to you, you know what I mean?"

I did know what he meant. I had no real grievance with the Food Bag lady. But I was a wisenheimer, and I just craved such encounters; it was satisfying to argue, to try to win a verbal contest with someone older, to flaunt adult terms like *age discrimination*. It seemed like something Alex P. Keaton or Ferris Bueller would have done.

I was aware that she was poor, that her life was no picnic, that she probably tried her best. I was at Food Bag enough to know what hours she worked, and I knew that nobody in my family worked those kinds of hours. There's plenty about the encounter that now makes me ashamed, especially my cavalier reference to my father the lawyer (I don't know when rank classism began to seem like a desirable trait or a natural accoutrement to my verbiage). I knew at the time that I was misbehaving. I would not have wanted my father to see me acting that way. Afterward, I felt worse about myself. Not only had I been cruel, I hadn't even prevailed. I had no credit card, no victory, just a creeping sense of embarrassment that I'd thought my plan was so funny. I got on my bike and pedaled hard, surging ahead of Derek, trying to outrace what I had done.

IV

Reading—the activity that preserves the sanity of so many precocious children—was complicated for me. When I was a little older, in junior high school, my father would occasionally recommend a book, such as Chaim Potok's *The Chosen* or Kurt Vonnegut's *Cat's Cradle*. In the meantime there was nobody, neither friends nor librarians nor teachers, to encourage my reading. The Montessori school had almost no books, and the children's librarian at the Forest Park library famously hated children, so with a few exceptions—for example, *From the Mixed-Up Files of Mrs. Basil E. Frankweiler*, which a friend handed me one day at school—I knew nothing of the Newbery Medal winners that, I learned in college, had been the favorites of many people my age. No *Jacob Have I Loved*, no *The Westing Game*, no *Bridge to Terabithia*. I encountered some of these young adult classics when I returned to public school for fifth grade; there, Scott O'Dell, Madeleine L'Engle, and Wilson Rawls were on the syllabus of the reading enrichment class for gifted students. Before then, when I was eight and nine years old, my reading was an endless, dispirited recycling of the Hardy Boys and Encyclopedia Brown, along with occasional, aborted attempts to read novels pulled from my parents' shelves.

Somehow, though, near the end of my third-grade year, I did discover Judy Blume. I do not remember how. At a school where we didn't read much, we definitely did not read Blume's books about menstruation, masturbation, and sex. She was after my parents' time, so they learned about Blume from me, not the other way around. But for about two years, beginning when I was almost nine, I read and reread, often a dozen times, every book Blume had written. And it was in one of those books, *Then Again, Maybe I Won't*, that I found a new template for acting out. I eagerly entered the world of practical jokes, Tony Miglione style.

Judy Blume fans will remember Tony Miglione for his wet dreams. Just as Margaret has her period, and Blubber her weight problem, Tony has his orgasms. Practically every night. He goes through a lot of sheets. He also has anxiety-induced stomachaches and a mute grandmother (she lost her larynx to cancer) who refuses to leave her bedroom—there's a lot of stress in the Miglione house, especially now that Tony's arriviste mother has uprooted the family from Jersey City and relocated them to the suburbs. New to town, Tony is befriended by Joel, whose older sister, the cheerleader Lisa, is the fantasy girl responsible for Tony's "nocturnal emissions."

But what captured my imagination in *Then Again, Maybe I Won't* was the game that Joel liked to play with Tony. When there were no parents around, Joel would pick up the phone and randomly dial phone numbers. When he reached somebody, he would ask for Denton F. Buchanan. Told that no such person lived there, Joel would hang up, wait a moment, and call back, asking again for Denton F. Buchanan. Told again that there was no such person, he would do it a third time. Then, Joel would call back one final time and, using a deeper voice, say, "This is Denton F. Buchanan calling. Have there been any calls for me?" And then he would hang up and laugh. In the book, Joel finally persuades Tony to have a go, which Tony does, reluctantly, using the name Peter Ira Grinch (because the initials spell *pig*). Before Tony can make the final phone call, pretending to be Peter Ira Grinch, he has a severe stomach cramp and runs to the bathroom.

Although the book makes it clear that Joel's actions are wrong, I was intrigued. Prank phone calling was an opportunity to be witty. I was sure I could outdo some character in a Judy Blume book. One night just after my tenth birthday, my parents went out with my youngest brother, Jonathan, and I took the phone with the very long cord from their bedroom, brought it into my room, and shut the door. Daniel was downstairs watching television. I dialed a number that started with our exchange, 739. I got the message that there was no phone at that number. I tried again, with a different final four digits. Again, no phone. Then, on the third try, it began to ring. These were the early days of answering machines, most people didn't have them, so it was nothing unusual to let a phone ring seven, eight, nine times. At last, a woman answered.

"Hello?"

I had planned my line carefully, and I delivered it in a breathless rush:

"You're on Channel Three right now! Go turn on the TV—it's important!"

And then I hung up.

As I sat on the floor of my bedroom, I felt an exhilaration better than anything I could remember. I felt dangerous. And I felt something else: effectual. Because of what I had done, that woman who answered the phone had probably run to her television and turned on Channel 3. For days afterward she might have wondered if she had in fact been on TV and barely missed seeing herself.

Such is the peculiar narcissism of the ten-year-old, anyway. Even if at first she had gone to her television, she had probably soon realized what had happened and then forgotten about it.

But I didn't. I had found something fun to do, and now it was time to refine the game. About a week later, the next time my parents were out, I took the phone and sat on my floor and dialed the phone number of a radio station I had found in the yellow pages. A man with a strong Puerto Rican accent answered.

"Hello?"

"Yes," I said, "may I please speak to the man in charge of news?"

"Yes, ma'am," he said, "I'm in charge of news." I was accustomed to being taken for a girl on the phone.

"You're the news director?"

"I'm a deejay, but I also do the news."

"I'm sorry, I need to speak to whoever is in *charge* of news."

"She's not in right now. I'm sorry."

"But I must speak with her. It's very important."

"What is this about?"

"It's *very important*." I slowly drew out the last two words, to make sure my point sank in. "I really must speak to her. I have a very important news story that your listeners will want to know about."

"Ma'am, this is a Hispanic station. We do all kinds of news, but is your story"—here he paused, struggling to come up with the right word—"is your story *especially* for Hispanics?" His voice went up, incredulously.

"Look," I said, "it's very important. It is. I really need to speak to somebody. Now!"

"Ma'am, it's seven o'clock at night. Nobody's here now. I'm the only one here. I have to go back to the booth. If you tell me what it is you are calling about, I can leave a note for our news director, okay? You tell me, you leave your number, I have her call you?"

As when the lady at Food Bag finally agreed to take my credit card, I was beaten. I no more had a good news story for the Hispanic deejay than I had a Master Charge. I hadn't even had the foresight to think up a story in advance, or to have a fake phone number ready. The man had, in essence, said to me, "It's your move," and I had no move. I was pathetic. Jason Bateman would have known what to say.

"Well, I'll think about it, and maybe I'll call back tomorrow. Have a good night." That was the best I could do.

Writing about these phone calls sounds anachronistic. I presume that caller ID has rendered mischievous phone calls a strange artifact of the past; for this reason, *Then Again, Maybe I Won't* must feel as dated as *Are You There God? It's Me, Margaret*, in which girls wear belts to keep their pads in place. In fact, phone calls as a medium for mischief were becoming passé even then. Across America, teenagers more gifted in electronics were using phone lines to commit a crime far more daring: hacking into computers. The popular culture was catching up to the coders and hackers, with movies like *WarGames*, in which Matthew Broderick nearly destroys the world with his computer skills, and *Real Genius*, in which Val Kilmer's Chris Knight and his little disciple, Mitch, break into a computer aboard an airplane and prevent a major arms escalation. Yet phone calls were the advanced frontier of my cleverness.

After the radio phone-in, I mostly stayed away from phones for a while, although on a couple of nights I went on marathons of dialing and hanging up, perhaps twenty phone numbers in a row, each time shouting some variant of "You're on TV, turn it on now!" or "It's urgent, go to your door!" Having felt foolish after my conversation with the Hispanic radio deejay, I limited myself to these short ejaculations, never waiting for a response. Sometimes, when it was over, I felt thuggish—the whole point of the phone-calling business was to glory in the power of words, not merely to harass people. In these final orgies of dialing and running, I kept expecting that the next phone call would be the exciting one, the one that produced the frisson I'd felt the first time. It never happened, so I gave up.

I focused my energies instead on using pieces of paper and a pen to terrorize a poor girl who had done nothing to me. Like the Food Bag lady, she just had the misfortune of being there.

Kelly was a student at Armory Street School, where she was briefly Derek's girlfriend. They were eleven, and given that I had never even had a ten-year-old's boyfriend/girlfriend relationship, I was deeply ignorant of what that kind of connection entailed between people a full year older. Something mysterious, I was sure, something to be desired—and my jealousy planted in me an antipathy toward this unseen Kelly, this older woman at a school across town from mine.

It was jealousy both of Derek for having a girlfriend and of Kelly for having Derek. Derek was steady in my life. I needed his friendship. And I admired him. He was tall and handsome, with curly blond hair, and one of the best baseball players in town, a homerun champion and a hero to his teammates, who would crowd him at home plate and offer high-fives as I, the tagalong friend, watched from the stands.

The girlfriend was, I should have seen, not much of a threat. Derek never saw Kelly outside of school, and just his telling me about their French-kissing opened up a new space for intimacy between us. But she seemed like a threat, and because I did not know how to admit that to myself, I redoubled my attachment to Derek. When they broke up after several weeks, I was secretly pleased, but I also proved my loyalty to Derek by taking the breakup personally, on his behalf, and deciding that Kelly was to blame. I had never really thought that girls were icky, and in fact had had minor crushes of my own, but I was easily persuaded by this turn in Derek's life that women carried the potential for evildoing. It seemed to make perfect sense to strike back at Kelly.

To get at Kelly I decided to exploit my least favorite customers on my paper route. The convolution of this plan made it especially appealing. I delivered the afternoon *Daily News* to about thirty families spread over four blocks around my house, and several of them were especially stingy tippers. Besides the cheapskates, there was another house with a black mark upon it, the Silvers', for although the elderly Silver was a kind man and generous tipper, his grown daughter, Andrea, would yell at me if the paper came late or wasn't placed just so on their doorstep. She was so abusive that my father had advised me to drop that household from my route. I decided to take my dad's advice, and I was looking forward to telling the mean daughter that she was being dropped, but when I rang the Silvers' doorbell the old man answered. He was bent over, and his eyes were watery. "What if I paid you extra?" he said. And it hit me just then that he needed his newspaper. He could barely walk, he lived with his beast of a daughter, and now I was taking away his daily paper. I felt a quickening of regret in my breast, but I couldn't think beyond my original plan, which I had promised myself I would stick to. "I'm sorry, I just can't" is all I told him, then I turned and walked toward the street as fast as I could without running.

It wasn't so long afterward that, on a night when Derek was sleeping over, I wrote out five identical notes with Kelly's phone number and the command, "You must call this number immediately!" Very late, after my parents were asleep, Derek and I sneaked away on our bikes and rode around the neighborhood, leaving the notes inside the screen doors of the Silvers and four other houses I had preselected, although I had to make a last-minute change when I saw lights on at one house. That was one of the great nights of my life. It was late fall, after midnight, and in my little slice of Forest Park the streets were ours. It was a neighborhood of old people, mostly with grown children. I lived amid a cluster of Colonial, Dutch Colonial, and faux-Tudor houses, most of them built around 1920, sitting placidly on quarter-acre lots. *Don't disturb us*, they seemed to say. *This is a respectable neighborhood.* The leaves were changing and falling, and one of them grazed my face as we cruised Olmsted Drive on our bicycles. Nobody had been awake to tell us to wear our jackets, and as we dragged our feet along the ground instead of using our brakes, the cold air was exciting.

Back at my house, Derek had seemed slightly bothered that I was taking the matter of his ex-girlfriend into my own hands, but he had developed an air of resignation about my exploits. I had made some of my phone calls from his house one afternoon, and he had just waited in the other room and watched videos on MTV. "You have this sadistic streak," he had muttered, and he'd sounded sad, as if he didn't really know me. That rebuke had prompted one of the only fights we'd ever had. I told him that I wasn't sadistic, just trying to play practical jokes, like Matthew Burton on *It's Your Move*. Derek was having none of it. "He has code-breaking machines, fancy gadgets, all this stuff! What do you have? Your telephone? *A pen and paper?*" He wasn't impressed. He didn't approve. But he rode with me on this nighttime mission, as a gesture of solidarity. In spite of his not comprehending me, he loved me, and wherever I went he would go, too.

A lot of what I did could be called youthful mischief, I suppose. But in truth I had become a bully. At the time, I would never have seen it that way. I didn't beat anybody up. I didn't stuff anyone in a locker. In school, I was the victim. But I was a bully in the only way I knew how. Kelly became my target, an especially easy one since I had never met her. It was revenge of the nerds, but Kelly hadn't done anything to merit my vengeance.

Another night, when my parents were out, Jonathan was sleeping, and I was awake with Daniel and a friend of his, I decided it was time to make an extra-daring phone call. Now, this was the era of the child-abuse scare: abducted children were on milk cartons, and fantastic stories about satanic rites at preschools were getting innocent people thrown in jail. Every public school student was given a talk about molestation and what to do if it happened. "Call a hotline," we were told. That night, I did. A woman with a warm, competent voice answered the phone.

"Hotline," she said. "May I help you?"

"My name is Kelly _____," I said, giving the first and last name of Derek's ex.

"Hi, Kelly. What did you want to talk about tonight?"

"Well, it's kind of embarrassing." I heard my brother stifle a giggle on the line upstairs, where he and his friend were listening in. I almost laughed, too, but I held it together.

"I'm listening," the nice lady said.

"My father . . ."

"Yes?"

"It's *really* embarrassing."

"Take your time, dear."

"Well, my dad . . ."

"Yes?"

"My dad, he . . ."

"Yes?" She sounded a little too eager, I remember thinking.

"My dad . . . he *touches* me." At this, I heard my brother giggle again, and the woman from the hotline must have heard it, too. I was sure that she was going to say, "Hey kids, this isn't a joke, okay?" and just hang up. But she didn't. She pretended not to hear the laughter, and she asked me to go on.

"He touches me," I said. *"Down there.* He's only done it a couple times, but I want him to stop."

"Can you tell me where you live?" she asked.

"No." That would be too much. I didn't want police to show up at anyone's door.

The only problem was, I had already given a last name. It was an unusual name, there weren't more than three or four families in the surrounding towns with that name, and it's unlikely that more than one of the families had a girl of elementary school age. In the days before caller ID, there was no way to tell that she wasn't the caller, that in fact a boy with a girlish voice and delusions of prankster grandeur had made the call from the telephone in his kitchen.

The next week, the police arrived at her doorstep and nearly destroyed her family. At the time, I had no idea what I had done. But six months later all my misdeeds visited me at once, like debt collectors colliding on my doorstep.

My return to public school after Montessori had, up to this point, felt triumphant. In early April 1985, my first year at New North Community School was almost over, and I was happy. I spent my days shuttling among the four subdivisions of Pod 2, one of the fifth-and-sixth-grade school's ten pods. Pods were large classrooms divided by crosses of bookshelves into quadrants of thirty people each. The 120 students of Pod 2 were a special group: not officially designated as "gifted," which would have cut against the progressive education philosophy from which the pods were derived, we nonetheless figured out pretty quickly that we were the school's good kids, the ones teachers like to teach. Some of us were academically advanced; others were just mature and eager to learn. And we were the only pod at New North that would all move, en masse, to another pod for sixth grade; Pod 2 would travel together, with its four teachers, to Pod 10.

That was a happy prospect, because I liked my classmates. I liked Demond Williams, a dandy who often wore three-piece suits to class and seemed to think of me, with my big words, as a fellow eccentric, worthy of his comradeship. I liked Jennifer Pilarczik, an amiable girl from a working-class neighborhood who at the end of sixth grade would invite me to the first adult-seeming party I'd ever attended, where there were no parent-supervised games but just a lot of friends hanging around, eating chips and drinking soda. I even secretly liked Tammy Duchesne, the other most ambitious student in Pod 2, even though I had decided early on that she was my nemesis. She was as smart as I was, but while I had no athletic ability she won citywide swim meets and, she said, ran a mile every day. Which meant that she won in an overall sense, both having brains and being good at sports, and I didn't like that. But even though in theory I hated her, I would have defended her to anyone from outside Pod 2.

And I was learning more than I had learned at Montessori. Mr. Luce's math lessons covered topics that were new to me, and when Mr. Rice, our English teacher, was working on grammatical concepts that he knew I understood, he encouraged me to sit in the corner and read ahead in our workbook. Other students found this curious but seemed to understand.

It was this contented school life, I think, that had helped me give up my criminal activity. For the first time since kindergarten, I liked going to school. After that brief, early misstep—the week in late September when I carried the briefcase to school—I had recovered gracefully, and by Christmas vacation I felt comfortable with my place in this small world. I was laughing a lot, and now, in April, I had just started my first week of Little League—on Derek's team, too—and that nagging need to show how smart I was began, at last, to abate.

So it was as a confident, law-abiding member of the fifth grade that I sat in Mr. Luce's class, that one bright spring day. The whole class had just returned from lunch and we had five minutes of free time before class began again. I was trading friendly insults with Gerald "Johnny" Mercy, a black boy from the North End who always wore perfectly ironed twill pants and Adidas sneakers; Billy Taylor, a hapless white kid whose hair looked as if he'd cut it himself—years later, I heard, his luck changed for the better after his mother won the Megabucks lottery; and Roberto Lopez, a boy with an unusually happy temperament whose dirty jokes always involved words like *douche* and *Kotex*, the meanings of which he patiently explained to me. It was from such a conversation that Mr. Luce extracted me.

"They want to see you in Miss Dryden's office," he said. Miss Dryden was the principal, a woman most students knew only from afar, at assemblies. She would approach the microphone in the large, professional-looking auditorium, with its proscenium stage and tiered seats that rose up to great heights in the rear of the room. Not one orange hair ever moved in the spherical bouffant on her head. She looked as contemporary as Lady Bird Johnson or Ann Landers. "Good *morning*, boys and girls," she would say. "Good *morning*, Miss Dryden," we would all reply. She lived with her twin sister, also the principal of a Springfield public school.

"What's it about?" I asked Mr. Luce, already afraid.

"Just go ahead down. I'm sure everything is fine." That was an unnerving thing for him to say, made worse by the extra solicitude in his voice. Ken Luce was my favorite teacher, an eminently decent man who talked a lot about his teenage daughter and genuinely seemed to like spending his days with children. There weren't many male teachers in the school, and none with his easy warmth. Just now, he seemed concerned for me. I could tell that he knew something I didn't, something that made him hope for the best.

I went downstairs to the main floor, then down another flight into the sunken, wide-open basement level that one could see when leaning over the railings on the ground level. From the outside, New North was a hulking, concrete assault of Brutalist architecture, a giant rectangular prism with no windows. It sat with cold disregard for Birnie Avenue, the poor, blighted street that most of its students walked every morning to school. I was one of the white students who was bused in, and I never got over my early-morning dread of the prisonlike building as the yellow bus approached. But once inside there was a futuristic, sci-fi feel to the corridors, atria, and walkways, like a hangar on the Death Star in *Star Wars*. Going to the warren of administrative offices in the basement was like descending into the beating heart of the building, and I felt an awesome fear as I approached the receptionist who guarded Miss Dryden's door.

"Mark?" She knew who I was—I had been invited to see the principal several times before, to accept citations and awards, such as spelling bee ribbons. "You can go ahead in."

I opened the door to find Miss Dryden sitting behind her desk, slowly signing some papers.

"Have a seat," she said, not looking up. "Your parents will be here soon."

My parents?

"What's wrong? Is everything okay?"

"They'll tell you all about it when they get here."

I was sure that somebody had died, and I thought immediately of my younger brothers, then eight and three.

"Is everyone okay? Is anyone hurt?"

"I'm sure your parents will tell you all about it when they get here." She kept her eyes on her paperwork.

I sat in Miss Dryden's office for five minutes before my parents walked in. They looked funereal, their eyes downcast and unwilling to meet mine, but I only knew for certain that something was wrong when my father said, "Thank you Miss Dryden. We're really sorry for all the trouble." My father took a dim view of Miss Dryden, whom he saw as a reactionary apparatchik, more concerned with order and deference than with education or the life of the mind. Only if something had really shaken him would he be excessively polite to Miss Dryden.

I followed my parents out to the parking lot across from the school. We got in the beige Plymouth station wagon and drove off. I hadn't yet asked what was wrong. Neither of my parents had looked at me, which was oddly reassuring: if they were mad at me, at least that meant that nobody was injured or dead.

When I was almost out of patience, my father finally spoke.

"Your mother got a visit from the police today." Always a quiet man, he was now scarcely audible from behind the wheel. I leaned forward in the backseat as far as my seat belt would allow. My feet were still two years from touching the floor.

"What?"

"Your mother got a visit from *the police* today." That's what I had thought he'd said, but that couldn't be right. Why? What had I done? And why was he referring to "your mother," a formal locution totally out of character for him? What had I done—and what role was he playing?

"Why?" I asked, and at this he glanced over his shoulder with a look somewhere well past annoyed, as if I'd drained all his patience. He didn't believe that I didn't know.

"Some *letters*?" he said. "You put letters in people's doors? Remember? Telling them to call some girl?"

My mother started to cry in the passenger seat, reaching into her purse for one of the tissues she always kept handy for her allergies. I was totally confused. I had a faint recollection of having put those notes in some people's mailboxes and inside their screen doors, but that was ages ago, last summer or fall. Was that even illegal? Why were the police involved? And how had anyone found out?

I had not made any of my phone calls or left any notes for the past six months, which was a lifetime to a ten-year-old. It was baseball season, and I was getting playing time in the outfield. My happiness at school and newfound sense of myself as a passable athlete had enhanced my confidence even in areas where I'd already felt pretty capable. I was reading longer books than I'd been reading a few months before, for instance, and was nearly through the last of

Gregory McDonald's Fletch novels, which I had started reading after seeing the Chevy Chase movie.

I was, in other words, older, wiser, and really in no mood to be punished for mischief committed by a younger boy.

But there was my mother, crying.

I said, "Yeah, Derek and I were fooling around, we might have put some joking notes in some people's doors, but what's the big deal?"

Then my father explained. He spoke methodically, as if focusing on being thorough would, for the moment, hold back his disappointment in me.

"Somebody from your paper route thought it might be you. They brought the notes to the police. The police got a sample of your writing from Miss Dryden, and they compared the handwriting. And the police also knew about the name and the phone number you had put on your notes—Kelly?—because they had been called to investigate a report of abuse or rape at her house. They had been out to her house, Mark. They went out and accused her father of abusing her."

He turned around in his seat and looked at me again. It was the same look as before, annoyed and exasperated, as if I should have confessed by now, as if by forcing him to continue with his story I was intentionally compounding his grief. The car was at a stop. I hadn't noticed that we were at Wendy's. "What would you like for lunch?" he asked. A cheeseburger with fries and a small Frosty, I said. My regular order. Wendy's was where my father sometimes took me for lunch on Saturdays, as a special treat. I felt sickened to be there on a weekday, in such ugly circumstances. My parents didn't believe in fast food on weekdays, and stopping there seemed a measure of how badly they'd been undone.

I was terrified of my parents, terrified of myself, and terrified of what I had done, in that order. It wasn't until we turned right off Dickinson and drove down Bronson Terrace to our small white house that I even thought to wonder about the consequences. What happened to a ten-year-old boy whose attempts at cleverness had brought the police to an unsuspecting family to investigate the father for child molestation?

Would I go to *jail?*

I wanted to know, but I didn't want to ask. Once we were inside the house, my father took me by the arm and turned me to face him. It was an unusually direct gesture, not like him at all. "They want me to bring you downtown," he said. "They didn't come and yank you out of class, which they normally would do. They came to me and Mom instead, and we're supposed to bring you to the police station."

"Are they going to put me in handcuffs?" My voice cracked. My life was totally ending.

"Not if we bring you there, no."

"Are they going to fingerprint me?"

My father rolled his eyes upward and bobbed his head toward one shoulder, then the other, as if looking for answers. This was a more familiar gesture, and all of a sudden he seemed less terrifying, less like an extension of the police. I had my dad back.

"They might," he said. The way he said it, I was sure he didn't want this to happen any more than I did. My mother was in the other room, probably still crying. She still hadn't looked at me. But to judge from his look and his voice, my father seemed to be returning to himself, becoming less severe and more compassionate. Maybe the world wasn't ending, I thought. Maybe it could return to normal. "But listen," he went on. "I'll go down there. You don't have to come. I'll go down and talk to them and promise that nothing like this will happen again."

"Nothing like this will ever happen again, I promise!"

"Okay, babe, okay. Just stay here."

Having left teaching, my father was now a lawyer with his own small practice. Most of his work was landlord/tenant law and employment discrimination. He fought for the little guy, didn't make much money doing it, but tried to make a difference. He also did some court-appointed work for juvenile offenders, and as the door closed behind him I realized that he was now representing me.

He was gone about an hour, and I was home with my mother in the middle of the day. I sat on the brown sofa in the living room. I was afraid to turn on the television. I was afraid even to open a book or look at the sports pages to read about last night's Yankees game. I feared that doing anything that resembled leisure activity would look disrespectful to my mother, who was in the kitchen being very quiet.

I went up to my room and lay on my bed. There was a book on my nightstand, right next to the lamp and my clock radio, which was tuned to 1600 AM for baseball games. I couldn't turn on the radio or pick up the book; it still seemed wrong. I lay on my bed and looked at the ceiling. I turned to my left to stare at my wallpaper until the repeating orange fleur-de-lis merged in my vision, every two becoming one. After an hour, I heard the front door open, then my father ascending the stairs to the second floor.

I ran out of my bedroom and sat at the top of the stairs. He stopped about two stairs short of the landing and looked down at me.

"I want you to know," he said, drawing out each word, "that this is *the last time I save you*. Do you know what would have happened if you were a black kid from the North End and did what you did? They would have thrown the book at you. They wanted you down there, to fingerprint, to arraign. They wanted you down there. But I told them that we would take care of it, and they said okay. But if you had been a *black* kid? Do you *understand?*"

I nodded. I understood. And I felt bad for my father. He was so visibly shaken, and I knew that I had done this to him: made him choose between his principles and his son. Asking the prosecutor to cut me a break could not have been easy for my dad, a man so profoundly allergic to dishonesty that he overpays his taxes. Aside from thinking about what destruction I might have wrought on Kelly's family, the hardest sin for me to contemplate was what I'd done to my dad, making him compromise himself like that.

The public schools' April vacation began two days later, and my parents sent me to Philadelphia to stay with my grandparents for the week. My mother gave me the news that night, a few hours after my father returned from the courthouse. "I just can't be around you right now," she said.

Of course, in Philadelphia I had as good a time as ever. I stayed up late with my grandfather to watch *Benny Hill*. I ate ice cream with pretzels and root beer after dinner. The whole week, neither my grandfather nor my grandmother mentioned my crime. I kept waiting for it, but midway through the week it occurred to me that my mother hadn't told them, either out of her own shame or out of kindness—she knew that their good opinion meant so much to me. After I got back to Springfield, my parents never spoke of it again. It was alluded to just once, on a Saturday after school resumed. My parents went out for the morning with my younger brothers, and before leaving my father said, "You won't use the phone, right? Unless there's an emergency?" I assured him that I would not.

I would never commit a crime again—no phone calls, no notes, not even lying if I could help it. For several months I tried to be wholly good, looking for any way to be helpful around the house, being irreproachably polite toward my parents and siblings. I felt terrible, and I even thought about calling Kelly to apologize, but I never did. I was scared of what would happen. At night, trying to fall asleep, I had violent, self-punishing fantasies of her father beating me to a pulp—and because I knew I deserved at least that much, I was ashamed that I was not man enough to show up on their doorstep and say I was sorry.

Mostly, though, I was confused. Had Kelly asked why I had done this to her, I would have had to answer, "I don't know." So instead of having that conversation, I just tried to be as good as I could. After a few months my parents began to trust me again, my crimes receded in time, and I began to forget.

Sixth grade had a sparse, parched quality to it. I tried to stay out of trouble. I watched a lot of television that year, mostly on NBC: *The Cosby Show, Family Ties, Night Court*. I liked *Growing Pains*, on ABC, and people told me I looked like the actor who played Mike Seaver's best friend, Boner. On Saturday nights, Derek and Adam had junior high parties to go to, but I didn't; I stayed in and watched *Solid Gold*, *227*, and *The Golden Girls*. On Sundays, there was *60 Minutes*, then *Murder, She Wrote*. I sometimes played chess with myself, turning the board around after each move.

Like many boys, I went through a period of sports infatuation, and mine was peaking at just about this time. Every year, Derek and I pooled our money and bought the complete set of Fleer baseball cards (they were more elegant than Topps, even if they didn't hold their value as well). We put them in clear polyurethane sleeves that we snapped into three-ring binders. I liked memorizing the statistics on the backs of the cards, then trying to figure out as I listened to games on the radio if a player's batting average was going up or down. Sports gave me a lawful way to use my words, too. Almost from the beginning, my love of sports fused with my love of talking. My goal was to be a broadcaster on TV, like Vin Scully or Joe Garagiola, or on the radio, like Bill White or Bobby Murcer. Every morning I would lay the sports page out on the kitchen table, pull up a chair, hunch over the page, and, as I slurped my Life cereal, begin to read the box scores aloud, turning the rows of names and numbers into announcers' patter: "Last night, Ron Guidry evened his record to four and four with a sterling ten-strikeout performance against the Bosox before an excited home field crowd at Yankee Stadium. He was backed up by some stellar performances, including a home run from the big man, the designated hitter, Don Baylor, who smacked it long in the first inning off the losing pitcher, Bobby Ojeda, who went six and two-thirds innings and saw his record drop to five and five. Butch Wynegar and Dave Winfield both had triples last night for the Yankees, an amazing and unusual occurrence, and that helped propel the Yankees to their twenty-second win, against the Sox, who themselves dropped to twenty-four and twenty-seven. Both teams will have to do much better in the remaining games before the All Star break if they hope to have any chance of being around in October."

The summer before seventh grade, as the Yankees battled the Red Sox for the Eastern Division title, my family went to the New Jersey shore for a week. I got up early every morning to ride my bike to the general store on Long Beach Island and buy a *Times*. I'd bring it back to our small bungalow and, while my parents still slept and my younger brothers—Daniel was now ten, and Jonathan was four—watched morning cartoons, I would go upstairs and lie down on the floor, the sports page spread before me, and quietly call games. When I was done giving the day's sports update to my fans out in radio land, I switched roles, becoming the guest on a call-in show, expertly fielding questions about the Yankees' chances in the coming years. "It's tough to imagine them doing it without better pitching . . . Guidry's not what he used to be, he's no Steve Carlton or Nolan Ryan, there are better pitchers out there . . . Dave Winfield is good, but the Yankees need more than power . . . now if this guy Mattingly can keep hitting the way he's been hitting, they might be onto something . . . I totally agree—you're right, Jim, and thanks for calling in . . . No, no, thank you, Jim. It's callers like you that keep me in this racket."

That fall, I began to write letters. I started correspondences with both of my grandmothers. I wrote to my Uncle Rick, who replied with a long, typewritten letter. I wrote to my Uncle Bob, and he wrote back, too. My cousin Jason, four years older than I was, sent me rambling, newsy letters that included reviews of all the record albums he had bought since he'd last written. When I was in sixth grade Jason got his driver's license, and from then on he made a point, whenever I visited Philadelphia, of fetching me at my grandparents' house to join him as he cruised East River Drive in his mother's car, its speakers blasting New Wave or Brit rock. He was a huge music fan, and his letters were dense and enthusiastic, like rock zines, filled with deep knowledge about bands whose names were made up of initials: U2, INXS, XTC, R.E.M., OMD, PiL.

I wanted to write letters like that, but I didn't know anything about music. So I began to write letters to the editor of the *Springfield Daily*

News. When I told my parents what I was doing, my mother, afraid of what I might write, asked me to use a pseudonym. I adopted the nom de plume Terry Bronson, a play on the name of my street, Bronson Terrace. The little box at the bottom of the letters section of our newspaper said that all letters must include the address and phone number of the writer, "for verification purposes." I didn't include a number or a street address, but of the five letters I wrote, four were published within the week. When this grew tiresome—fooling the newspaper had proved too easy—I wrote one letter, in opposition to the death penalty, under my own name. It was published, and I was proud when several friends at school told me their parents had seen it. But when my father reported back to me that his friend Michael had seen the letter and found it "cute," I was embarrassed and never wrote to the paper again.

I still have a letter that I wrote to Mary Crist, the director of the Ames Hill Center for Gifted Children, a program that ran on Saturday mornings during the school year and as a summer camp in July and August; I had taken computer classes and chess lessons there as an eight- and nine-year-old. I continued to get the course catalog, and when I visited after a hiatus of a year and didn't like what I saw, I felt called to share my displeasure with Mrs. Crist. I must have never sent the letter, because my mother found it in a box twenty years later and, laughing, presented it to me, saying, "Do you remember this?"

Dear Mrs. Crist,

I would like, as a friend of Ames Hill, to say that Ames Hill's enrollment has taken a sharp dive. I hope that you take into consideration what I am about to say.

I will set the time. Two years ago, a cool Saturday during the peak of Autumn, 1983. Several pre-teen-aged youngsters blow up the S.S. Maine in Mr. Nolte's Historic Military Simulations class. A frog is created in Miss Silverman's LOGO course. Dinosaurs are drawn with Mrs. Koscher. Mr. Rich teaches BASIC while photography is taught by yet another Ames Hill ex. All during this a reject finds a friend; a loner learns to like; a gifted child finds a new mentor.

I will set the time. One year ago, a rainy winter Saturday, 1984. So-and-so sits through the chess course, repeated for the 15th time. Courses of the same caliber as "Making Block Letters" are taught to restless kids with perfect attendance due to parental persistence [and] persuasion. Joe is called to be informed that a favorite course is being canceled due to lack of popularity.

Favorite teachers have left. An institution that I was with all through grade school is now largely a pre-schooler's delight and a computer camp. Friends that I looked forward to seeing again next semester are now replaced by non-gifted, immature 7-year-olds with an IQ of sub-100.

The decline of Ames Hill is even evident through your own literature. Once a nicely printed 12 page booklet, it turned into a computer-printed leaflet, which is now a single piece of paper without even a photograph from Ames Hill's good days.

I suggest that you look at your Spring '83 and Summer '83 curriculums and try to bring back the same teachers, courses, and even booklets from those years. I could guarantee a rise in enrollment.

Change is only good when it's for the best.

I had not signed the letter, and my mother must have talked me out of sending it.

I directed my pen elsewhere. In the mid-1980s, Chips Ahoy was running its advertising campaign promising "Betcha bite a chip." Once, when my mother brought home a bag of Chips Ahoy, I tore it open and bit into a cookie—*and did not bite a chip.* I dug around in the cabinet under our kitchen countertop and found a yellow legal pad. "Dear Chips Ahoy," I wrote, and went on to inform Nabisco of my chipless bite. Two weeks later, I received a letter in the mail: "Dear Mr. Oppenheimer: Please accept our sincerest apologies. While Chips Ahoy attempts to include sufficient chips in every Chips Ahoy cookie to ensure that any reasonably sized bite encounters a chip, it is inevitable that some unforeseen chip-clustering may, on rare occasion, occur. And in such instances, it is Nabisco's policy to guarantee a replacement, not just of one cookie but of the entire package." My coupon for a free package was enclosed.

Now *here* was an activity to make Matthew Burton proud. It was legal, it required wit and skill, and it was potentially devious. I discovered to my delight that food companies had no interest in contesting a customer's claim; indeed, they were astonishingly eager to give me free product. In the next month I made claims for a new canister of Quaker Oatmeal (I had found a blackened oat in my oatmeal), a new six-pack of Coca-Cola (the soda in one of my cans had been suspiciously flat), and a new pint of Häagen-Dazs coffee ice cream (the flavor had been just slightly off in my last serving). All of my claims were met with solicitous reply mail and free stuff. What could be better?

It helped my good cheer that I didn't have the wide-angle view of the world necessary for a generalized ennui. By sixth grade, some of my classmates were starting to get that view, that understanding that some decisions have permanence, that although life is long the future can quickly be set in place, that one can do more than just live out one moment until the next arrives. Those classmates were the first to show signs of disaffection, even outright rebellion. A year or two later, in junior high, they would change their hairstyles and find music that suited their temperaments: angry metal, Goth despair-pop, decadent New Wave, whatever music seemed to them sufficiently jaded or weary. But I, after years of sadness, had just found a precariously balanced happiness, and I was not willing to ask any questions that might complicate my mood.

I did feel an occasional, barely perceptible envy. Some of my friends seemed to have found a passion. I liked pretending to be a sports commentator or writing letters to get free stuff, but I can't say that either activity excited me the way that playing baseball excited Derek or stage acting excited Wendy Burke, whom I met doing children's theater the summer after fifth grade. The mid-1980s were a time of fads, too, and my classmates always seemed to be feeding a new craving—Cabbage Patch Kids, Reeboks, sticker collecting—that I didn't feel. I was not interested in clothes or collectibles. I just loved the evanescent pleasure of using many words and using them well.

Although I didn't know it yet, there was an activity for young people like me. The next year, in seventh grade, I found it.

V

As the end of sixth grade approached, I discovered that I was afraid of Forest Park Junior High, my neighborhood school. Derek was already at Forest Park, and the talk I heard from him and his friends terrified me. They spoke of school dances where students necked under the bleachers; of notes passed in class conveying intelligence on who liked whom; and of study halls in the library during which students escaped behind bookshelves to continue what had begun under the bleachers at the dance. I was not ready for this scene.

I couldn't be sure that Wilbraham & Monson Academy, a hard-luck school for grades seven through twelve, would be less sexually pressurized, but it seemed a chance worth taking. Remembering that a boy a year ahead of me at New North had gone on to "the Academy," I asked my parents if I could apply. I arranged my own visit, picked the day for my tour, and went to classes with the old New North boy, T. J. Woodward. The junior high was the misbegotten afterthought of the school, just five rooms located in the basement of the main dormitory, and there were only about ten students each in the seventh and eighth grades. But it seemed less libidinous than the public junior high school, if only because there were fewer students per teacher and everyone seemed carefully watched over. I found that surveillance reassuring—less chance that couples would be making out all around me. As it happened, I matriculated with a class of seven boys and three girls, which nicely realized my hopes. With only three girls, there was no serious expectation that a boy would partner with any one of them.

There were two reasons besides the hoped-for gender dynamic that I was eager to attend the Academy. First, I would be allowed to take classes with the high school students—I could start algebra in seventh grade, for example. Second, and more important, the school had a dress code. Boys were required to wear a coat and tie, and girls wore skirts and blouses. When I first visited the Academy in sixth grade, it did not escape my attention that the boys were dressed like Alex P. Keaton and Alan Pinkard, my TV heroes. And the preppy aesthetic seemed to suggest a more civilized culture, perhaps one with a high regard for the spoken word. At the Academy I would find boys and girls like me, children for whom neither athletic prowess nor sexual precociousness, but rather eloquence and intellectual sophistication, were the measures of true worth.

When I arrived that fall, the classmates I actually got were mildly disappointing, too much like me in all the wrong, adolescent ways: confused, frightened, desperate for popularity but unsure how to attain it. And the boys, especially, complained incessantly about the dress code, which they honored as shabbily as possible, with ill-fitting blazers and indifferently knotted ties. The first month of school I walked around feeling faintly ridiculous, proud of my dapperness but embarrassed that I'd expected others to share my pride.

On the bright side, there was an Academy debate team. I knew about scholastic debate from *Family Ties*. ("Oh, we had a meeting at the debate club that ran a little long," Alex tells his father in one episode. "Kept arguing over what time to stop.") My first week at the Academy, checking the bulletin board for announcements of after-school activities, I saw that there was a debate team meeting that afternoon. It was meant for the high school, but middle schoolers were allowed to participate. So at three-fifteen I crossed Main Street to the high school side of campus, trudged up the tall hill, and presented myself in Mrs. Mercier's classroom in the basement of the small, redbrick building known as Old Academy.

The Academy was not a particularly good school. The small boarding population comprised many students who had been discipline cases at their old schools or who couldn't get along with their parents; still others were wealthy foreigners (a lot of Thai, I remember) sent abroad to improve their chances of acceptance by an American university. In general, you could say that some of the Academy's students were there because they were too good for their old school, more because they were too bad, and the rest because somebody, the child or the parent, had ambitions they felt the public schools couldn't support. We were not a student body with brilliant futures. But the ten other students who joined the debate team that fall—all from the high school, nearly all seniors—were among the most interesting characters on campus.

At the Academy, students were required to do some activity in the afternoon, and the debaters were all unified in not wanting to play sports. We were a diverse, eccentric bunch. Two seniors, Jeff Crane and Todd Sabin, were part of the school's small but enthusiastic heavy-metal clique. Jeff had shaggy blond hair down to his shoulders, Todd had beautifully feathered brown hair that hung down his back in a male version of the Farah Fawcett look on *Charlie's Angels*, and they could both be found between classes smoking in the school's regulated smoking area, a painted-white square in the corner of the parking lot next to Mattern Hall. Members of the class of 1987 were the last to be allowed to smoke, and they could do so only in that hundred-square-foot spot, and only if their parents had sent letters of permission to the dean. About twenty seniors had smoking permission, Jeff and Todd among them. They'd be there in the coldest weather, wearing denim jackets over their blazers, lip syncing to Jimi Hendrix. They wanted to *rock*, and they both knew they'd been born ten years too late.

There was another pair of allied seniors, and they prayed to a different rock god. Charles Wainwright IV was tall and thin like a pole, his hair was peroxide blond, and years later, when I became a Smiths fan, I recognized in what I remembered of Charles an aspiration to the asexual, or perhaps pansexual, decadence of Morrissey. Charles was pretty and worldly and bitchy. Marc Schlossberg was rounder, with reddish hair cut in the shelf style popular at the time: a bowl cut on top, with the few inches about the neck shaved close. He seemed slightly more punk than Charles, in a Mancunian way that makes me think he listened to Joy Division or, later on, the Stone Roses. But the best cultural referent for describing Charles and Marc is *Less than Zero* (the movie more than the book). Charles and Marc acted like the Andrew McCarthy character—bored, rich, distracted. They didn't seem to think anything mattered. During debate practice they sat next to each other, making catty comments and laughing silly laughs. They shared an '80s affectation that one doesn't see anymore, its dangerous edge rooted in an effeminacy that is no longer transgressive.

Todd and Jeff were nice in the way of headbangers, bikers, and truckers everywhere: they knew that people expected them to be rough and rude, and so they took an especial pleasure in being kindly. Marc was a follower, mild and blasé. Charles was cruel in the way of sissies who were once pummeled but now, through age and perseverance, have been freed from their own prison and can look around for revenge. I was twelve years old, they were seventeen. To spend afternoons with them . . . it was thrilling.

Mrs. Mercier, our coach, was an English teacher, very well read, and she spoke French, too. She was Catholic, and one got the feeling that she had been taught by nuns who had taken grammar seriously; for her, good English was a moral concern, for it led to clear thinking. And what was debate but clear thinking clearly expressed? In her classroom in the basement of the Old Academy, she somehow brought the headbangers, the rich bitches, the forgettable others, and the seventh-grader together in common purpose: thinking about big ideas.

Every two weeks we were paired in different teams of two and sent to the library to research a new topic. In the pre-Internet days this meant a bipartite division of efforts: one partner would look through the old, wooden card catalogs, finding the one or two books in the Academy library that pertained to the death penalty, abortion, or just-war theory, while the other partner would flip through the *Reader's Guide to Periodical Literature*, looking for germane, recent articles that could be found in the library's small magazine collection.

I remember how comfortable it was, freshly embarking on a new topic during the off weeks—the benevolent lulls in the cycle, the debate heats still a week in the future. In a time before the ubiquitous click-click of keyboards, with the library nearly empty, most of the student body on the playing fields, just our small corps pulling books and magazines from the stacks, poring over them at an oak table in the center of the room, whispering to each other and occasionally being hushed by the librarian, always in tones that modeled the proper degree of quiet, we slowly enlarged our knowledge, so that what had been a mystery on Monday was, by Friday, an area of mild competency—and, after the weekend, would become a locus of hard-earned opinion as we stood in the school chapel and fought for our sides in formal rounds of debate. Those off weeks were my first experience of the pleasures of slow, accumulated knowledge— what I imagined my parents and their friends possessed. I felt my mind stretching itself toward something like adult wisdom. I mimicked the gestures that I thought went along with my new, aspirational adulthood, taking a tactile pleasure in the business of going to and from the stacks, leaning over the table and flipping to the relevant page of a magazine, conferring with my debate partner of the week—Scott Dixon or Monica Maslowski or Joe Manuli—as I unbuttoned my top button and loosened my tie.

It was on those afternoons that I discovered *Vital Speeches, Facts on File, Who's Who*—those wonderful compendia that even today can distract me in a library; the sight of their bindings on a shelf draws me from whatever search I've come to do. It was also dur-

ing this time that I got to know the range of opinion magazines—
and that the *Nation* was more liberal than the *New Republic*, that
National Review was conservative and residually Catholic. I know
other former debaters who say the same thing: that these after-
school bursts of debate topic research were their earliest introduc-
tions to the country's intellectual scene.

It was a testament to Mrs. Mercier's calming influence, and to
her mastery of classroom dynamics, that I generally felt safe around
these much older students. But Charles soon had it in for me—more
than anyone since my old teacher Lisa—and Mrs. Mercier could not
always protect me. When the group was batting ideas back and forth,
Charles took particular pleasure in shooting me down, and he was
good at it. I don't remember his seeming particularly intellectual—I
am certain, based on his cultivated air of anomie, that he was at best
an average student—but he had a cutting wit and a perfected style
of condescension.

We'd be going around the table in Mrs. Mercier's classroom,
each student offering his own take on, say, what to do about welfare dependency. I'd say something like "The poor are victims of cir-
cumstance, and it would be unfair to cut their support, especially
because their children would suffer." And Charles would roll his eyes
and say, with an intentional, barely detectable lisp on the second
word, "Oh, *suffer* the children!" Everyone would laugh, even if none
of us really knew what he meant—an ignorance that of course added
to my mortification. Just like that, he had made me seem ridiculous.
He had not defeated my point, or even rendered it absurd. He had
just made me appear small.

I tried to fight back, in small ways. Once, after he had lobbed a bit
of ridicule at me, I decided not to look away. I stared at him, narrowing my gaze to let him know how I felt. Even after the laughter died
down and Mrs. Mercier was moving the discussion forward, I continued staring at Charles. He stared back at me. At first, I even tried
not to blink, but I quickly adjusted my expectations: I could blink,
so long as I otherwise held his gaze. He continued to hold mine. This

went on for about a minute. I knew I was losing. He had a hint of a smirk around his mouth, and the set of his red lips, which looked painted on, said that while this was life-and-death for me, it was just good fun for him. I tried to bow out manfully, by waiting until Mrs. Mercier had said something that I could plausibly respond to. I raised my hand—which must have looked strange, since my eyes were fixed on Charles, rather than on Mrs. Mercier at the end of the table—and when she called on me, I looked at her and began to speak.

Score one for him.

The only time we faced each other in an intramural debate, Charles destroyed me on cross-examination. We were debating the death penalty—it sometimes seems that most scholastic debates are about the death penalty—and I had been assigned the affirmative side, arguing in favor of it. The whole debate club had been preparing this topic for a month, and now we were in the school chapel, a Gothic structure with wooden pews, a carpeted altar, and a solid oak lectern from which we could speak. The two teams were sitting in the front pew, on opposite sides of the aisle, and the rest of the club was there as the audience, scattered throughout the cavernous room. I had just finished my speech, and Charles rose to cross-examine me. He ran his hand over the contours of his closely cropped, blonded hair, buttoned the top button of his blazer, and began to list men's names:

"Timothy Evans—do you know him?"

"No," I said.

"Joe Arridy—know him?"

"No." Where was he going with this?

"These men," Charles said, "are just two of the dozens of men in the twentieth century to have been conclusively exonerated after their executions. They were, Mr. Oppenheimer, wrongly convicted, and then killed by the state. Do you, Mr. Oppenheimer, want there to be more such men?"

"Well, I think those are exceptions and—"

"—just answer the question, Mr. Oppenheimer."

That contrivance, which we know so well from television courtroom dramas—"Just answer the question"—is actually not heard in the best high school or college debate. In front of a sophisticated audience, the questioner would seem afraid: What is it that he doesn't want the other speaker to say? Why the need to cut him off? What's more, it can be easily disarmed. The proper way to handle oneself under such questioning is to say what the questioner wants to hear, and say it proudly and vigorously—a technique I would master later, in high school. "Of course not!" I should have thundered back at Charles. "Wrongful convictions are a scourge!" And I should have added, "Surely we can agree on that much!" thereby suggesting that the questioner is suspect for asking so foolish a question— maybe *he* is the one who doesn't take the execution of innocent men seriously enough!

Instead, I fell into his trap: "No, but—" I said, allowing him to cut me off again with a curt *"Thank* you, Mr. Oppenheimer. We have your answer." And then he sat down, while I stood pouting, all eyes on me. It was about five seconds before I sat, and during that time it was as if I were on display as Exhibit A, the Defeated Debater.

Yet even as I was being undone by Charles Wainwright IV, I was excited in defeat. I wanted to keep debating. I wanted revenge against Charles, I wanted to win back Mrs. Mercier's respect, I wanted to show that I was nobody's little pushover. I wanted to be good at this. Above all I just wanted to keep going. I wanted to accrue many more debate memories, so that this one humiliation became just a sorry prelude to a long, grand career. This was what I was made to do.

With Thanksgiving vacation and the end of the fall term came the end of intramural debate club. When we came back to school in December, only four of us signed up for debate again, but now we constituted a traveling varsity team. Winter was the season for the Connecticut Valley Debate League, which held meets every Wednesday afternoon for three months at schools up and down the Connecticut River. The Academy was the only traditional prep school in the league; our opponents included public schools such as Holyoke High, East Longmeadow High, Chicopee High, and its rival, Chicopee Comprehensive, as well as Catholic schools such as Holyoke Catholic.

The Connecticut Valley league was in many ways typical of debate leagues across the country, peopled by striving boys with suitcases and the prim, officious girls they dated (think of the Reese Witherspoon character in the movie *Election*). In solo oratory there can be suavity, but not in debate—there is too much emphasis on winning, and winning, at least in American debate, depends on a fastidious, neurotic attention to detail. Debate rarely looks effortless, unless there is an extreme mismatch between the two sides. When all four debaters in a round are skilled, they talk fast, they grimace, and they obviously care who wins. Debaters are not, cannot be, *cool*. Even at an elite, academically competitive school, the most popular kids are never debaters; it is just not an elegant way to pass one's extracurricular hours.

Our debate league was independent, not part of either of the two big national organizations, the National Forensic League and the National Catholic Forensic League. But for this independence, I probably would have hated debate, and my life from junior high through college would have turned out very different. This is because the big national leagues use a style called "policy debate," a variant of the "Oregon style," codified by J. Stanley Gray, the University of Oregon debate coach in the 1920s. In Oregon-style debate, there are two teams, an affirmative and a negative, each with two debaters. The First Affirmative speaks for about eight minutes (more or less, depending on league rules), arguing in favor of the resolution. He or she is followed by the First Negative, then the Second Affirmative, then the Second Negative. After each person speaks, there is a brief period of cross-examination, when the speaker is questioned by the opposing debater who is not due to give his own speech next. In other words, after the First Affirmative speaks, he is grilled by the Second Negative; then the First Negative gives his speech. And so forth. At the end, each speaker has a few minutes to give a closing argument, or rebuttal. Every speaker thus gets to speak twice, be cross-examined once, and cross-examine an opposing speaker once. This style worked well for fifty years, but beginning in the early 1970s policy debaters—as they call themselves in the large national leagues—changed it to something hardly recognizable as debate: in order to cram in as many different arguments as possible, policy debaters now talk superfast, pausing every few sentences for a deep breath and then starting again at top speed. What's more, they use jargon, like *DA* or *disad* for *disadvantage*, that makes their debates indecipherable to the nondebater, and even to someone like me, a debater not used to their style.

Although it used the Oregon style, the Connecticut Valley Debate League, being independent, was free of policy debaters' overlay of fast talking and jargon. We didn't attend the big national tournaments where judges had come to expect the dozens of arguments per speech that speed-talking made possible. We were never infected with those bad habits from other parts of the country. Our debates thus sounded radically different from most American interscholastic debates: they were intelligible to anyone who happened by.

In the winter of 1986–87, the league's topic, which we debated twice every Wednesday afternoon, was the desirability of the Strategic Defense Initiative, the "Star Wars" missile-defense system about which President Reagan was so enthusiastic. My partner, Todd, the long-haired dude with the nicotine habit, and I were on the negative side, opposing Star Wars. Todd and I had nothing in common, and he was five years of hard living ahead of me, but we both sincerely believed in our side, which isn't necessary but does help.

As a debate round began, Todd and I would be seated on one side of a classroom, our desks pushed together, facing our two opponents sitting across the room. The judge, a coach from a neutral school, would be seated at the back. After the judge called the round to order, the First Affirmative, from the other school, would stand up, walk to the front of the room, his or her back to the blackboard, and read a prepared eight-minute speech in favor of Star Wars. "Good afternoon," he or she would say, "friends, colleagues, and of course Honored Judge." He or she would then launch into the definition of the terms, a set piece that, according to the rules, is the First Affirmative's responsibility: "We are here to debate the resolution, 'Resolved: That the United States should invest significant funding in the Strategic Defense Initiative.' As is my duty as First Affirmative, I will begin by defining the terms. By *United States* we mean the government of the United States. By *significant* we mean a lot. By *funding* we mean money." And so it would go, the First Affirmative finishing the definitions and then listing, in the six or so minutes remaining, enough horrifying facts about Soviet expansionism to make the case for a missile-defense system. Then I would cross-examine the First Affirmative speaker for three minutes, after which Todd would walk to the front of the room and read his prepared speech.

Todd's speech never varied, no matter what the First Affirmative had said. Mrs. Mercier made Todd the First Negative, and me Second Negative, because going later in the round is more improvisational. The more people who have already spoken, the better the odds that the round has been sidetracked into new territory, or is off on an unexpected tangent. For a good analogy, think of a courtroom: the opening arguments are easier, for both lawyers, than the closing arguments. A lawyer has all the time in the world to prepare an opening, but perhaps only hours, at most a day or two, to prepare the closing, which must sum up a much greater body of material. Some high school debaters and coaches do argue that the better speaker should go first because the first impression is so important, and if the two partners are almost equally good, that may be right. But when there's a real mismatch in skill, most will agree that you should put the lesser debater first, so he can always use a prepared speech, and save the better debater for last.

Nobody in the league expected me and Todd to win much. To begin with, the Academy was new to the league; we had no reputation preceding us. Moreover, my partner, like many bikers, metalheads, and other toughs who cultivate an angry look, was basically shy. He mumbled, too, and as a supremely nice guy had no killer instinct. He was a late '60s, Hendrix-burning-the-guitar metalhead, in love with the beauty and power of music; he walked around with an intense but absentminded stare, his eyes dreamily focused far away, as if always wondering what guitar chord would be the perfect accompaniment to the moment at hand. He was smart, and in our last debate of the season, with weeks of practice behind him, he outscored me in our best round. But for most of the season he seemed ill suited to a rapid-fire contest of verbal wits.

And nobody looked at me and figured I'd be much of a threat. In a league of high schools, the Academy was the only school with a junior high as well, so I was the only twelve-year-old in sight. I was also a particularly short twelve-year-old, still three years away from a meager growth spurt, so I basically came across as a ten-year-old kid. With his long hair, ragged clothes, tobacco odor, and low, sultry voice, Todd was the recalcitrant hood whom teachers figured they'd hate; I looked like the teacher's pet, or maybe the teacher's windup doll. We were an unlikely combination, and when we started winning I half suspected that it was on shock value alone.

But it surely helped that I was a very advanced talker. "Our opposition has presented what seems to be a very tight case today," I would say, addressing the judge. "But on close inspection, we will see that not all is according to Hoyle." From that point on, it never mattered that I had slightly misused "according to Hoyle," or that I would go on to misuse "Hobson's choice." It would be years before I knew that the biblical *Job* was not pronounced *job*. But in the Connecticut Valley Debate League, I managed to impress people as a surprising, precocious, pocket-sized curio of an intellectual. "Our opposition might want to consider the notion of *stare decisis*," I would say, "a notion very well ratified by the Supreme Court." (Well, true enough, sort of, though oddly put.) The judges, some of them barely out of college and many of them lured into coaching by the meager bit of extra pay, nodded with approval. I did my research, had good quotations from reputable magazines to back up what I said, and so generally had our team in good shape by the end of my speech. If Todd was on his game, we had a pretty good shot.

As the season wore on, two teams developed reputations and got whispered about in the halls between matches. One was me and Todd. According to the growing lore, I was a boy genius and he was a mad, drug-addled genius. The other team was a boyfriend and girlfriend from East Longmeadow High School. East Longmeadow is a middle-class town, less wealthy than Longmeadow but a big step up from Springfield, Agawam, or Chicopee. This twosome carried themselves as if they were the debutante of the ball and her escort. Her haircut and perm, though probably purchased for ten dollars at the Eastfield Mall, looked more big-city and fashionable than any of the other girls', and he wore a suit rather than a blazer and pleated khakis. Between rounds, they could be seen ducking into small alcoves between rows of lockers to steal twenty or thirty seconds of deep tongue-kissing. I remember once hurrying late to a round, half walking and half running, and it was only once I had blown past the gap in the lockers that the smell of her perfume hit me, and with it a realization of what I had subliminally caught in my peripheral vision: the two of them jammed into each other, his hands on the back of her head, pulling her to him tightly. I got excited, then confused, and forgot my room assignment.

Todd and I weren't scheduled to face the East Longmeadow duo until early February, near the end of the season. So I had time to ask around about their case, and their badly beaten opponents were eager to give us as many pointers as they could. "Read Ben Nova," one victim of their onslaught told me. "They quote a lot of Ben Nova." I consulted with other teams who had lost to East Longmeadow, and there was a consensus: Ben Nova was their main source, and if we could impeach his expertise, we might prevail.

So in the week before our East Longmeadow match, I set out to research this Ben Nova. I had not planned to dive back into the book stacks; between Thanksgiving and Christmas, before we returned in

January to begin the season, I had researched the topic carefully, and I had note cards filled with facts, figures, and quotations from *Time*, *Newsweek*, the *Economist*, the *New York Times*, and even government research papers that I had gotten by calling my congressman and asking an aide to send me everything they had on Star Wars. In high school debate, all facts tend to be treated with equal seriousness, and so long as you have a bit of research to rebut your opponent's research, the judge doesn't care if his is from the *Times* and yours is from *National Review*. So you pile it on.

Yet in all the clippings and photocopied encyclopedia articles we had found before the season, there was no Ben Nova. The government directories listed no staffer named Ben Nova. The card catalog at the Academy had no books by Ben Nova. When I went to Waldenbooks, they found no Ben Nova in *Books in Print*. Yet I was quite certain that Ben Nova was the name I had been given. He was apparently a world-renowned expert on the Strategic Defense Initiative—so why did he seem not to exist? Was it possible that the East Longmeadow team had *invented* him? If I could prove that, we'd definitely score an upset.

When the day came to face East Longmeadow, I put on my double-breasted Saks Fifth Avenue blazer, a blue button-down Oxford cloth shirt, and my yellow power tie with black polka dots. I tapped my foot nervously throughout the school day, and I didn't notice when my teachers called on me in class. In my mind, the season had come down to that afternoon's match. Todd and I had already lost twice, and at 9–2 the best finish we could hope for was third. With two matches to go, we could stretch to 11–2. But there were two undefeated teams left (East Longmeadow was one of them), and they were facing each other in the final week, meaning that one of them, at least, was guaranteed at worst a 12–1 finish, which we could not equal. So I was playing for the glory of the underdog. If we won, I would be the boy who brought down East Longmeadow.

And my partner's well-known lassitude would only increase my glory—I would be the pint-sized hero who single-handedly defeated the slickest, most polished team in the league, overcoming the debility of having a slacker for a partner. I would, at last, be praised for my ability to talk, celebrated for it even, like the boys I admired on the television shows that I watched. I would be like Alex P. Keaton in his jacket and tie, arguing politics and becoming famous for it.

But to do this, it would help to know: Who the hell was Ben Nova?

That afternoon, in an overheated classroom at Minnechaug Regional High School, the boy from East Longmeadow stood up to give the First Affirmative speech. He was genial, with a big smile that surely had won him many class officer elections at his school. "Good afternoon," he began, "friends, colleagues, and of course most worthy, wise, honored judge." Worthy *and* wise *and* honored? Smiley Boy said the words slowly, laying it on thick. After defining the terms, he listed his goal for the case—to make America safer—and began to give three arguments for why Star Wars was needed. And sure enough, there was that name, that mysterious source we had been warned about. Except this great expert, the one he seemed to quote every ten seconds to prove the incontrovertible need for a missile-defense system—and the obvious truth that the technology existed to build an effective one—was named not Ben Nova but Ben *Bova*.

As First Negative, I did not get to cross-examine the boy. That job fell to Todd, who did not seem to be taking any notes about what questions to ask. Usually I could manage to think up three or four good questions to write down and pass him on a piece of paper. Against most opponents, my questions were good enough to fluster the bewildered boys and girls who never really understood the speeches their coaches had written for them. But Smiley Face—he looked unflappable. So, on a hunch, I wrote down just one question to slide across our table to Todd. "Ask him," I wrote, "who the hell is Ben Bova?"

The boy from East Longmeadow finished his speech—"For all these reasons, Judge, we ask for a decision in the affirmative"—and sat down. He immediately turned to his girlfriend, and in his hopeful eyes I saw that he sought her approval, not the other way around.

She put her hand on his and squeezed. He took a sip from his can of Tab and waited out Todd's thirty seconds of prep time before the cross-examination began. When the time was up, Todd stood, and so did our nemesis. Todd's face was barely visible behind his curtain of long brown hair, and before he spoke he cleared his throat, hocking up a nice loogie of cigarette phlegm. In his skinny tie, thrift-store tweed jacket, and work boots, he looked like a worker trying to get up the courage to challenge the boss.

"Hello," Todd said at last. He was holding the note card on which I had written his one question, and was squinting at it as if he had already forgotten what it said.

"Hello," the boy replied, with a heavy top note of smarm.

"Um, so, I have a question."

"Yes, please."

"Who is Ben Bova?"

"*Well*," our opponent began, as if he had been asked that question in every prior round and had finally perfected his response, "as I said, Mr. Bova is the author of *Assured Survival: Putting the Star Wars Defense in Perspective*, a book released in 1984 by the publisher Tor. It was well received and a bestseller. Mr. Bova is also the author of many books, and he holds degrees from leading universities."

"Is he a scientist?" Todd improvised. It was a good question.

"Well, he's a leading scientific expert."

"But is he an expert on, um, Star Wars?"

"The Strategic Defense Initiative? Yes he is, he is an expert. He has done an extraordinary amount of research and he is one of the leading experts on it."

"How do you know?"

"It's well-known. It's—it's just a fact. He's very famous, you know."

And so it went for three minutes, Todd trying vainly to crack Smiley Boy's crunchy, moussed outer shell. I might have passed him the note card with the initial question, but I soon realized that Todd hadn't needed it. He'd smelled this guy's rotten inner core from the start, with the heightened sensitivity that the criminal has for the narc. Todd had been picked on and kicked around and condescended to by enough self-satisfied preppies that he knew them better than they knew themselves, and he knew this one was a phony. Ben Nova, Ben Bova—whoever it was, it didn't sound right.

But Todd couldn't quite break this guy. If he had broken him, we would have learned what I learned years later, when I began thinking back over my debate career. By this time there was an Internet, and I wasn't dependent on the bookstore at the mall or our poorly stocked school library. It was easy to discover that Ben Bova is indeed a prolific author . . . but mainly of science fiction. He held no advanced degree, although years later he got a doctorate from California Coast University, "a pioneer in distance learning since its founding in 1973." Yes, he is the author of *Assured Survival: Putting the Star Wars Defense in Perspective*, but if Todd or I had known better we would have revealed that for what it was, not a scientific treatise but an amateur's enthusiastic tract.

Smiley Boy and his girlfriend beat us, although not as badly as I had feared. They were the Connecticut Valley champions that winter, and at the awards banquet they celebrated by holding their trophy aloft and giving each other a quick but energetic kiss on the lips. I wondered, twelve-year-old that I was, if the kiss was long enough, and if their mouths had opened wide enough, for tongue.

The debate season ended in late February, and after the school's March break we returned to rosebuds and melted snow. Fall term seemed far gone. But I still remembered how Charles Wainwright IV had humiliated me, and I wanted revenge. Unfortunately, the most convenient way to get it entailed a regression to my fifth-grade self.

The *Atlas*, the Academy's official student newspaper, was dry and safe, basically an advertisement for the school's sports teams. All the action was in the *Beast*, an anonymously produced two-page broadsheet featuring satirical articles, parodies of the *Atlas*, and a gossip column that printed items dropped in the cardboard box on top of the radiator in the foyer of the library. For one day every two weeks, when stacked copies of the new *Beast* appeared in front of the dining hall, the Academy became a school in love with reading. Groups of students crowded together over lunch tables, straining to read a copy someone had just brought in. The items were contributed anonymously, but no real effort was made to conceal the identities of those being talked about. All that was omitted was a last name: "JAMES, you're looking even heavier—lay off the extra Jell-O in the dining hall!" "AMY, you're so hot. Why do you date that loser??"

I didn't have any crushes to announce, but I did have an injury to nurse. Soon, every issue carried some taunt, submitted anonymously by me, directed at Charles, who had been so mean to me the previous fall and who continued to mock me every chance he got: winking at me in hallways, smiling devilish smiles. One item referenced his close friendship with another senior, Tony: "CHARLES, are you and Tony JUST friends?" Tony was the most effeminate man at school, a regular user of mascara and eyeliner who wore a long black overcoat that he buttoned up to the top and cinched tight with a belt around the waist. Tony was very nice to me whenever I saw him, which was usually when he was walking with Charles, my nemesis. From a hundred feet away I would see the two of them coming, and I would know what to expect. As I passed them, Charles would say "Hi, *Oppy*," showing a mock affection, and then Tony would give me an understanding look and say, "Hey, Mark." That always made me feel better.

Why was I gay-baiting Charles? Lots of reasons. It was 1987, before good liberal kids knew that homophobia was as bad as racism and sexism. And I hated Charles. And I was twelve.

Still, I wish I could take it back.

Although I don't know how he knew, Charles knew that the anonymous slurs were coming from me, and two weeks before his graduation he got his revenge. Running through the middle of campus was a small brook, no more than five feet across and a couple of feet deep, called the Rubicon, into which Academy students were occasionally thrown as part of one sports team initiation or another. But it was also the chief site for the ritual humiliation of geeks, dweebs, losers, nerds, and poindexters, so I tried not to walk too close to its banks. One day, as I was walking toward Rich Hall, a building at least one hundred yards from the Rubicon, I felt myself hugged from behind and lifted off the ground, and then I heard the familiar refrain: "Hi, *Oppy*." As Charles turned around and began to carry me across Main Street, I was surprised by how much strength he had in his thin arms. He had pulled my arms tight to my sides, and after struggling briefly I realized there was no way I could get out. So I took to verbal persuasion: "Come on Charles, what's the big idea? I mean, what are you doing? Okay, just stop it, all right? Whatever it is I did to upset you, please just put me down, all right? Put me down! Okay, you *asshole*, put me down!"

"But *Oppy*," he said, in his queeny voice, "I *love* you. I'm *gay*, you know, and I want to *fuck* you, Oppy. You know me so well, Oppy, and now it's happening, at *last*!"

"What are you talking about?"

"Now *Oppy*, let's not pretend you don't know what I'm talking about! I *love* you, Oppy!"

It wasn't until we had crossed the street and begun our march toward the Rubicon that I noticed the cheering section following us. About five other seniors were walking behind and to the other side of Charles, laughing at every comment he made and at my desperate, fruitless bursts of struggle. When we finally got to the Rubicon, two of them came around to face me and each one grabbed a leg. As Charles held my arms and his two henchmen held tight to my legs, they swung me three times and finally let go. Somehow I managed to partially right myself in midair, so that as I hit the water my legs and knees got below my torso. I landed upright, more or less, drenched below my waist. As Charles and his friends walked away, cackling wickedly, he called after me one last time, "Oppy, I *love* you!"

I was fully prepared to avoid Charles until his graduation, knowing that when I returned to school in the fall he would be gone from my life forever. My father, ever the lawyer for the little guy, had a different plan.

"I have an idea," he told me in his office, where I was hanging out one afternoon, a couple of days after the incident. His shirtsleeves were rolled up and his tie was loosened—the exact picture I have of him at the end of a day's work.

"What's that?" I said.

"We should sue him."

"Sue who?"

"The guy who threw you in the river—what's his name?"

"Charles."

"Charles. We should sue him, and we should sue the school for not doing anything about it."

My father then told me about the conversation he had had with J. William LaBelle, the dean of students at the Academy. He had called Dean LaBelle and explained what had happened to me. LaBelle had promised to talk to Charles about it, and he had called my father back later in the day. There was, he'd told my father, not much he could do. Charles was a senior, he was graduating, he was done with his exams. A suspension wouldn't mean much. The dean was sorry for what had happened to me, but there just wasn't anything to do.

This professed impotence in the face of injustice infuriated my father. If there was one thing he hated, it was a bully, and to his mind the test of an institution was whether it sided with the victim. His son was young and small and had been humiliated by a pack of bigger, older boys, and there had to be a proper response to that.

"We could sue for pain and suffering," my father said to me.

"Well . . ." I thought it over for ten seconds. "I don't think so. Let's just let it be."

"You'd get the money," my father said. He was really hoping I'd agree to sue, or else he would never have goaded me with the promise of material rewards. He was a deeply unacquisitive soul.

"No. No, let's just let it be. He's graduating. It's fine."

My father shrugged. "Okay." He started to roll down his sleeves.

Next he would put on his blue blazer and drive us home, where I would try to screw up the courage to tell him why I really didn't want to sue. I felt terrible that he had gone to all this trouble, calling the dean and then beginning work on a legal plan of attack. Because if he had known why Charles had made a victim of me, he would not have been so quick to leap to his son's defense. I was worse than a normal criminal: I was a recidivist, a backslider. It was two years since the episodes with the notes and the child-abuse hotline, and in the meantime I had tried to be a scrupulously good child. My gossip items in the *Beast*, the bit of criminality for which Charles had exacted vigilante justice, scared me now, because as I looked backward a few months after the commission of the acts, I realized that here I was again, back in the aftermath of a spate of ill-considered cleverness: me and my poisonous pen, causing mischief, hurting people. Charles was a bad guy, but that did not make it any better.

Back at home, a few minutes before dinner was ready, I took my father aside and told him that I had been dishonest. He asked me what I'd been dishonest about.

"Remember when I said I didn't know why Charles had thrown me in the Rubicon? That wasn't true. It was because of notes I had put in this newspaper about him." I tried to explain it all—Charles's having been mean to me in the fall, the *Beast*, the anonymous gossip items. By the end of my rambling description, I think he understood, more or less. He filled his cheeks with air and blew out slowly, his all-purpose gesture of befuddlement bordering on exasperation.

"Well, thanks for telling me," he said. And we left it at that.

In the fall of my eighth-grade year I returned to school with a sense of liberation, the fruit of knowing what to expect. I'd survived the first year. Charles was gone. And I had made a good friend who, although not on the debate team, shared my love of verbal conflict: Jim Cherry, an avowed Republican in the class ahead of me. The son of schoolteachers from nearby Somers, Connecticut, Jim was a fellow committed preppy, from his penny loafers to his tweed jackets; he was the only other boy I knew who enjoyed, rather than resented, the school's dress code. In addition to being aesthetic soulmates, we shared a love of politics. This was the end of the Reagan era, and Jim and I would hang out in his bedroom, play video golf on his Apple IIe, and debate the wisdom of purging single mothers from the welfare rolls. As he issued proclamations about the virtues of the free market and Democrats' unfitness to govern, Jim had a blithe confidence in his persona. He did for the political geek what Jason Bateman on *It's Your Move* had done for the high school practical jokester: he took a nerdy type and made it cool.

Jim played soccer in the fall, so he couldn't join the debate club, but I signed up again, excited to meet the new prospects. The club had lost almost all its members to graduation, a fact that pleased me more than I'd expected. It was a relief that Charles and Marc were gone, of course. But I was surprised to find myself equally relieved that the metalheads were gone, too. Todd and Jeff, as classmates of Charles and Marc, had reached an accommodation with them over the years; I realized that even if they had never joined in the cruelty toward me, they had offered passive, tacit acceptance. Maybe they were just too out of it to care one way or the other, but they were part of a senior class that I had learned to fear, and it was freeing to walk around campus never seeing any of them. It was a sign, too, that I was a year older. I was coming up in the world.

The debaters that fall were an easier group for me to be around. Juniors and seniors mostly, none of them was especially close to any of the others; they all seemed unsure of what they were doing in debate, as if they had found their way there not through any anti-sports ethos, or burnout solidarity, but just because they couldn't figure out what else to do with their autumn afternoons. They included Elke Marosits, a pretty, silent girl with blown-dry blond hair; Scott Pinstein, one of the first teenage boys I knew to wear a stud in his left earlobe, a style that somehow looked very tough on him; Peter Juliak, who as a seventh-grader made me feel like an old hand; and Scott Dixon, a senior and the Academy's leading thespian.

By nature Scott Dixon was an actor, not a debater; the Academy put up plays only in the winter, so in the fall debate was the most performative activity he could find to fill his afternoons. He didn't care about debate, not the way I did. But in his indifference he still influenced me: the best debaters are both thinkers and performers, and while I'd met some thinkers, Scott was the first pure performer I'd ever met. He was jolly, with a rubbery face, like Jim Carrey's or Bill Irwin's, capable of a whole range of theatrical affects: sorrow, delight, skepticism, condescension, amusement, and the most ego-shriveling disdain. In so many ways—telling a joke, needling Mrs. Mercier for her insistence on perfect grammar, doing a flawless imitation of a classmate who had cut debate that day—Scott made us laugh. He did voices, he did accents, he punned. Once he had the whole group going on fish puns: "What's that tuna you just played on your guitar? *Cod*, that was awful!" But he was never mean. The few times we sparred in intramural debates that fall, Scott cracked jokes only at his own expense.

Scott was the first person to teach me, by example, that persuasion is more an art than a science, and that the art relies more on being well liked than on being well read. When Scott did debate, even in these intramural club rounds, everyone wanted him to win. He was very smart, but it wouldn't have been fatal if he were not: flaws in his reasoning could be overlooked, incorrect facts could be forgiven or assumed to be misheard. After all, this was *Scott*! When I debated, it was as if I were in a tight jacket and everyone was waiting for me to pop a button; when Scott debated, he was in a roomy robe, comfortable with himself and comfortable to look at, and people assumed he had all sorts of tricks up his sleeve. He knew intuitively what our president at the time, the former actor, also knew: people vote for the man, not the argument.

I had, I believed, found my partner for the upcoming interscholastic season; if I could go 9–4 debating with Todd, just think what I could do with Scott. We would vanquish all comers. But shortly before Thanksgiving break, Mrs. Mercier received word from the league secretary that there would be no Connecticut Valley debates in the winter of 1987–88. For reasons that were never explained to her, the league was on hiatus. I tried out for the school play instead, and I was cast in a small role; I liked acting, and now I was meeting a whole new group of students from the upper school, which was exciting. But I missed debate.

In April, my French teacher, Mr. Richards, called me into his office to say that it would be a waste for me to remain at the Academy for high school. The Academy, he said, was a mediocre place and not getting any better. He was leaving for a job at St. George's School, in Newport, Rhode Island, and I should get out, too. He thought he could get me into Andover, the famous prep school, which he had attended and where his parents still worked. I should think seriously about his offer, he said. And I should have my parents come talk to him.

There must have been some panic afoot, some reason for the administration to fear that students and teachers were about to defect in droves, because the same week that Mr. Richards told me to flee, my English teacher told our class, apropos of nothing, that "great things" were in the works for the Academy, and that those of us who stuck around would be there for an exciting time. It was strange, because no one had said anything about leaving, and most of my classmates looked no further into the future than next weekend, when Jeff Lavoie's older brother might buy them some packs of smokes. The word must have come down at some faculty meeting that students were to be urged to stay. But Mr. Richards was fed up with the school and had decided to tell his favorite students what he thought.

At Yale, my father had known many alumni of top New England boarding schools, and he had not held them in very high regard; they were, he thought, preppy kids from the right families, not necessarily very industrious or intellectual. Still, Mr. Richards convinced him that the Academy would not serve me well and that any number of New England schools—like Andover, Exeter, or Deerfield—would be better fits. I told my father, when we spoke later that day, that I agreed. I had noticed that some of the best young teachers, like Mr. Richards, were going elsewhere. And as I looked at the seniors, four years above me, I noticed that even the smartest of them did not seem to be going to colleges I had heard of. Why were *none* of them bound for the Ivy League or Stanford or the University of Chicago?

But the schools that Mr. Richards had mentioned to my father were all far away, especially by New England standards. Residents of Dallas or Los Angeles might think nothing of a thirty-mile commute, but my parents were not going to drive forty minutes each way to Deerfield Academy, north of us in Massachusetts. Andover was close to two hours away, Exeter farther still. And I did not want to leave home, even if my family could have found the money. I knew that I was young in precisely the ways that would make boarding life difficult. I was still afraid of drinking, morally opposed to smoking, and intimidated by girls. At one of the two junior high dances the Academy sponsored during my two years, I pretended to have injured my leg earlier in the day, so I would have an excuse not to dance.

I was, I think, generally afraid of experience. Today, whenever I hear an Aerosmith song on the radio, I think back to the summer of '87, when Mike Kalish, whom I met at a three-week day camp at the Jewish Community Center, invited me to go see Aerosmith in concert. Mike's dad owned a local car dealership that sponsored concerts, and Mike, a big rock-and-roll fan, had made sure his dad sponsored this one. I wasn't much for hard rock—the poppy Aerosmith of the *Permanent Vacation* album seemed really, really hard to me—but "Rag Doll" was on the radio and MTV all the time, and I had to admit, it was catchy. But when Mike told me he had an extra ticket to the Aerosmith concert at the Springfield Civic Center on the first of November, I immediately said, "I think I'm busy that night." He looked puzzled. "You already know you're busy on November 1?" he said. Yeah, I told him, I was sure of it, I was busy. I couldn't tell him the truth, which was that being around all those kids who smoked and drank, and especially their loose-looking metal-chick girlfriends, scared me. Eight months later, thinking about boarding school, I got scared in the same way. Too dangerous.

The only school on Mr. Richards's list that was less than half an hour from home was the Loomis Chaffee School, a boarding and day school in Windsor, Connecticut. It was already April, past the application deadline, but my parents made an appointment for a tour. I had my parents call the Academy to say I was sick—some gasp of loyalty within me didn't want the dean to know that I was considering a defection—and we drove twenty miles south, across the border, to visit Loomis.

And I loved it, loved everything about it. The students had the confident look of people who would go on to good colleges. They were more attractive than Academy students, and within their more relaxed dress code—no jacket required, but no jeans allowed—Loomis students seemed to wear their clothes languorously and confidently, like gentlemen and ladies. I sat in on two classes, and I could tell, listening to these boys and girls speak, that they had done the reading. They were educated, or they aspired to be. A tousle-haired kid in khakis, wearing a Patagonia fleece to ward off the early spring chill, reading a translation of the *Iliad* while hurrying late to class: that's who I wanted to be.

At the end of the day, I had an interview with Fred Seebeck, an English teacher, water polo coach, and part-time admission officer who three years later would be my dean. Loomis had theater, he told me. And good sports teams. "Chess?" I asked. No, he said, but I could always start a club. "Debate?" Yes, he said, a very good debate program.

At the end of the interview we walked out of his office to meet my parents. The freshman class was already filled, Mr. Seebeck cautioned them. We were late in the process. But, he added, with what I thought was a wink, a spot for a day student might open up over the summer. I should definitely apply. He couldn't make any promises, but he had a good feeling about me.

VI

My first month as a freshman at Loomis, I was enraptured. I was busier than I had ever been, more tired, and getting worse grades, but I didn't care. At the Academy I had been the best student in the middle school, winning the prize in every subject area at eighth-grade graduation, while at Loomis I would never, ever be the best student—Harry Tsai was taking calculus as a freshman! But there was so much here besides schoolwork. I was the only freshman cast in the fall play, *The Foreigner*, and I got to spend the next three months rehearsing with sophisticated, upper-class cast mates like David Case and the very beautiful Kristin Lowe. David was a hilarious, self-deprecating theater nerd who complained about how pretty girls always went for "athletes with big dicks"; Kristin was the kind of pretty girl he had in mind, except that she was very sweet and didn't seem to be dating anybody. I struggled with my Algebra II class, and I was scared to ask for help from Mr. Haller, an old-fashioned bachelor schoolmaster with a terrier named Taffy, who accompanied him everywhere. Mr. Haller posted the completed Sunday *Times* crossword puzzle on his bulletin board every Monday, and he once told me that in the 1960s he had left the teaching of history, his original subject, because students had begun demanding to know "why" things happened. In Mr. Knapp's English class, I got my first ever B, complained after class, and was told in no uncertain terms that work that cut it in junior high wouldn't cut it here.

My new schoolmates seemed like graduates of some special training camp to which I had not been invited. For one thing, they were as attractive as the people I'd remembered from my campus visit the previous spring: fit, clear-skinned, always smiling. Students at the Academy had worn clothes that expressed disdain—they told the school what they thought of its dress code by barely staying within it—but fashion at Loomis was more enthusiastic, in an unabashedly preppy way. Instead of cheap J. C. Penney blazers, Loomis boys wore thoroughly broken-in, wrinkled khakis, L. L. Bean moccasins, frayed Oxford cloth shirts, fisherman's sweaters, and those peculiarly named official shoes of prepdom, the blucher and the Weejun. There were a few sartorial rebels, the occasional Goth or Deadhead, but their ensembles, too, were carefully chosen, meant to flatter. And people stood taller, literally—there was no desultory slouching. Holly Mason, a junior whom I met on Student Council, had the most graceful posture I had ever seen. Perfect hair, too, and an easy, unhurried walk. I imagined that anyone who could date her would be instantly happy.

At the time, I was so glad to be at a place that encouraged success, where doing the work was expected and even the wisenheimers were quietly admired, that I didn't care about, or even notice, the contradictions and hypocrisies of prep school life—the absurdity, for example, that tattered pants and wrinkled shirts were signifiers of privilege, or that it was cool to wear old shoes held together with brightly colored gaffing tape. Only those with enviable class prerogative could have the audacity to assume that others would understand their upside-down system, in which poor stood for rich, dishevelment was cultivated, and one was attentive to looking indifferent. But everyone there seemed to get it, no matter one's origins. Loomis drew boarders from around the country, and its day-student openings were coveted in the wealthy Hartford suburbs, where lawyers, doctors, and insurance barons moved "for the good public schools" that they hoped their sons and daughters would not have to attend. So my freshman classmates entered prep school already prepared: by the "pre-prep" elementary and junior high schools, such as Renbrook and Cardigan Mountain; by the soccer and lacrosse summer camps where they had honed their skills; and by the suburban social education that had taught them how to be ambitious without letting it show. They were especially gifted at leisure. On the main quadrangle on a sunny fall day, somebody would place his stereo speakers in his dormitory window and blast, say, Bob Marley's album *Legend* onto the courtyard, and the students below would bob their heads to the bass line as they studied. Boys would lie faceup on the green grass as their girls lay perpendicular to them, heads on the boys' stomachs, squinting at Signet editions of Shakespeare held up with two hands to block the sun.

I didn't even think about debate until October. Life seemed so full. The play was rehearsing two hours every afternoon, and I was slowly learning to manage the four hours of homework every night. So it was a small shock one Friday to pick up the *Daily Bulletin* to read a tiny item that said, "ATTENTION DEBATERS: First meeting of the year today after lunch in Gilchrist Auditorium—we'll talk about teams for this Sunday's practice tournament. For information see Mr. Robison, B. J. Chisholm or Kevin Moran."

That afternoon, like every day that year, I had lunch in the New Dining Hall, where freshmen and sophomores typically ate. (This was an unspoken rule, enforced entirely by tradition: juniors, seniors, and any underclass girl who was dating a junior or senior boy ate in the Old Dining Hall, a dark, oaken room whose windows faced the picturesque Quad, the heart of the campus; freshmen and sophomores ate in the New Dining Hall, which looked new and somewhat cheaper and faced the campus's less attractive buildings.) After I had bused my tray, I nervously approached a table of sophomores and asked where Gilchrist Auditorium was. "Science building," one of them said, and pointed through the wall of glass windows at the south end of the dining hall. After I arrived at Clark Science Center and found my way to Gilchrist, I poked my head nervously through the doors, saw about half a dozen students standing around a bearded, rabbinic-looking teacher, and figured this must be the debate team.

I had arrived late, and the meeting was about to disband. The teacher, Mr. Robison, was calling for volunteers for Sunday's tournament at Kingswood-Oxford School in West Hartford. "It's extemp, no prep needed, anyone can come," he said. As people began to clear their trays and head out for fifth period, I approached him. "I'll go," I said.

My parents dropped me off at Loomis early Sunday morning so that I could ride over in the van with my new teammates. Four of us went, and I was partnered with Kevin Moran, a junior and one of the co-presidents of the debate team. Lynda Duna, whom I'd immediately liked when, on the first day of school, she'd told me that the boys at her junior high had been too stupid for her, was also going, partnered with another freshman, Mark Murphy. Lynda and I would be among the dominant debaters in New England for four years, but that morning I just hoped that I wasn't about to embarrass myself.

I was relieved to discover that I was able to get right back on the bicycle, even after a year away from competitive debate—and with new styles to learn, too. Tournaments in the Debating Association of New England Independent Schools, known as DANEIS ("dan-ice"), came in several varieties. There were Oregon-style tournaments like the ones I had known in junior high school; there was parliamentary debate, in which topics were announced only half an hour before each round and judges paid more attention to speakers' reasoning and eloquence than to researched facts; there were public-speaking tournaments, where instead of debating we competed in heats of impromptu speeches on topics we might see just two minutes before going onstage; and every spring there was one Lincoln-Douglas tournament, the only event in which we debated one-on-one rather than in teams of two.

Even though I remembered enough to know what I was doing, it was reassuring to have Kevin as my partner. The Kingswood-Oxford tune-up tournament was parliamentary, so while its basic structure of two-against-two arguing was familiar to me, there were subtle differences. Kevin was the first person to teach me the parliamentary lexicon that would soon be my second language: British terms like "Mr. Speaker" instead of "Honored Judge," "government" instead of "affirmative," and "opposition" instead of "negative," and, in place of cross-examinations, the option to stand up and interrupt the opposing team to ask a "point of information" or, if misquoted, to declare a "point of personal privilege."

Kevin was an ideal guide. He had Scott Dixon's wit and easy charm. His logic and reasoning were always sound. And he had the self-possession that I would come to recognize as the singular trait of the "fac brat." His parents both worked at the school, and he had grown up in a house on campus; like other faculty children, he had a sense of belonging that preceded whatever popularity he might win among his classmates. He had been at play in those green fields for years. Talking with him in the van that morning, on the way to Kingswood-Oxford, I instantly felt safe, because the secret social knowledge that Kevin seemed to have would make it hard to lose a debate.

And I was not alone in my impression: there was no Loomis student, I soon realized, about whom there was a greater consensus. *Kevin was a great guy.* A few years later he would have drawn comparisons to Bill Clinton, but they would have been off. As a short, very blond, very cute sixteen-year-old, Kevin lacked the future president's threatening edge of sexuality. He was probably the most popular boy in the whole school, but he didn't date. (Whereas you would never leave your sister with Bill Clinton, you would happily introduce your sister to Kevin.) He was fashionably preppy, but not intimidating about it, probably because his hair was cut modestly short; he lacked the soccer manes, and the arrogance, of some of his more aggressively beautiful classmates.

Kevin and I finished third in that tournament, my first in high school, but we won several together before he graduated. The victory I remember best came on January 22 of my freshman year, at Loomis's own tournament, which was prepared Oregon-style, the topic mailed to all the league schools two months in advance: "Resolved: That the use and sale or distribution of a number of drugs which are currently illegal and widely abused should be legalized." After three extemporaneous tournaments in the fall, I was excited to be able to prepare again, as I had for the Star Wars debates in junior high. I began to research drug legalization with a particularly freshman zeal. To gather information on the more relaxed drug laws of Western European countries, I embarked on a project of writing letters to various foreign embassies in Washington. I mailed my requests for information in early December, shortly after the invitation announcing the Loomis topic was mailed to other schools, and by Christmas break I had received generously sized pamphlets describing the Dutch, Swedish, and German legal regimes regarding narcotics. When I presented my haul at the last debate team meeting before break, Kevin's team co-president, an earthy, hippieish senior girl named B. J. Chisholm, looked at me and said, "You wrote *letters?*" I detected both admiration and an equal measure of annoyance, as if I were trying too hard.

Seventeen schools came to the tournament, including the Roxbury Latin School, a small boys' day school outside Boston whose students were a mix of suave upper-class schoolboys and working-class Catholic kids who actually had the Boston accent; the Hotchkiss School, from northwest Connecticut; Deerfield Academy, from western Massachusetts, famously described in *The Headmaster*, John McPhee's book about the legendary Frank Boyden; and St. Paul's School, of Concord, New Hampshire, then the wealthiest school per student in the world—before the recent crash, its endowment was over $400 million, for just over five hundred students.

Unlike the large tournaments hosted by the National Forensic League and the National Catholic Forensic League, which take place over two or three days, prep school tournaments were one-day affairs: three preliminary rounds followed by an exhibition round between the top two teams, with the winner taking the first-place trophy. Usually the exhibition round took place at about five o'clock, and although it was considered a faux pas, some coaches, on hearing that none of their twosomes was in the exhibition round, loaded the boys and girls into the van and drove off, asking that any lesser trophies they might have won be mailed to them or brought to a future tournament for a handoff. The classier move was to stay and watch the finals, which about ten of the schools did that evening.

So it was a small crowd on hand to hear the announcement that, after three rounds, the two highest-scoring teams, the two teams who would compete for the winners' trophy, were from St. Paul's School and Loomis Chaffee.

Kevin and I were well prepared, and not just because of our prodigious research. Every other Friday during lunch, the team met for what amounted to a biweekly philosophical salon. If the upcoming tournament had an announced topic, Mr. Robison led us through rigorous discussions of arguments and counterarguments, prodding to see which held water and which had logical leaks. As he thought out loud, he was filled with a visible, contagious glee. His voluminous, unshaped, red-flecked brown beard aged him considerably, made him look much older than his mid-thirties, but his laugh took the years off again: the combination of that sound coming from that beard gladdened everyone. A team meeting, coming at the end of a long, tiring week, felt like an escape to someplace fun, informal, and occasionally hilarious—Mr. Robison was not above making fun of other teams' coaches and debaters, and he was never above making fun of himself. If we were talking about a topic, whether drug legalization or universal health care or nuclear disarmament, he expected us all, the dozen or so students who might be there, to discuss the question as equals. If he jumped in with a suggestion, we were free to call it stupid or silly. His arguments were rarely less than brilliant, however.

Debate coaches come in three kinds, roughly speaking. The history or social studies teacher gravitates to debate, Model Congress, and mock trial because he likes talking about current events and catching students up on the world around them. The English or drama teacher enjoys the performative aspect of debate (especially in public school leagues, in which more tournaments have such events as dramatic interpretation and interpretive reading). And then the philosophy teacher, like Mr. Robison, is interested in ideas. This is the best kind of coach.

Mr. Robison gave us tools that other coaches just did not have. Sometimes, the tools were just terminology, ways of putting into words ethical concepts that we might intuit but needed help articulating. A classic example, especially widespread in high school debate, is utilitarianism, the belief (to oversimplify) that the best action in any given situation is the one that creates the greatest happiness for the greatest number. So, for example, a utilitarian might argue that if by shooting one very unhappy person you're able to greatly improve the lives of a thousand other people, then go ahead and fire the shot. Jewish or Christian ethics would not, of course, support this conclusion—the commandment not to commit murder is nonnegotiable. And Immanuel Kant, as Mr. Robison taught us, had a secular form of deontology, or duty-bound ethics, which proceeded from premises different from religion's but was equally hostile to the "consequentialist" calculus of utilitarianism.

So what did it matter that Mr. Robison could explain to us teenagers the difference between utilitarianism and deontology? Take a topic like abortion. If you're debating the pro-choice side, you're likely to make an argument along the lines of "Yes, abortion isn't desirable, but when you consider how awful an unwanted pregnancy can be for the mother, and for her mother, who ends up taking care of the baby, and for the people harmed if the unwanted baby grows up to be a criminal, then you have to think maybe aborting is the right thing to do. Or at least it's *sometimes* the right thing to do, and the mother should be able to decide when that is." And the pro-life debater gets up and says, "Look, my opponent conceded that this is the taking of a life, so how can that be a good thing? Killing is always wrong. And if we allow this killing, where will it end?" This is a debate that to many people sounds pretty trite. And if the judge in the room feels that way, he doesn't want to sit through an hour of it. He's heard these two sides, they both have some truth in them, so what is going to elevate one debater above the other?

In high school debate, the answer often comes down to philosophy. If one debater can rise above this back-and-forth, using the language of philosophy to describe what's really being argued over, then all of a sudden the debate seems much more sophisticated, and that debater is likely to win.

"What we have here is a conflict between utilitarian ethics and a more Kantian ethics," a debater might say, never having read Mill or Kant but having got a good ten-minute primer from Mr. Robison. "And while I respect my opponent's utilitarian impulse, in the end I submit that that's a poor philosophy. We must be a country of laws, and those laws have to be undergirded by universal principles, and one of them has to be 'Thou shalt not kill.' Otherwise, we open ourselves up to all kinds of arguments: Shall we kill people we deem to be polluters? What about people who make violent TV shows that may, in some indirect way, lead to violence? No, Kant warned us about this. We must act as if everyone were to act thus, he said. And he was right."

That oversimplification would not hold up in a graduate seminar, but in a round of high school debate it wins the day. And for good reason: by invoking timeless principles (even while name-dropping philosophers he may not fully understand), the student makes the implicit point that debate is about the life of the mind and is preparation for a lifetime of cogent thinking. Everyone in the room, even the losing team, feels better when the argument is lifted to the plane of philosophy. Mr. Robison helped us do that lifting.

As a former champion debater, Mr. Robison was also very handy with both pragmatic speaking tips—*Don't pace. Use humor, but don't be mean. Look at the judge.*—and the kind of useful systems that make difficult reasoning seem manageable. For example, according to the taxonomy Mr. Robison had used when he was a debater, and which he shared with us, any affirmative argument for a policy change could be classified as one of three types: "needs," "goals," or "comparative advantage." A needs case, which some debate coaches call a harms case, argued that the change in policy was needed because of harms inherent in the status quo. A goals case simply presented the policy change as useful for achieving some desirable goal. And a comparative advantage case made a more modest claim than either of the other two: the policy change might not be necessary, and it might not fulfill any lofty goal, but, all other things being equal, it offered a comparative advantage—a somewhat better world than the one we live in.

As Kevin and I had prepared our case for drug decriminalization we had followed Mr. Robison's system. We could argue a needs case: that the war on drugs was so costly, leading to so much illegal trafficking, driving the price of drugs up, causing addicts to commit more crimes, in an endless spiral of destruction, that the United States needed to decriminalize drugs immediately. (Or at least decriminalize the least harmful drugs, such as marijuana, to free up resources to stop the spread of more dangerous drugs, such as crack.) Or we could make the case that decriminalizing drugs would help us reach some worthy goal, for example, creating a more hospitable climate for addicts to seek treatment. Finally, we could say that while there was no need to change the laws, and while it would be hubris to think that a new legal regime would realize any particular goals, on balance things would be somewhat better if the laws were changed: crime would go down, drug use wouldn't go up that much, and we'd save lots of money. There would be a comparative advantage. (We went with that argument.)

But Mr. Robison's most urgent message for us, his signature teaching, was a blend of the philosophical and the pragmatic, a dictum that would make us better thinkers and, not incidentally, would help us win debates. "Seize the moral high ground," he told us, over and again. "Seize the moral high ground." Often, seizing the moral high ground was simply a matter of talking earnestly about what was at stake, reminding the audience that high school debate was not just scholastic sport but also a forum for figuring out how to do the right thing. In other words, we could surprise the audience by making them aware that, sitting in the auditorium and rooting for one side or the other to win, they had forgotten the real costs being discussed.

When the first St. Paul's speaker stood to address the crowd, the sunlight was already gone from the windows lining the Loomis chapel, and the students scattered sparsely through the pews were lit only by the chandeliers from above. But there was a warmth in our diminished numbers, as if we were a hearty group united by our perseverance, or maybe by a shared indifference to the January cold.

The St. Paul's team consisted of Guillermo Cisneros and Sophie Backus, and although Kevin and I had not faced them in the preliminary rounds, we had seen them stalking the hallways with their music stands. St. Paul's debaters always brought music stands on which to set their sheaves of paper, and they were so often victorious that debaters from other schools got a sense of foreboding whenever they walked into a room to see their opponents setting up music stands. The speeches they placed on those stands were read verbatim, as were their rebuttals at the ends of the rounds. Their resistance to whatever their opponents had said—*how could they have written their rebuttals before they knew what to rebut?* we wondered—never seemed to count against them: most opponents were so scared by the St. Paul's team's confidence, smooth delivery, and air of inevitability that they pretty much folded by the middle of the round.

I had an advantage. Unlike Kevin, and unlike many of the debaters in the audience, I had not spent several years losing to St. Paul's debaters, so I did not know I was supposed to be afraid. And as a freshman, I had nothing to lose. When all the competitors assembled in the Founders Hall chapel to hear who would be in the finals, I did not expect to hear my name read. And when I did hear Mr. Robison read aloud "Loomis A, Kevin Moran and Mark Oppenheimer, versus

St. Paul's A, Guillermo Cisneros and Sophie Backus," I felt a brief chill of nervousness, but mostly I thought that here was an opportunity to pick up where I'd left off in seventh grade. And this time, I had Kevin Moran as a partner. I had finally been promoted to the big league.

Loomis was a "switch-side" tournament, in which every team debated twice on one side and then switched sides for the third round. In the exhibition round, the winner of a coin toss got to pick its side. The St. Paul's team won the toss and elected to argue in the affirmative, for the decriminalization of drugs. That had been Kevin's and my predominant side—we'd argued twice for decriminalization, once against it—so this was an advantage to St. Paul's.

And they did look formidable. As he rose to deliver the First Affirmative speech, Guillermo Cisneros was the picture of self-assurance. Standing in the middle of the stage at the lectern, he was beautiful, and beautifully tailored—Latin aristocracy, to be sure. Sophie looked every bit his female counterpart, a poised, self-certain thoroughbred.

In my rebuttal, after a vigorous debate marked by a rather cool courtesy on both sides, I quoted Charles Rangel, the pugnacious Democrat who still represents Harlem in Congress. He was, and remains, a forceful opponent of decriminalization who believes that making drugs more easily available would be tantamount to the "genocide" of his people. Beginning with Rangel's observation, I argued that all four of us in the debate had lost sight of the personal nature of the topic. I could hear Mr. Robison: *Seize the moral high ground.*

"These are real people we're talking about!" I said, holding my hands about a foot apart and bringing them down for effect on "real" and "people." "It's all well and good to say that legalizing drugs may lead to 'only' another few thousand overdoses a year, and then to be happy about the reduced overcrowding in the prisons. But those are *real people*, those few thousand more people who will die because drugs are all of a sudden cheaper and more available. Those people have families—mothers and fathers and brothers and sisters, relatives who will miss them, whose lives will never be the same again without them. They aren't just junkies and cokeheads to be tossed overboard, people who won't be missed. To the contrary, they are lives worth saving." Standing at my lectern, I looked to my right, where Guillermo and Sophie were seated at their desks. "*Some* people may just apply a utilitarian calculus," I said, inclining my head in my opponents' direction. "*Some* people may figure that overall, if the prisons are less crowded, or if we save money on law enforcement and can spend it elsewhere, then that's a net gain for society. And maybe it is, in some cold, impersonal way. But I can't be as cavalier about the lives lost.

"Honorable judges, my partner and I have demonstrated that the harms identified by the affirmative team, while very real, will not be adequately met by the affirmative plan. What's more, there is no comparative advantage to adopting their plan—we only incur suffering in different sectors of society. But most important, honorable judges, we have shone a spotlight on an aspect of their plan—their deadly, rather cruel plan—that makes us loath to adopt it. Just as you, honorable judges, should be loath to give them a victory. Thank you."

There was one speech after mine, the Second Affirmative rebuttal, in which Sophie did an excellent job refocusing the judges on the facts before us: the money wasted in an ineffectual war on drugs that was overcrowding our prisons, fueling gang wars, and creating a surge in petty crime. She was right, of course—the drug war *is* stupid. The facts were on their side, and they knew it. Given Guillermo's and Sophie's confidence, and the crisp efficiency with which they had presented their case, I decided, as the debate ended and all four of us shook hands, that our being declared the victors was against the odds. There was a loud clamor of applause, surprisingly loud for the small number of debaters in the big chapel, and as we descended the stage I looked out at the crowd, found the other Loomis freshmen, and sent them a hopeful smile. The St. Paul's debaters found the rest of their team, and Kevin and I filed in next to the other Loomis debaters, who squeezed our shoulders and clapped us on the backs. "You guys *killed* them!" "Nice *job.*" "You will *definitely* win." I sat down and bounced my knee nervously while the three final-round judges debated in the hallway, out of earshot.

As it turned out, our teammates were right. When the trophies were awarded, the judges had declared Loomis the winner of the exhibition round. Kevin and I had done it. And we both won speaker trophies, me for second place and Kevin for third. Along with Heather McGray and B. J. Chisholm, who had twice debated the negative and once the affirmative, we were the top four-person team. Lynda was the second-place novice speaker, and the novice team of John DeSimone and John Carton had gone undefeated. As Mr. Robison read the results, he manfully tried to hold back a big smile, but it broke through both his restraint and his beard. He couldn't help himself. We'd made him proud.

The ballots for an exhibition round were always filled out more cursorily than ballots in the preliminary rounds. Final rounds were judged by panels of three, so there wasn't the same need for a single judge to justify his decision, and, what's more, final-round judges were encouraged to do their work quickly, so that the trophies could be awarded and teams could get on the road. So there was scant writing on the yellow triplicate sheaves that Kevin and I were handed, and only one of the three ballots had a comment specifically directed at me. In the box allotted to the Second Negative speaker, in scratchy handwriting made less legible by the special press-through ink, a judge had written: "Don't try so hard to pull at our heart-strings."

Even allowing for the hurried nature of final-round ballots, it stung. That judge, like the other two, had ruled for me and Kevin; obviously our reasoning had been strong, or we would never have beaten such tough opponents. But in trying to seize the moral high ground I had let my style descend into maudlin and sentimental showmanship, and I had irked this judge. And on reading his comment, and reflecting back on my speech, my style irked me, too. I had tried to force sympathy from my audience, rather than just trusting that my speech would generate it. None of the other three debaters had seemed so crass and debaterly. Not Guillermo or Sophie, and certainly not Kevin, who always trusted his connection with the audience, whether an audience of one or of five hundred. The judge was hinting at a lesson integral to the sprezzatura, the effortless grace, that I had yet to master—*don't try so hard to pull at our heart-strings; good oratory lets the evidence and arguments speak for themselves*—and I never forgot the advice.

My freshman year, I won trophies at Exeter, Loomis, Hotchkiss, Stoneleigh-Burnham, Kingswood-Oxford, and Deerfield. Tournament Sundays were my favorite days, the van my favorite place in the world. During the morning rides we would sleep or listen to music on our Walkmans. I always seemed to awake five minutes before we pulled up to the school. And these old New England schools, they had the grandest driveways, a quarter mile or half mile long, separating them from the small towns they gingerly inhabited. At the end of the driveway we wended through the campus, past tennis courts and freshly mown soccer fields; from the big van windows we might see a lonely runner, up early, circling the fields' perimeter. After we'd parked the van, I'd jump out simmering with anticipation of the day and speed-walk to the double doors of the classroom building. I loved making an entrance. Inside, as we passed coaches and debaters from opposing teams, balancing their bagels and cups of coffee atop stacks of books and binders, I would call out to them, a little too eagerly, as if I were the mayor of some small town instead of just a freshman new to these parts. "Hi, Mr. Hansen!" I would say to the Roxbury Latin coach. "Hey, John, how are you?" I would ask a Deerfield Academy debater. "Hope we get to face each other today!" And because I had beaten him at a previous tournament, he might interpret my friendliness as smugness, but I didn't mean it that way. I was just in my element, and it felt good.

On the return trips, doubling back on Interstate 91 or the Massachusetts Turnpike, we would boil over with energy from the tournament just ended. Mr. Robison let whoever was riding shotgun control the radio, and all the rest of us hung like elementary school children over the benches in back, gliding in and out of conversations. On campus we weren't all friends, but as a team we were close, and there was definitely respect all around. I was proud to be winning trophies with these guys, *for* these guys.

That year, my greatest triumph, and the team's, came in April, at the Kingswood-Oxford tournament—not the tune-up at the beginning of the year, but Kingswood-Oxford's traditional one-on-one, Lincoln-Douglas tournament, in the style named after the famous debates in 1858 between Abraham Lincoln and his opponent in the race for U.S. Senate, Stephen A. Douglas. The topic in 1989 was a quotation made famous by Barry Goldwater: "Resolved: Extremism in the defense of liberty is no vice." (Goldwater went on to say, "and moderation in the pursuit of justice is no virtue," but that wasn't part of the topic.) This was a typical Lincoln-Douglas, or "L-D," resolution, pertaining to an abstract question of values rather than a specific policy or political question. Mr. Robison thought it was a great topic, and when we met to discuss it, he wasn't cracking jokes. His voice slowed down, and he spoke with an intense curiosity, his eyes fixed above our heads, each word touched with an aspect of the quizzical, as if he was letting us watch him in the process of discernment—a reminder that, to the true debater, there are no pat answers, everything is in a shade of gray, and the debater most comfortable with that lack of clarity is actually the most forceful.

"I think," he told his assembled debaters, gathered around the table, "I think that this might be seen as a question of first principles. What the affirmative is basically arguing, and what the negative is arguing against, is that liberty is the most important thing, so important that it outweighs the potential downside of extreme acts. We could look at it as a question of act utilitarianism versus rule utilitarianism. The act utilitarian says, 'Always do the act that most greatly increases happiness,' but the rule utilitarian says, 'You can't know enough about the consequences of any act to correctly guess whether it is likely to increase utility. So it's better to figure out which rules, generally followed, will tend to increase utility.' It ends up sounding a lot like deontology or even religious ethics, but it's not, because the goal is still utility, not some duty to God or fellow man. So as a rule utilitarian, your rule here might be, 'Do that which protects liberty'—and that means that if you have to kill someone to protect liberty, then you do it. The act itself seems anti-utilitarian, but you're following a pretty good rule for increasing utility: Don't let anyone curtail your liberty."

The next week, a few days before the tournament, Mr. Robison found me between classes and showed me a letter he had written a few years earlier to another one of Loomis's most cerebral teachers, Bert Thurber. Mr. Robison had asked Mr. Thurber, who had worked in government and now taught classes on the American presidency and on communism, to talk with one of his debaters about an upcoming debate topic: whether government was ever justified in being dishonest. After Mr. Thurber had spoken with the student, Mr. Robison wrote him a private letter about some finer points that had come up. Though the letter dealt with a question very different from extremism in defense of liberty, Mr. Robison saw similarities, and he thought the letter to Mr. Thurber would help complicate my thinking.

"Dear Bert," it began. "I appreciate the time you spent with me and Erwin talking about the issue of dishonesty and government. Below I give a sketch of my argument from which I conclude that there are possible states of affairs where dishonesty by the government (or any other agent) is necessary. . . .

"First, I agree with those moral philosophers who like Hare affirm that moral principles override any other principles of practical judgment; second, I believe that moral conflict is possible, i.e., that two ethical principles can prescribe incompatible courses of action; third, I hold that there are ethical principles which are higher than that of honesty and, hence, which in case of conflict override honesty (which is only to say that I don't take honesty to be the supreme moral principle); fourth, there is nothing to exclude that the government as a moral agent could be faced with a situation where the principle of honesty and some higher ethical principle are in conflict; in which case, given my first premise, it would not only be acceptable, but indeed, morally obligatory to be dishonest. . . .

"I know that you were trying to leave moral considerations aside (as I suggest my affirmative debaters should do as well) but I honestly can't, because I really do find moral principles overriding in any consideration of practical judgments. Therefore, I can't accept the absolute status you give to honesty."

Mr. Robison also shared with me a grad school paper in which he had argued that any useful rule utilitarianism ends up with rules so specific that they are actually describing acts, rather than general rules—in effect, he wrote, rule utilitarianism collapses into act utilitarianism. This argument ran contrary to the tack he suggested we debaters take at the tournament, drawing a distinction between act and rule utilitarianism, but he knew that I was getting excited about this topic, and he was enjoying this ongoing conversation.

I know I didn't fully understand all the supplementary reading he gave me. I certainly was not moved, for example, to ask who this "Hare" was, and if Mr. Robison informed me he was the moral philosopher R. M. Hare, I definitely did not inquire any further. But his point was not to ensure that I understood any philosophical system, or even that I knew the names of any philosophers. He was just trying to get one of his debaters to think philosophically.

I was now an amateur philosopher—and the speech I prepared for the debate proceeded accordingly. First, I wrote an introduction in which I argued that liberty is the most important value and explained, pointing to historical examples of people losing their lives for liberty (the American Revolution, people fleeing communist East Germany at risk of getting shot, etc.), that it's an obvious choice as something to value above all else. Second, I introduced in the speech the idea of utility, saying that it's a useful concept for analyzing the rightness of particular actions. (At this point, I expected, my opponent would begin to quake and sweat.) Third, I explained the distinction between act utilitarianism and rule utilitarianism. (At this point, my opponent's head would, I was sure, shoot off the top of his spine.) Fourth, I concluded by saying that, proceeding with an appropriate understanding of rule utilitarianism, it made sense to defend liberty at all costs, no matter what, "so that it's clear, Honored Judge, that extremism in defense of liberty is no vice!"

(Any questions?)

And Mr. Robison's philosophical coaching paid off for my teammates arguing the negative side, too. They had to think about it this way: Your opponent has just concluded a pedestrian speech listing all the good reasons to condone extremism. "If you aren't extreme in favor of liberty, you'll lose to tyrants who are totally extreme in taking it away from you!" "Sometimes you have to be willing to take extreme actions, even laying down your life for a cause, otherwise where would we be?" And the dreaded Holocaust reference, stock in trade of young, inexperienced debaters everywhere: "When the Nazis were trying to deprive Jews of their liberty, imagine if all the Jews had gotten really *extreme* in defense of themselves? Like, if there had been *lots* of Warsaw Ghetto uprisings?" Now, as negative, you stand up and begin this way: "Honored Judge, worthy opponent. I'd like to thank my opponent for a fine and thought-provoking speech, filled with good, topical examples. Unfortunately, I don't think she has given a proper philosophical grounding to her argument. We are compelled to ask: What is her ethical system?"

And then you use the same utilitarian language, but favoring the act instead of the rule: "It seems that my worthy opponent has thrown in her lot with a crude rule utilitarianism, according to which we can count on certain rules to maximize happiness, or perhaps liberty, in the world. But what if following these rules means committing barbaric acts, thus reducing utility in the short term? Or what if utility isn't the proper goal at all? What if liberty isn't? What if the preservation of life is?" And so forth, chipping away at the affirmative's defense of extremism, using the language of philosophy to take away the force of her examples. After all, nobody wants to defend the loyalists in the American Revolution, still less the Nazis. It's a debate that's hard to win if both sides are arguing by example. Lift it to the plane of philosophy, however, and your opponent is suddenly lost, and your cool, rarefied reason will prevail.

Although Mr. Robison was, in the estimation of many at Loomis, an eccentric genius, he looked hopelessly normal compared to his fellow debate coaches. If adults seem to children like a whole other genus, no species of adult was stranger than *Homo rhetagogicus*, the debate coach. (And in England I would learn that the coaches' strangeness obtained regardless of their country; the English and Canadian coaches were every bit as marvelously queer as their counterparts in New England.)

They were an extraordinary collection of pleasing oddities, the kind of men—and they were almost all men—whom it was impossible to imagine settled in civilian society; indeed they seemed unemployable anywhere off prep school grounds. They were too deficient in hygiene, too prolific in opinions, too prolix, too absentminded, too prurience-minded, too slovenly, too fastidious, too loud, or too soft to move well in polite company. But they were smart and dedicated and utterly concerned with the life of the mind. I miss them.

I remember only three female coaches. The rather formal Jean Berg coached the girls of Winsor School, in Boston. The more exuberant Julie Hill, who for a short time was the Exeter coach, was pleasantly plain her first year of coaching and returned the following year with newly frosted hair and a thick layer of makeup. Finally, there was the grand Linda Martin, who coached at Balmoral Hall, a girls' school in Winnipeg, Manitoba, that sent teams to the same Canadian and English tournaments that Loomis attended. She was an aristocrat of the Canadian plains—her father had been a Tory chief judge of Manitoba and a close political ally of Prime Minister John Diefenbaker—and matriarch of a powerful debate clan: her sons, Campbell, Jock, and Cal, were all champion debaters for

St. John's–Ravenscourt, the brother school to Balmoral Hall. Mrs. Martin's favorite topics were her sons' glory, her father's lost glory, and the inflated reputation of former prime minister Pierre Trudeau; she descanted on all three matters with perfect diction and in a flat Canadian accent.

But the great majority of coaches were men, and I remember their guild comprising two kinds: bearded and stout. Among the bearded: Mr. Robison; Geoff Buerger of the Forman School; and Joe Pollender, a legal librarian and former collegiate champion who assisted with judging at large tournaments in the Boston area. And the stout: E. Lawrence Katzenbach III, of St. Paul's School, a man of truly authoritative girth; Phil Hansen, of Roxbury Latin, who possessed a slight paunch, the kind that I always thought would look good festooned with suspenders; and Bob Googins, of Kingswood-Oxford, reputedly a fearsome college athlete in his time, now gone soft. I often wondered at the limitless possibilities of a hypothetical coach who was hirsute *and* fat—had such a man existed, his teams would have been unstoppable. These looks were tributes to the men's greatness, perhaps inseparable from it. At most New England prep schools, where the ideal master is both fit and wholesomely clean-shaven, an unruly beard like Mr. Robison's was the mark of a free spirit, and a nice paunch was a sign that its bearer did not take the athletic fields too seriously. These were not coaches who *happened* to be fat or bearded—they were coaches for the same reasons they were fat or bearded. For all the tuition we paid, very few of our teachers were eccentrics, gadflies, or original thinkers; those who were often coached debate.

Some other coaches I remember well:

Christopher "Kit" Brown was a Yale alumnus, a classicist and lover of English literature who coached at Salisbury, a perfectly respectable school with the misfortune of being just miles from Hotchkiss, one of New England's finest schools. One can only imagine how much success the energetic Mr. Brown would have had if he had taken the reins of the Hotchkiss team from the doddering old Rob

Dyer. Mr. Brown was prematurely gray, and his shaggy hair flopped from side to side as he bounced around the halls at a tournament, coaching his boys and girls to another seventh-place finish. Mr. Dyer, whose sparse, unruly white hair made him look like a Gentile version of Albert Einstein, had scarcely any more success, despite having far more accomplished students to work with. Being experienced but unsuccessful coaches, Mr. Dyer and Mr. Brown were both asked to judge an unusual number of final rounds, since their own teams were never competing.

Max Gorsky, the Deerfield Academy coach, had a thatch of bristly hair from the same dye lot as Mr. Buerger's red beard. (If one had merged the two men, the resultant beast would have been something like a hirsute Scottish caber tosser with an aggrieved Russian temper.) Gorsky always seemed annoyed. In between rounds, he would stand outside, under the archways of doors if it was raining, dragging deeply on his cigarettes and muttering inaudibly. He was a Russian teacher by trade, and one got the sense that he had been forced to coach debate, perhaps because his unreformed smoking habit rendered him a poor choice to coach a sports team. That he did not want to coach debate did not, however, make him a failure at the job; some of his speakers, like the very beautiful Kendall Moore, were strong debaters, quite inspired to win for the team. Dark, angry, brooding, and stuck in the wrong place and time, Gorsky was eccentric, but his eccentricity had a coherence that made him seem like a leader.

Dr. Paul Bassett coached the girls of Stoneleigh-Burnham, a single-sex school in western Massachusetts, known to the Deerfield boys down the highway as Stoneleigh-Burnout. The slur on the school's name excited me whenever I heard it used. It made me think of girls sent off to boarding school after being caught in their parents' horse stables dragging on a joint with one hand and servicing the horse groom, a very lucky local boy, with the other. In reality, the Stoneleigh girls were sweet and maternal, and they were devoted to their coach, whom with an earnest, ardent affection they called "Peebs." He had a bowl cut of brown hair and a quiet, tight-lipped seriousness, as if debate were a very grave matter. Stoneleigh-Burnham hosted the only tournament in New England that focused just on public speaking, with no debating at all. Along with Dana Hall outside Boston, another girls' school, and Kingswood-Oxford, Stoneleigh was one of the only places that kept alive a merry old event called triple-speak. A triple-speak competitor is given a word and immediately has to begin an oration based on that word. One minute later, another word is shouted at him, and he has thirty seconds to seamlessly integrate that word into his talk. Then, a minute later, a final word is called, and in the final minute of the speech the competitor must use the third word and then conclude as elegantly as possible. Dr. Bassett never looked as if he would much enjoy triple-speak—or impromptu speaking, or any of the other events his tournament featured—but he coached and officiated with a dogged consistency, and he got more out of the girls than the school's nickname led us to expect. Twenty years later, he is still coaching.

The three leading statesmen of the league were Mr. Robison, Mr. Hansen, and Mr. Katzenbach. All had been coaching since the early years of the league, which had been founded in 1978. Although very different men, they recognized in each other a shared commitment to the formation of young people, and to the art of debate. That would have been enough to sustain the mutual fondness, but they also shared similar passions for the humanities, and each had done graduate work toward a career other than high school teaching: Mr. Katzenbach had graduated from Harvard Law School and Mr. Hansen from Harvard Divinity School, and Mr. Robison had nearly finished a doctorate in philosophy at Brown.

Each had his familial struggles, too. Mr. Hansen, a bachelor, took in foster sons, many of whom had troubled pasts. Years after he retired from coaching, Mr. Hansen moved to Maine, where several of his sons, as he always called them, moved to be near him. When I first met him—when my primary relationship to him was debater to judge—I found Mr. Hansen a little too prim to be likable. Today I see

him as an admirably old-fashioned type, the unmarried schoolmaster, reserved but compassionate, who devotes his life to boys, takes a
special interest in those who need him, and more than compensates
for having no sons of his own.

Mr. Katzenbach was, like Mr. Robison, a single father, coping with
his own worsening diabetes while raising his daughter, Allita. He was
fiercely devoted to his only child, so much so that when Allita was
denied admission to St. Paul's he quit and moved to Deerfield Academy. I so much associate him with St. Paul's that I forget that when I
first met him he was the Deerfield coach, a job he held for only one
year: St. Paul's admitted Allita from its wait list, she never attended
Deerfield, and the next year her father returned to St. Paul's. Mr.
Katzenbach had an open, almost flirtatious personality that con-
trasted with Mr. Hansen's emphatic privateness. Very big, preceded
into a room by his sebaceous smell, Mr. Katzenbach wore a loosely
knotted tie and, always, a red and white St. Paul's scarf. He would
clap boys on the back but allow a respectful perimeter around girls,
as if not to invite suspicion. Many of his debaters were girls—more
of them, it seemed, than on rival teams, making me wonder if he had
a particular interest in outreach to co-eds. Once, I remember, he told
me that the best teams "have a boy and a girl—the tension is good
for the team."

There was something of the overgrown adolescent in Mr. Katzenbach. He was brilliant but a show-off, and the traditional critique he
gave to debaters at the end of a round was, while always extremely
generous and helpful, and inevitably dead-on, an obvious showcase
for his own intellect. He was a braggart, never letting anybody forget that he was Princeton and Harvard Law. He had an ironic stance
toward his foibles—he knew he was a braggart, and while he was
proud of being at St. Paul's, he was ashamed of being proud of it.

This conflicted, childlike side of his personality was displayed very
vividly before a final round in which I had to face the St. Paul's team
of Eliza Griswold and Lucy Barzun. About two minutes before the
round was to begin, Mr. Katzenbach walked up to me, smiling. "Do

you know who Lucy's grandfather is?" he asked. When I said that I didn't, he told me that her grandfather was Jacques Barzun. When I said I didn't know who that was, he instructed me: "One of the twentieth century's greatest intellectuals," he said. And then he volunteered that Eliza's father was the Episcopal bishop of Chicago.

Mr. Katzenbach vouchsafed this knowledge in a conspiratorial tone, as if he were awed and expected that I would be, too. The idea was that we were just two proletarians from the valley, him and me, who had arduously ascended the hilltops to peer at the nobility. I think there was sincerity in this pose: he was a high school teacher from a family of high government officials. Though descended of a signatory to the Declaration of Independence, he had no money, or so he said. But there was a disingenuousness, too. If he was trying to forge an alliance based on our shared inferiority, he was also trying to give his debaters—those to whom we were inferior—a psychological advantage in the debate round about to begin. And because it's the truly privileged who most eagerly gab about their lack of privilege, I immediately grasped that although he was insisting he was with me, he surely knew he wasn't like me. There was a bit too much magnanimity in his buddy-buddy manner; he believed that he had once had status but had allowed it to deliquesce, or at least accepted that it had.

They each did their job as best they could, using whatever tools they possessed. The coaches who were history teachers loaded their students down with Roman examples from Gibbon, or with fine perorations half stolen from Churchill. Mr. Katzenbach liked bringing everything around to his legal training; his students were likely to cite legal precedent, and they spoke as if giving closing arguments in court, without much humor, with no mischief in their eyes, but with a smooth and serious polish to their well-rehearsed speeches. Mr. Hansen taught social studies, and his students always gave examples from foreign countries. And Mr. Robison—he had philosophy, so that's what he gave us. By the end of freshman year, I was, although still a beginner, learning how to think.

* * *

It was the second weekend in April, at the Kingswood-Oxford tournament, that I became aware how powerfully Mr. Robison's coaching had taken hold. The Loomis debaters all had winning records. I went 3–0 in the preliminary rounds, after which, while the preliminary scores were tabulated, the debaters competed in quick public-speaking events, I chose impromptu speaking, gave what I thought was a pretty good speech on the quotation "Workers of the world unite," and then returned to the auditorium to hear which debaters would be in the final round and what their new topic would be. I was one of the two finalists, and I would face Jon Bonanno, of Deerfield, in the exhibition round.

I don't remember that final round at all, but I recently found it mentioned in an old copy of the *Log*, the Loomis school newspaper. "Debate Team Continues Winning Streak" is the headline, and the article is by my friend Thacher Kent, who happened to be one of the debaters that day. "The topic," he writes, "which [Oppenheimer and Bonanno] had fifteen minutes to prepare, was a quote from Martin Luther King, Jr.: 'Resolved: That if a man does not have a cause for which he is willing to die, he is not fit to live.' Mark was given the negative side and annihilated the other contestant, using logic, the Constitution, and his opponent's own words against him. There was no question as to who had won, but Mark's victory was confirmed at the awards ceremony when he took the award for top speaker. . . . Loomis Chaffee won the top school award, with ten wins and only three losses. That makes three consecutive top school awards for Loomis Chaffee, an unprecedented feat in this league."

VII

The victory at Kingswood-Oxford had me in good spirits for my first international championship, in England the next month. In March, Mr. Hansen, who was the league secretary in perpetuity, had approached me between rounds at a tournament. "How would you like to go to England?" he'd asked. The previous year, 1988, some coaches from private schools in Canada and England had started a tournament to bring together high school debaters from the English-speaking world, and this year they had asked if our league would send some American speakers. The Hotchkiss tournament in February had been designated a qualifier for England, and as the leading scorer there I was now invited to the 1989 World Debate and Public Speaking Championships, to be held in May at the Reading Blue Coat School in Reading, England.

I wanted to go. I had never been so excited about anything in my life. But I would have to find the money for plane fare. My parents had just had their fourth child, my sister, Rachel, and they were already paying more than ten thousand dollars a year for my tuition, so they weren't excited about sending me on a debate junket to England. Fortunately, when my headmaster, the bearded, bald, brilliant, and merry Dr. John Ratté, agreed to cover half the cost from his discretionary fund, my parents said they would cover the other half.

I was less worried about missing classes than I was about missing track practices; it was easy to catch up on history reading, but it was hard to get back in shape after a week away. Like the Academy and most other prep schools, Loomis required students to do a sport every term. In the fall, I had taken group tennis lessons taught by one of the gym teachers, and in the winter I had wrestled—I could make the 119-pound weight class, so was useful to the junior varsity squad. Now, in the spring, having failed to make the JV tennis team, I had become a runner. Distance running is the last refuge of the uncoordinated: some runners are more gifted than others, have bigger lung capacities or better strides, but mostly you get good just by working hard. I immediately loved track because, as I discovered, runners were the misfits of the athletic world: intellectuals, eccentrics, obsessives, and mystics. The seniors on the team, especially, were unconventional and inspiring—our best runner, George Peacock, would have acid flashbacks at the end of a long run when the clouds realigned themselves just so. The other freshmen on the team became my good friends; we shared the absurdity of being brains who at last were forced to use our bodies, only to discover that this new form of exertion was not so bad. When the delirium hit on mile seven or eight of a long run, we would be talking about Kurt Vonnegut or Tom Robbins. Our coach, Mr. Glazier, entirely approved: he was a long-haired, wild-eyed math teacher in his late twenties who would expound at length on the beauty of geometry.

And he was only too happy to let me slip off to England. But before I left, G (as we called him) wanted to hear more about this debate competition that would take me away from the team for a whole week. One afternoon, two or three days before I was to leave for England, G pulled up alongside me as we were nearing the end of a long run, then asked me to explain to him and the rest of the JV distance squad what it took to win at debate. He was a math guy through and through, and dyslexic at that, so reading and writing, or a word-based activity like public speaking, seemed exotic to him. The varsity runners were far ahead, and the small hill on the approach to Chaffee

119

Hall was taxing our lungs, but between deep breaths I tried to explain to my coach, my fellow freshmen, and a few slow sophomores why going to England was worth missing a whole week of practice.

"It takes amazing precision," I said, trying to sound very authoritative. "Everything you do affects how the judges see you. It has to do with what you wear, how you hold your head. A debate tournament isn't just about talking a lot or even just about arguing. You have to anticipate what the other side is going to do. It's like reading their minds, then coming up with the appropriate response, even before they know what they're going to say. It's like playing chess—you always have to be thinking moves ahead." My friends nodded, and through their fatigue some managed to let out grunts—"Unh-hunh"—to indicate that they got what I was saying.

We were running in tight formation, ten of us proceeding up the hill at a rate of eight minutes a mile. Nobody brushed against anybody. Especially at the end of a long practice, runners in a pack are no more likely to collide than cars going eighty miles an hour, mere yards from each other, on a freeway. What's dangerous is not speed but change in speed, and when each runner is locked to the pace, pulse steady, breathing constant, it becomes a pleasure rather than a burden to be alongside each other. Like a school of fish or a flock of birds, the pack is an organism: leadership may change—first one runner, then, while no one is watching, another. I was trying to explain, more portentously than I would have wished, that debate, like running, was beautiful. Winning required precision, and precision required a good eye and ear, not just the cold power of reasoning.

"It's, like, you have to be *so* careful what you say! Do you know what I mean?" They all nodded again, and those that could grunted. "You have to be really careful. One misstated word, one *um* or *like*, and that could be the point you get marked down that eventually loses you the round, and then the tournament."

"Really?" G was running comfortably and turned his head to look straight at me as he spoke; our legs kept moving forward at the same pace. "One wrong word and that's it?"

He was impressed. I had made debate sound as dramatic as a race to the finish—a contest in which times differed by mere hundredths of a second, in which the slightest misstep rendered years of training for naught. In my fantasy debate tournament, audiences watched rapt to see if a debater would pull out the victory with a lean at the tape, and they held their breath as they turned to the official clock. I was describing for my coach and teammates debate as I hoped it would be in England. Or, rather, I was describing who I hoped *I* would be in England.

On the New England debate circuit, I had at last come to feel simply proud, without ambivalence, of my gift for talking; I was using my words to win fair, tough competitions, to bring glory to a school and schoolmates whom I loved and who seemed to love me back. But, like many people who have success at an early age, I did wonder if it was coming too easily. As I became devoted to debate as a sport—and as I decided it was a noble civic activity—I began to suspect that my success so far was the result of beginner's luck, or, worse, brute power brought to bear. (*Don't try so hard to pull at our heart-strings.*) Like a chess player with an eidetic memory, I might be powerful but not necessarily artistic. Was I an elegant debater? Was I edifying to watch and hear? Was I subtle? I could win, but I hoped I could win beautifully.

We ran through the meadows that cut along the Connecticut River, between the woods to our left and the cornfields, leased to a local farmer, on our right. The formation was loosening now, runners going more at their own pace, lapsing into their own interior worlds. I was thinking about England.

I took an overnight flight to England with Mr. Hansen and Matthew Collins, the other American competitor. Collins, a Kingswood-Oxford senior, was three years older than I was, and his demeanor toward me was cool, bordering on surly. He was big and broad, and he had a deep voice with an angry edge. He sounded like a football coach whose team was down by twenty points at halftime. He seemed very proud of his combination of intellect and muscle, and he never wanted anyone to forget either half of his one-two punch. He never actually called me a wimp or a pussy, but I kept expecting him to.

I was growing to like Mr. Hansen and enjoy his courtly, old-fashioned affect. With his beige tweed jacket and his necktie, and his short hair parted perfectly in the middle, in the fashion of the 1920s, he looked like a less pugnacious H. L. Mencken. In truth he was a professor from another era shuffling into the 1990s. It made sense that he was the coach at a boys' school, one that still required Latin of all its students, no less. In retrospect, I appreciate that he was willing to suffer my arrogance, certain that it was a freshman foible with an expiration date; when he gave comments at the ends of rounds in which he'd been my judge, he always offered me gentle proddings toward humility, and as I became a more likable debater over four years I suspected that he took some pride in the part he was sure he had played. And although I didn't think we needed a chaperone in England, I soon was glad that Mr. Hansen was there. Matt often looked as if he wanted to put me in a headlock, and I was sure Mr. Hansen's presence was all that restrained him.

As we disembarked at Heathrow, Matt kept his distance, strutting out of baggage claim like a man on a blind date with a sure thing. When he got to the receiving area, where limousine drivers held up signs for their parties, Matt slowed down, allowing us to catch up. After five minutes we found the man holding the white placard that said DEBATE TOURNAMENT. He showed us to the parking lot, where he led us to a van stenciled with the words READING BLUE COAT SCHOOL. We climbed in, the quiet Englishman sent by the school started the motor, and I promptly fell asleep.

I awoke as we pulled up to the school's main building, a grand brick edifice facing a wide green lawn. Inside, we were taken to the cafeteria, where other competitors and coaches were sitting in front of their trays, slurping broth and eating sandwiches and french fries. The Blue Coat students were on school holiday, so except for the debaters the big room with its high ceilings was empty. I went through the line and got some food, then sat down with some Canadian boys and began to eat. The food was mostly bland, but the vanilla pudding was tasty and seemed an acceptable breakfast. We were all jet-lagged. Hardly anybody talked. It did not feel like a gathering of great speakers.

After breakfast, we were escorted to a large hall, busy with smiling Brits; this was where we were to meet the families who would be billeting us for the week. After my name was called, I stepped forward and was introduced to a boy named Graham McMillan, who was waiting with his mother, Barbara. I have no memory of the car ride back to the McMillans' house, nor do I remember falling asleep in a small bedroom when I got there. What I remember is waking up in the dark in my pajama pants and T-shirt and stumbling downstairs, where I was greeted by Graham, his younger brother, their mother, and their father, Peter, a tall man with a broad smile who said, "Good morning, Mark!" It took me a moment to realize that he was kidding, that it was not morning but about nine o'clock at night. I liked Mr. McMillan at once. He had a warm Scottish accent, with a heavily rolled *r*, and his wife and children, though English, seemed to acquiesce in his provincial informality. They were all in their stocking feet, standing in the large kitchen drinking tea with another man, a family friend whose name I forget. He had a pointed, narrow face, and his bushy eyebrows stuck forth from his brow like awnings over his eyes. He handed me a cup of tea and began asking me about myself, and soon we were in a long conversation about international politics, a topic to which I was quite inadequate.

This mischievous friend soon goaded me into confessing that I did not understand why any country would want a king or a queen. The McMillans watched as their two guests, one an old bachelor and the other a boy adolescing before them, debated the merits of the monarchy. Early in the conversation I was worried that my hosts would be offended, and I tried to back off, but the man with the eyebrows kept pressing his case. His voice shot up an octave on words he really wanted to stress; he had a delightful patter, with that musical range that Britons have, so much more evocative than our American monotone.

"Well as *I* see it, having a queen can do *worlds* of good and no harm at *all*. I mean, she provides continuity." He pronounced it slowly, with an aspirated *t*, a yod with the *u* sound, and an octave-higher third syllable: contt-in-*yoo*-i-tee. "You see, she is there as prime ministers come and go. She's been queen since right after the war, since Churchill's third term until now"—these were the waning days of Margaret Thatcher's ministry—"and she's known them all: Eden, Macmillan, Wilson, Heath, all of them. And she's a smart woman, not the most brilliant, but smart. And so she can offer some sense of historical contt-in-*yoo*-i-tee, and they can go to her for advice. I don't know if they ever do, but they can, you see.

"Now, if Elizabeth were a dullard—and perhaps she is a dullard, I don't *really* know—but if she's a dullard, then the prime ministers, who by and large are really quite intelligent men, can simply ignore her, they can ignore her entirely. But if she is clever, they can pay attention. And if ever we had a monarch who was quite clever, then I'm certain that person would be a statesman for the ages, a true asset to the political *or*der, consulted by every prime minister, able to give memorable speeches, a uniter of the land—which is part of what she *does* do, you know, unite the Commonwealth countries! Now Elizabeth is not that kind of statesman, or stateswoman, you know, but she is not bad! And so why *not* keep her, I say!"

He seemed to be finished, and all four McMillans and I looked at him with some admiration, but he had more to add:

"And by the way, I know how people always ask—and the English ask it just as Americans do, you must know—they always ask if having a monarch is worth the cost. But you know, at this point much of the money is *hers*. They are a wealthy family; it is *their* money. I sup*pose* there are those in the Labour Party who would have us rob the queen and Philip of their money, and the children too, but that does not seem *right*. And do we support them somewhat? Is there a subvention? Well of course. Just think of what having a queen does for our tourism revenue! And it is a job, you know! Being the living, breathing embodiment of the hopes of a nation is not easy!"

It was a splendid peroration, and by the time the man with the eyebrows was done speaking I was ready to join the Queen's Guard at Buckingham Palace.

I came to enjoy the McMillans very much. I was to stay with them once more, a year later, when I returned to this tournament at Reading Blue Coat. And that second year they once again had a guest besides me, a white-haired American woman who gave me a deliciously violent shoulder massage while she talked about the virtues of Unitarianism. Both years I played football—soccer—with the young McMillans, and Graham became my first non-American friend. But what I remember best about my two weeks over two years with the McMillans was the man with the eyebrows and the soft spot for his country's political system. Being an Oppenheimer, I had already been present for hundreds of deeply felt political argu-ments among cocksure adults. But that man spoke with a marriage of deep feeling and careful reasoning, admixed with a touch of ironic self-deprecation, that seemed distinctly un-American. It was oratory, really, delivered right there in a kitchen in provincial England. I was sure that this would be a very fine week.

The competition began the next morning. I was one of about thirty entrants from a dozen countries, including Canada, the United States, Australia, England, and Cyprus. We each had to compete in four events: parliamentary debate, impromptu speaking, interpre-tive reading, and either persuasive speaking or after-dinner speaking. Since receiving my entry materials in the mail three weeks earlier, I had pored over each event description as if scrutinizing the rules for an unfamiliar foreign sport, like cricket or curling.

Parliamentary debate I knew: two against two (I'd be randomly paired with partners from other countries), no cross-examination, and the topic announced only half an hour before the debate, so a premium on wit and oratory, not research or facts. "Parly" was an English event that my small American league had embraced, but the remaining four events had apparently traveled the other way: all were slightly modified versions of events that I knew were popular in American public and Catholic school leagues, but which appeared only rarely on the prep school circuit. In interpretive reading, one selected a passage from a work of literature, gave a thirty-second introduction, and then read for eight to twelve minutes. One was not allowed to use any props, so we were judged purely on how we used our voice, in categories such as "inflection" and "clarity." Impromptu speaking, which was occasionally done in New England, was like the National Forensic League's extemp speaking—a daredevil event. The competitor reached into a hat and picked out a small piece of paper with three topics written on it; the topics might be sayings or slogans, famous or obscure. For example: "A house divided against itself cannot stand." "It takes two to tango." "Go ahead. Make my day." After two minutes for preparation, the competitor had to stand and deliver a speech, inspired by one of the three topics, lasting no less than three and no more than five minutes, aided only by whatever notes he could scribble on a 3x5-inch note card. (Yes, 3x5—the rules were clear.)

And then there was the choice of persuasive speaking or after-dinner speaking, a choice that divided the field into two kinds of public speakers: those who tried to be funny and those too scared to try.

Persuasive speaking, like the National Forensic League's original oratory, was a solo prepared event. One delivered an eight-to-twelve-minute oration, attempting to persuade the audience of some policy position—"The United States should voluntarily give up nuclear weapons," say. After-dinner speaking was also a prepared event, so it lacked the edgy danger of impromptu speaking, but it was the sexiest event: like humorous interpretation in the American league, it showcased the cut-up, the comedian, the young orator eager to seduce an audience with his most shameless pickup lines, even at the risk of getting shot down. The after-dinner speech lasted from four to six minutes, could be on any topic, and was delivered as if to entertain a hall of conventioneers well lubricated with port. The event guidelines were explicit that this speech was to be humorous—"wit, humour, and absurdity are all equally welcome"—and the final round was held not before the closing banquet but right after it, before the coffee, dessert, and awarding of trophies. This was the only event, I was to discover, in which one's fellow competitors might influence the judges: whichever finalist got the bigger laughs at the closing banquet was likely to win the judges' ballots.

There were, then, two events I'd had to prepare for in advance. For my interpretive reading, I had selected John F. Kennedy's inaugural address. It was suitably short, and it was distinctly American. The United States had not yet invaded Iraq (not even the first time), we were still generally esteemed throughout the world, and I embraced the notion of sailing to England as the boy patriot, washing ashore with the words of a great president—a president from my home state!—on my lips. For my persuasive speech, I had written an extended version of the affirmative case for drug legalization that I had presented at the Loomis tournament in January. It seemed a topic ill suited to England, where the "drug war" was not as aggressively fought as in the United States, but with little time to prepare it made sense to recycle my drug research.

Why had I chosen persuasive speaking rather than after-dinner speaking? I had intuited that a fourteen-year-old American probably would not match up well in a battle of wit, humor, and absurdity against a bevy of seventeen-year-olds from England and the Commonwealth. I'm not sure how I knew this, but I was right. It's not just Americans who find Britons particularly funny—as I was to learn, Britons find themselves very funny, too. We think Monty Python is uproarious, but they think Monty Python is even more uproarious than we do. Americans find it easier to laugh at a joke told in an English accent, and the English do, too. This all goes double for Scots, who are twice as funny as Americans but think themselves four times as funny. (It helps that in Scotland even high schoolers occasionally fortify themselves with beer or whiskey before starting their workday, or rather their schoolday. Truly. I saw this my junior year, when I debated in Scotland.) I would have been poor competition for the English boys and girls, with their posh accents and their pre-Oxon wit. In this element, I was at best a plodding policy wonk, and it seemed wise to accept that fact. So I gave the drug speech.

I ended up making the out rounds, or playoff rounds, in only one event, interpretive reading. I had prepared well, even reading up on the rhetorical devices Kennedy used, such as chiasmus, the reversal of word order in clauses like "Ask not what your country can do for you, but what you can do for your country." And my recitation of Kennedy's inaugural address seemed to hold a special appeal for the middle-aged ladies, mostly local parents and retirees, who constituted the bulk of the judging pool. They remembered Kennedy—he was probably the last American president they had adored—so hearing an earnest American boy of fourteen read back to them the words they had thrilled to in their bachelorette years held an irresistible appeal. And although we were only shortly past the halcyon days of the Reagan/Thatcher love-in, Kennedy's pledge of devotion to his allies still had the ring of the new: "To those old allies, whose cultural and spiritual origins we share, we pledge the loyalty of faithful friends. United, there is little we cannot do in a host of cooperative ventures. Divided, there is little we can do—for we dare not meet a powerful challenge at odds and split asunder." I have a distinct memory, from one of the preliminary rounds, held in a drafty aerie in the main academic building, of finishing the speech and seeing the three ladies of the judging panel erupt in vigorous applause. The only other people in the room were the six other interpretive readers, and they looked either bored or nervous, but the old ladies of the judiciary were elated. One of my ballots in this event read, simply, "Bravo, Mark!"

In the other events, I lagged the field badly. In debate, my knowledge of current events, always sufficient to impress judges back home, was paltry compared with the Europeans' and Canadians'.

(The first lesson an American learns in international debate is how little we know of the world. Prime minister of Australia? Most Americans can't even name the prime minister of Canada.) My persuasive speech, which in its original, debate form had been so effective against the team from St. Paul's, fell flat in England, probably in part because non-Americans, being from saner countries, cannot fathom the bottomless stupidity of our drug war. Europeans would like drugs to be even more legal than they are, but given the liberal drug regimes under which they already live, it's hardly a pressing concern.

As for impromptu speaking, I just was not witty enough. Actually, that's not quite right—impromptu speaking only seems to be about wit. The truth is, very few people, given a topic and two minutes to prepare, can deliver a speech with any real, spontaneous cleverness. People who are funny on their feet may have some requisite quickness of mind, but what they really have is the ability to sell themselves: a mix of timing, facial expressions, stock bits that fit many situations, perfectly calibrated nervous energy, and loads of confidence. A good impromptu speaker makes you believe that he is being witty; in fact, he is only being funny, and that's good enough. Comedy is one part good material, three parts salesmanship. In an impromptu speech, you may get lucky and come up with an original angle or a couple of good lines, but the best competitors never count on it.

I learned the importance of salesmanship from Rob Goffin, that year's winner of the impromptu-speaking championship as well as the overall title. Rob, like so many of the best Anglophone debaters in the past twenty years, was a student of John Robinson, the coach at St. John's–Ravenscourt School in Winnipeg. (The place you'd least like to visit has produced the people most able to persuade you to come.) Mr. Robinson's debaters were always well coached, rehearsed to a high sheen, but Rob was the most impressive. Maybe it's just that I saw him when I was a freshman and he was a senior, but even adjusting for freshman hero worship, Rob was astonishing.

To begin with, he was awfully well dressed. He wore a double-breasted navy blue chalk-stripe suit, cut in the English style, with double vents in the back. Rob was the only teenager I had ever seen attempt such clothes. He carried a leather briefcase, too, yet somehow didn't seem preposterous. Had he opened his mouth and spoken pure drivel, I'd still have wanted to be Rob, just for his style. But as it happened he was the most articulate person of any age whom I had ever encountered.

That impression holds even though I can recall only one specific Goffin riff from the entire tournament. It came during his winning speech in the impromptu-speaking finals. After his two-minute preparation time had expired, he ascended the stage, took a final look at his one permitted note card, ostentatiously stuffed it deep in his jacket pocket, and began:

"Ladies and gentlemen, Mr. Chairman, honored judges. I'd like to tell you a story. I was home in bed one day, under the covers, on school vacation." Goffin stood stage right, as I recall, but he occasionally took small, purposive steps to his left. With his wavy brown pompadour, red cheeks, and reed-thin build, he projected a radical cool; he had the look of a white jazzman. But when he spoke he vibrated with energy. He was Chet Baker meets Robin Williams. "I just wanted to settle in for a long morning of sleeping," he continued. He was speaking slowly, almost languorously. From this buildup, we knew that something was going to disturb his sleep. "Finals were over. I had earned a holiday. My parents were off at work, nobody was home. This was going to be my day. I was in a half-dreaming state when all of a sudden the doorbell rang. I looked over at my clock radio. It said eleven A.M. As I got out of bed, pulling on my robe, I thought to myself, 'Dear God, what could *anyone* possibly be doing awake this early?'"

And at that, everyone in the crowded auditorium, all the assembled debaters, parents, teachers, administrators, and judges, laughed a collective laugh, a laugh that bounced off the wooden ceiling and paneled walls. Was it a brilliant line? No. There was, however, an undeniable punch to this punch line, one that none of his spectators missed.

To begin with, Goffin's delivery had been impeccable. Nothing in his buildup had telegraphed the payoff: when he let on that 11 A.M. seemed early to him, we were surprised, from our heads to our viscera. His slight emphasis on "anyone" had in fact been a sleight of hand, making us wonder for a split second who was at the door, leaving us sucker-punched when we realized, just a moment later, that he had described 11 A.M. as *early*. What's more—and here we venture into the realm of mystical good luck, for I don't think Goffin intended this effect—he had made a joke that was funny in different ways to different members of the audience. To the teenagers, eleven-as-early was funny because *it's so true*—it's funny in the *Seinfeld* sense, the recognition of a commonplace, so that everyone can smile in agreement. To the adults, eleven-as-early was funny in the hokey, Dan Barry, *Family Circus* sense, a shared complaint that parents have about their children, or teachers about their students. It's funny not only because it's true, but also because *Hey, we can commiserate*. Finally, because most of the world doesn't distinguish between Canadians and Americans, eleven-as-early struck the audience as a hilarious bit of testimony from a typical American slacker, the laid-back dude whom the whole world loves (such as, from the very year of Goffin's triumph, the title characters in *Bill & Ted's Excellent Adventure*).

Having won us over with that line, there was no way Goffin could lose us. We were his. Remember, impromptu speaking only seems to be about wit. Eleven-as-early is not witty, not even particularly clever. But delivered to the right people, with the right timing, and with supreme confidence, such a line persuades the audience that they are in the presence of a true wit, even a true orator. From then on, every line is given the benefit of the doubt. All the jokes seem funnier, because we trust that they're the work of someone funny. We believe in the man, which is more important than believing in the message.

In Goffin's speech, it turned out that the man at the door was a salesman. Goffin's topic, which he eventually worked his way around to, was "Clothes make the man," and the salesman was relevant because, according to Goffin's metaphorical take, salesmen embodied the power of style over substance, clothes making the man. "We need to *learn* from salesmen," Goffin said, as he neared the end of his five minutes. "If we can learn their secrets, using charm and style and savoir-faire to achieve our ends, then no matter who we are, we can do more good. No matter what our cause, we are better prepared to achieve it."

As he walked offstage to wildly appreciative applause, I wondered if Goffin sensed his own perfection: how in his paean to style over substance, he had shown more style than substance. If I noticed it, starstruck tyro that I was, it could not have been lost on the more senior debaters and judges in the room. It might only have been lost on the orator himself, a boy to whom speaking was so instinctive that it defeated analysis. We were in the presence of a true natural.

When I got back to the United States, my friends all asked if I was disappointed that I hadn't won the tournament in England. I was surprised to answer, truthfully, that I wasn't upset. It was exciting to realize that, as I had suspected, there were better speakers, much better speakers. I was fourteen years old, and it was okay that I still had a ways to go.

I was also beginning to feel less anxious about words. As a young child, speaking had been a pleasure but also a compulsion; there were times when I just couldn't stop talking or arguing or explaining (even as my tearful mother pleaded with me to be quiet). As I got older, I learned more self-control, especially in the aftermath of my legal troubles. But it was only once I found debate, in junior high school, that the urgency of talking, its needy quality, began to abate. Channeling my words into a sport was cathartic; it seemed to loosen some neurotic knot in my chest, and I became a far more relaxed, and generally quieter, person. That was especially true after England, where I heard words used more elegantly than ever. The trip had been such a pleasure; over there, I'd seen how public speaking could both be a sport and an art. Winning was so utterly beside the point.

Finally, I was happy to be home. Even if I was not returning a champion, it would be good to be back on the New England circuit. There was one more tournament before the year was out. Three weeks later, this short item ran in our school newspaper, the *Log:*

DEBATE RACKS UP MORE WINS
by Thacher Kent

May 24, 1989

Loomis Chaffee had another successful debating tournament at Deerfield, Sunday, May 7. . . .

The topics for the debates were varied, including such resolutions as, "Technology is a wolf at the door" and "He who will have no judge but himself condemns himself." The topics for the third round were promised to be a little "lighter," but no one thought there was much difference between them and the others.

Unfortunately, the scheduled exhibition debate was canceled due to time limitations, so the debaters headed to the dining hall for dinner and the distribution of awards. Roxbury Latin took the top overall school, but Loomis Chaffee took a good deal of the other trophies, including the top advanced four person team, won by Heather McGray, Dan Donshik, Mark Oppenheimer and Kevin Moran. They also won the first and second two person team awards. Mark Oppenheimer was awarded the top speaker award, and Kevin Moran got second. Adam Donshik also did very well for his first debate.

The same victory was described with an authoritative succinctness in the Loomis Chaffee *Daily Bulletin:* "For the fourth consecutive tournament LC was the top team in the advanced division." If it wasn't quite DiMaggio's fifty-six-game hitting streak, it was still unprecedented in prep school debate. But then the school year ended, the week after the article appeared.

That summer, I earned spending money by answering phones at my father's law office. I didn't see much of Adam, who was now on to girlfriends. Lynda had parties in her basement recreation room, and we watched tortured, romantic movies, like *Say Anything*, and ironic, sophisticated movies, including a lot of Woody Allen. About once a week, Derek and I got one of our mothers to drop us at Showcase Cinemas, in the strip-mall land of West Springfield; *Batman* was the big movie that summer. In August, I attended two weeks of tennis camp at Williams College, where all the cool kids had spray-painted the *Batman* insignia in black on their white tennis strings. I followed the Yankees in the newspaper and on the radio, but it felt more like a duty than a pleasure. As the summer waned, I began to feel a bizarre new sensation: the aching desire to return to school—and to my friends, and to debate.

VIII

The arrival of the new school year felt promising. Although only a sophomore, I had been elected a co-president of the team, with Kevin, and we had a good crew, with a strong senior class, a sophomore cohort led by me and Lynda, and some very enthusiastic freshmen. I don't remember many of the debate tournaments the first half of that year, I think because the glory was spread among so many of us. Looking back at old copies of the school's *Daily Bulletin*, in which results of the weekend's debate tournaments were always printed on Monday, I see that five Loomis debaters contributed to our wins at Exeter, Dana Hall, and an international tournament hosted in October by Roxbury Latin.

But in January of sophomore year I participated in what was to be my favorite round of debate ever—my funniest, loosest, most slaphappy and spirited round. It took place at MacDuffie, a private girls' school (now co-ed) in Springfield. Here's how the *Springfield Union-News* covered the MacDuffie parliamentary tournament the next day:

MARK OPPENHEIMER

DEBATERS DO IT FOR THE SAKE OF ARGUMENTS
17 TEAMS COMPETE IN TOURNAMENT
by William Freebairn

Staff Writer

January 29, 1990

There were 87 hour-long, heated arguments at the MacDuffie
School in Springfield yesterday, but most participants went home
friends when it was all over. More than 100 high school students
participated in a day-long extemporaneous debate tournament
involving 17 private preparatory schools in three rounds of debating. And while the arguments were largely friendly, some adults
and students were upset by comments in the final round they said
were sexist and offensive. . . .

For most of the day, debaters argued away in formal face-offs on
such topics as "The most dangerous food is a wedding cake," and
"Nothing that is morally wrong can be politically right." The tournament, sponsored by the debate club at MacDuffie, is one of the
largest for the private prep schools, organizers said. . . .

The two top teams going into yesterday's final debate were a
team from Phillips Academy, in Andover, and one from the Loomis
Chaffee School in Windsor, Conn. The topic chosen was "The most
exquisite pleasure is giving pleasure to others," and, in the course
of arguments, the Andover team expressed support for prostitution,
arguing it was a "noble, worthwhile" profession which requires little effort. "If sex is good, then wouldn't more sex be better?" asked
one Andover debater rhetorically.

Debaters from Loomis opposed the Andover argument, saying prostitution is a form of slavery, and is far from safe for most
women. Speakers for both sides made wide use of sexual innuendo
and humor in their comments to a mostly appreciative crowd.

After the debate, which all three judges scored for Loomis,

136

some in the audience expressed concern about the arguments. Julie Hill, debate coach for Phillips Exeter Academy in New Hampshire, said the language used by Andover debaters in the discussion was offensive and sexist.

Hill said she felt officials should have steered the debate in other directions.

"They got too explicit and illicit and went overboard," said Sia Battle, a debater from the Dana Hall School in Wellesley.

Mark Oppenheimer, a 10th grader who was half of the winning Loomis team, agreed that the debate took a turn for the unseemly. "In an exhibition round there is a tendency to play to the crowd," said the 15-year-old Springfield resident.

[MacDuffie team a]dviser [Ted] Lyman said he thought it would not be appropriate to cut off debate that grows tasteless. "Once you give people the liberty to speak, which is what debate is, you have to let them speak within the framework you set," he said.

In that final round, John DeSimone and I faced the Andover team of Doug Kern and Chris Deem. Years later, Kern was a standout college debater at Princeton, but in high school I thought of him as the brilliant but intense redhead who between rounds would lecture everybody on the virtues of libertarianism. His partner, Chris, was a loud, louche kid with wild blond hair and a real swagger, and together they were the perfect team to argue in favor of prostitution: Doug argued on libertarian grounds, and Chris cracked a lot of jokes about sex. That the audience included many MacDuffie students— girls' school students!—seemed to please Chris tremendously, and he did his best to scandalize them. Doug and Chris had five main arguments in favor of the motion, arguments that Chris summed up in his Second Affirmative speech:

"First," he said, stepping from behind the lectern and gesturing with his legal pad in his right hand, "legalizing prostitution would be an economic boon for many women who need the money but right now stay out of the business for fear of jail. . . . Second, it would be

137

an economic boon for our government, which would take prostitution out of the black market and bring it above-ground, thus making it taxable. Why should the only people making money from the world's oldest profession be the whores and their pimps? . . . Third, prostitution provides a genuine service, helping lonely, hard-up men everywhere satisfy some basic human needs. . . . Fourth, by helping those men satisfy those needs, they become more productive members of society, spending less time in peep shows or hunting down illicit prostitutes in bad neighborhoods—now they can just place a phone call to their service of choice, entertain a fine lady in the comfort of their own home, and then go back to selling insurance or manufacturing widgets! . . . Finally, let's face it: some prostitutes enjoy the work! By making their work legal, and thus making it safer and even bringing more women into the profession, we can maximize sexual pleasure not just for the men, but also for the women— for the whole world!"

It was while listening to this last point that I saw my opening. If the Andover boys had conducted the whole debate at the johns' expense, playing up these poor losers' need for safe, legal sexual relief, they would have been tough to beat. But by suggesting that prostitution was actually fun for the women, they left themselves open to charges of misogyny, ignorance, and just plain heartlessness.

The trick to beating them would be to match their humor while also seizing the moral high ground. As I rose to speak, the hundred members of the audience, a mix of coaches, fellow debaters, and curious MacDuffie girls, seemed to favor Andover. Chris had given a winning speech, and it didn't hurt that he was handsome. He would be forgiven his poor judgment, unless I made sure that he paid the price. But if I gave a speech that was all moral censure— "How dare my opponent ignore the difficulty of the prostitute's life, the oppressions, the lack of choices . . ."—then I would just seem like a fifteen-year-old Gladstone, lecturing from on high. I would seem like a prude. It was crucial that I be funny first, *then* appeal to morality.

"Honored judges, worthy opponents." I was speaking from behind the lectern, my partner at a desk stage left, the Andover debaters seated to my right. "The fine gentlemen of the opposition have given us five reasons the House should legalize prostitution. If even one of them had merit, I would be worried." I enumerated their reasons, giving about one minute to each, improving on their wit as best I could. "The thing is, you only gain productivity if the prostitute is mediocre—then you can go right back to your job. But if she's really *good*, you purchase an extra hour. You go again. You *lose productivity*. . . . And might I also ask how the right honorable gentlemen from Andover know so much about the virtues of prostitution, anyway? Is *this* the secret to straight A's at Phillips Academy?" The audience was laughing, and I was feeling a contact high from the freshman girls blushing in the front row. Was I losing track of time? I checked my watch—still a minute to go. Good. If I didn't leave time for the peroration, and wrap it up with a big, royal seizing of the moral high ground, nothing would be assured. Being funny like them was only playing for a draw, and could well end up a loss. Time to move in— big joke, then turn serious:

"As to their last contention, Mr. Speaker, that women *enjoy* prostitution—why, I think I can rebut this lame assertion rather easily." I again stepped from behind the lectern, moving right and stopping directly behind Doug Kern's poof of curly red hair. He turned his head around, looking up at me, but I kept my eyes fixed on the audience. "Ladies and gentlemen, boys and girls, I give you *Doug Kern*! If you think for one second that prostitutes enjoy their work, you have not considered that they have to sleep with men like *Doug*." Everybody laughed—and they had permission to laugh, because it was the Andover debaters themselves who had suggested that prostitutes are in it for the kicks. Chris rolled his eyes, while Doug just buried his face in his hands.

Then, after the laughter had died down, I said: "The thing is, ladies and gentlemen, that while we can laugh at the absurdity of the affirmative team's arguments, we can't laugh at the horror of prostitution. To us, sitting in a comfortable, heated auditorium on this cold January day, it's all just a game—who can win this debate? Who gets the trophy at the end? But to women out there walking the street, it isn't funny. It's their lives. So while I have some sympathy for the libertarian arguments they bring up—after all, I don't like government intrusion, either, and I think basically we should be allowed to do as we please—I can't travel down this road with them. I can't so cavalierly endorse the trade in human flesh. The humans involved matter too much. After all, what's the desired goal? Pleasure for men? Well, yes, that's a good thing. But so too is equality between the sexes. So too is women's control over their bodies . . ."

I did not frame the question in terms of some grand philosophical principle. I never used the word *utility*, never talked about distributive justice. But I managed, I think, to use philosophical thinking to go funny early, then claim the moral high ground, just as Mr. Robison taught us. It's not always easy to claim the moral high ground; you have to take your audience with you, persuade them that it's actually more gratifying to let go of their laughter, take a deep breath, shift in their seats, and then get serious. To avoid mere preachiness, it helps if the serious turn is couched in big, edifying questions, the biggest of which is always some version of what philosophers call teleology: the good being striven for. *What is the desired goal? What are we really after?*

Mr. Robison was an exceptional coach, and I knew that we were lucky to have him. Some debaters got no coaching at all. Years later, I asked Doug Kern what his high school experience had been like. "I was always quite envious," he said, "of your situation and the situation of a lot of people, who had dedicated faculty members who showed up year after year and gave smart suggestions." Andover, he said, never had any better than a nominal adviser, a teacher who would okay their expenses but had no interest in teaching the team anything. With better coaching, Doug told me, they might have avoided the MacDuffie debacle.

"I remember you kicked our ass, and quite deservedly so," Doug said. "It was a lame topic, a one-joke topic where you tell the joke and then there's five long minutes left. And you watched those minutes tick down so slowly: five, four, three, two . . . I remember you asking me in cross"—I had probably asked with a heckle, since there is no cross-examination in a parliamentary tournament—"if it was such a good suggestion, why didn't I do it? I got on the self-deprecation kick and said, 'Well I don't have the equipment,' which was my one good laugh line.

"I knew we were going to lose, I knew Deem wasn't going to be as funny as he thought we were going to be, and then it was like watching the iceberg hitting the *Titanic*."

Deem had screwed up, but he and Doug might have survived to win the round had John and I done no more than match them joke for joke. We knew we had to share the joke, but then move beyond it—and that's what debate was teaching us. We were supposed to move from competitive, often immature grandstanding to intellectual questing. It might not have been obvious from our one-hour tangle with Andover about the merits of whoring, but even in such prurient, glandular moments, we were learning how to think.

By February of my sophomore year, the Loomis debate team had won or tied for the win at six tournaments in just a year and a half. I had been all over New England; to Canada, for a tournament in the fall; to England, the spring before. I was proud of the trophies, and also of my growing reputation at school for being someone who mattered off campus (I felt that I shared some special, unspoken status with Hillary Anderson, a fellow sophomore and a world-class gymnast—she too would miss class to disappear for long weekends, and in those days before the Internet we would hear only whispers of big titles she had won).

But for me the best part of debate, beyond even the intellectual growth, was the thrilling discovery that I had found community. At my school, and at schools in other states and foreign countries, I was developing a network of friends who loved the art of the speech; when we saw each other there was instant camaraderie. Our shared connoisseurship gave us a powerful sense of fraternity.

I remember my peers—Rob Goffin, Jock Martin, Naomi Schaefer, Robert Haskell—and I miss them. Rob is now making money on Wall Street, I hear. Jock, who was from Rob's high school, is teaching drama at their alma mater. Naomi, who debated for Worcester Academy, in Worcester, Massachusetts, is an editor at the *Wall Street Journal*. Robert was for many years a fashion journalist, and he is now finishing medical school. People think that all debaters become lawyers, but in my experience many of the best do not. The best debaters are eccentrics, and nobody knows where time will take them. Kevin Moran is working for the State Department in Afghanistan. Shira Springer, who was a year behind me at Loomis, covers the Celtics for the *Boston Globe*.

Then there was Lynda. At that first meeting in Chaffee Hall, on the first day of school, we bonded as fellow book people, word people, the kind of kids who would end up doing debate. She was from Vernon, Connecticut, a working-class bedroom community where small cars are parked in the driveways of small houses. Her parents were an ex-nun and the man she'd left her order for. A tall, broad-shouldered blond with far-set eyes and translucent skin, Lynda could have been just another popular girl, but she wasn't demure and she wasn't flirty. Some Loomis girls refused to eat in front of boys—that was not Lynda. She talked in bursts of purposive energy, using long sentences and a handsome vocabulary. She had emerged from junior high ready to conquer high school, and that obviously meant more to her than getting a boyfriend.

I grew to marvel at Lynda's dedication and mastery: she dove into every new interest with the resolve to own it as soon as possible. She joined the debate team and became a star debater; she went to Spain the summer after sophomore year and returned a dedicated

Hispanophile, pledging that she would major in Spanish when she got to college; junior year, she started dating (Jordan Oland, a junior, was her first), and from then on she announced each new boy as the love of her life. She did nothing half-assed. After college, when she became a lesbian, she became a lesbian social worker active in pro-choice politics.

And then she married a Republican man who had had a crush on her at Cornell. She now works at an investment bank in Boston.

As for Webster McDuff, he ended up just where we all thought he would. "Duff," a day student from West Hartford, was about 90 percent as articulate as I was, at least as creative, and twice as charismatic. He was also more self-destructive than anyone I had ever known. An avid reader of fantasy and horror novels—Clive Barker was his favorite writer, and he had a particular fondness for Barker's *Imajica*—Duff was a general connoisseur of escapism: what his literature couldn't give him, he got from copious amounts of drink and drugs. He enjoyed theater, too, and was a gifted actor. I'll never forget the dismay of Mr. Nields, the theater director, as he realized in the spring of our senior year, when Duff was doing brilliant work in rehearsals for a one-act play, that he had busted Duff for drinking in the parking lot outside a school dance at the beginning of the school year. "Fuck," Mr. Nields said, talking casually to me and the other students in the directing class, "I can't believe he's the guy I had to bust for being drunk outside Chaffee. He's so fucking good." Duff now lives in California, where he surfs and designs video games.

Lynda, Duff, and I were a representative sample of who debated at Loomis. All three of us wrote for the *Log*, our school newspaper, at one point or another. Lynda gravitated toward Model Congress, then late in high school did a bit of theater. Duff wrote for the *Loom*, the literary magazine, but was never the extracurriculars maven that Lynda or I was. He spent a lot of time alone, at home, reading his novels and listening to gangsta rap—it was in his bedroom that I first heard N.W.A.'s "Fuck tha Police." If for me debate was about oratory and philosophy, and for Lynda about current events and policy, for

Duff it was about the theater, finding another stage on which to perform the grand opera that was his life.

No school had a bench as deep as Loomis's. Our second-string debaters would have been stars at any other school. There was John DeSimone, whose perfect part on the far left side of his straight black hair seemed to signify honesty itself, or perhaps obsessive compulsion. He was totally focused on doing the right thing—earning good grades, treating people as he'd wish to be treated. As Michael Kinsley said of Al Gore, John looked like an old person's idea of a young person, and I was not surprised to learn that he is now practicing real estate law in suburban New Jersey. I'd want him for my lawyer. Then there were John Carton, with his turtlenecks and his foghorn voice; Sarah Hennigan, who our sophomore year dated John DeSimone; Suzette Smikle, a shy West Indian girl with a lilting, barely audible voice who grasped debate intuitively and began winning right away; Cary Franklin, who years later became a Rhodes Scholar; Thacher Kent, who was to drop out of Williams College to join a cult in the woods of western Massachusetts, a cult that was on the front page of the *New York Post* in 1996 after many members were caught stockpiling weapons in Brooklyn; and Adam Donshik, now an actor in Los Angeles who once appeared on *Party of Five*.

Some of them are on Facebook now, posing for pictures with their young children. Others have vanished: Where have you gone, Trevor Robertson? We debated together once, you got near-perfect SAT scores but had a C average, and now nobody can find you. Rebecca Tovey, beautiful English lass? Duff and I were both in love with you. David Cohen, from Toronto? You always did interpretive readings of Elie Wiesel's *Night*, playing the Holocaust card—which everyone knew was a cheap, tear-jerking move. I miss even you.

At the end of sophomore year, I was invited back to England, for another run at the world title. After I was home from the tournament, this article ran in the *Log:*

DEBATERS RETURN
FROM WORLD CHAMPIONSHIPS
by Lynda Duna

May 25, 1990

As the Chamber Singers and the visitors to the Soviet Union have done previously this year, two members of the community traveled overseas extending Loomis Chaffee's reputation for excellence. Senior Kevin Moran and sophomore Mark Oppenheimer competed, with impressive results, in the World Debating and Public Speaking Championships held in Reading, England, from April 29 through May 2.

Mark Oppenheimer, the youngest competitor in the last two years, was the highest American finisher, placing fifth overall. He also earned first place honors in the impromptu speaking category, defeating the overall winner from Canada, talking on "The grass is always greener on the other side." Oppenheimer is the first American to place in the top five at both major world competitions, the first being the International Independent Schools Public Speaking Championships held earlier this year, where he won two divisions, again the first American to accomplish the title. . . .

The day after his return from England, Mark became the first person ever to win the Deerfield Debate Tournament two years in a row. He was victorious from a field of over a hundred speakers and coupled with senior John DeSimone, the second place speaker, to be the first place advanced team.

Commenting on the tournament [in England], Oppenheimer said, "While placing so well was a great personal thrill, the true triumph was having Loomis Chaffee's good reputation spread abroad."

That last line of mine, about winning for my school, was not a total lie. I took an underdog's pride in Loomis's success. I was aware that

145

those who didn't know Mr. Robison would expect Andover, St. Paul's, or Exeter to have the superior team, and it was exciting to humble those more famous schools, with their grander reputations and famous alumni. But as in cross-country running—another sport in which you perform alone but win as a team—debate could be an emotional seesaw, with school spirit on one end and the drive for individual glory on the other. Rereading that article, from my sophomore year, I winced when I got to the end, because while at Deerfield I really did want the team to win—the New England circuit brought out the team spirit in me—in England the week before, on my second trip to Worlds, I had put personal pride first, with rather ugly results.

As the article says, I was a finalist in impromptu speaking; the other finalists were Kevin Moran, from Loomis, and Atul Verma, the eventual winner of the whole tournament, from St. John's–Ravenscourt in Winnipeg. It was the last night of the competition, unusually muggy for England in May, and no event could have made me sweat harder than impromptu. In the prepared events, like persuasive speaking or interpretive reading, everyone would do well enough, and the best boy or girl would win, but impromptu was an event you could really *lose*. You could draw a blank. You could take one look at the topic on your slip of paper—"A stitch in time saves nine," maybe, or "The answer is blowing in the wind"—and have *absolutely no idea* what to say. I had seen Rob Goffin win this category so brilliantly the year before, stringing together his comic set pieces, making them seem natural and spontaneous, wrapping everything up in a perfect five minutes. I even remembered the sheen of his double-breasted wool suit. I remembered his briefcase. I had no briefcase, was wearing my father's old green tweed blazer, and could not imagine summoning that startling Goffinian confidence.

But none of that would matter, if the right speech was delivered to me. That's how impromptu speeches come—they're delivered, like unexpected gifts. You look at one word, maybe *stitch* in "stitch in time," and after a panicked three or four seconds the adrenaline and testosterone combust and you somehow remember that hilarious story about the ER doctor who didn't know how to suture your cut . . . and after that humorous lead-in, why not launch into a story about the American health-care system (the whole world likes an American who can laugh at his own country—it goes against their expectation that we're all jingoists) . . . and claim the moral high ground at the end by coming out for universal health care . . . but then, in the spirit of impromptu, just as the five minutes are coming to a close, *limp* off the stage at the end, as if your wound never did heal. And there it is: A stitch in time saves nine!

But if the gift doesn't come, you flounder. Your mind swims, you try anything. You turn the words around like letters on a Scrabble palette. You try out a bad pun: "Would it be funny to riff on a stitch in *thyme?*" You dismiss the pun, realizing there's nothing there. Then, suddenly, you hear the chairman of the room call "Time!" and as you head to the stage, you grasp for a way to start. When you get up there, you take a deep breath—the bright lights are in your eyes, you can't see the audience, but you know they're there, can hear their expectant silence—and you begin by holding up the slip of paper and stating the topic: "Ladies and gentlemen, a stitch in time saves nine!" You pause, and if nothing comes to you, *still* nothing, then you commit that most criminal of debate felonies: you repeat the topic. "Yes in*deed*, a stitch in time *does* save nine." And at that moment you sound for all the world like a liar asked a question he cannot answer, praying that if he restates the question with shifting emphases he'll figure a way out of this one: "What was *I* doing with her in that restaurant yesterday? What was I *doing* with her? Is *that* what you're asking me?" If matters are truly bad, you never find a good train of thought, so you run out the clock making mealy comments about the topic: "A stitch in time saves nine . . . Now there's a hackneyed expression. I mean, really, what does it mean? It apparently comes from a time when people were still stitching. Who stitches anymore? Are there any seamstresses in the house. Hello? Seamstresses, where are you?"

Five minutes of that—that's what you're afraid of.

So I was relieved when I looked at the slip of paper and saw "The grass is always greener on the other side." I knew that expression, and I even had a story about it. Derek had once used the phrase when we were twelve years old. We were talking about who had the better house for sleepovers. I said that I always enjoyed going to his mom's house, where he had Atari, cable television, and a foldout sofa in front of the TV, and where I could escape my siblings; he said that he liked my house because—well, he couldn't say exactly why, but he just did. "It's just that the grass is always greener on the other side," he finally concluded.

I sat down in my chair at the front of the auditorium, and rested my one note card on my knee. As I began to compose a speech, I was optimistic that the Derek story would lead to something good. But after thirty seconds, a full quarter of my prep time, I wasn't getting anywhere. I needed a story with broad significance, some anecdote that would open onto a global truth. The story about me and Derek and sleepovers seemed close, but I could not figure out the next step—some comment about family life? The eternal pleasure of sleepovers with friends? No, it wasn't there.

Another minute passed. I still had nothing to say. Behind me, the other students and the coaches were talking, keeping their voices low, at the level of a polite, deferential murmur. I began to let my mind wander; I found myself trying to pick up scattered words from their conversations. My prep time was slipping away.

And then it came: the story I needed to tell was about envy, the kind inspired by the amenities at Derek's house, only bigger, amplified. I needed to tell a story about a rich friend who seemed to have everything—money, summer house, clothes, girls—but who turned out not to have what mattered most, the love of his parents.

"Time!" the chairman called, but it was okay, because as I ascended the stage I knew what story I was going to tell.

"The grass is always greener on the other side," I said, as I made a show of folding up the slip of paper and placing it in my blazer pocket. "You know who taught me that? My friend J. Stillman Hanson. You wouldn't have heard of J. Stillman Hanson, but you might have heard of his family, the Rockefellers. One of the wealthiest families in the world, owners of banks, oil, shipping, real estate. J. Stillman Hanson, a senior at my high school, stands to inherit all of that. Ever since I first met him, I was jealous. Wouldn't you be?

"I remember the time I first visited his house. It was a mansion so big that there were rooms even he had never seen—and he grew up there! There was a movie theater, a bowling alley, tennis courts. The maids' quarters had maids' quarters!" That line surprised me as it came out of my mouth—it was a gift. It got a laugh, and when I started in again I felt the words coming more easily: superlatives about his family's wealth, the splendor of their house, their social prominence. Tales of black-tie events in their ballroom. Visits with presidents and royalty.

These were all lies, by the way. I knew Stillman, a Loomis senior, only slightly. He was the varsity soccer goalie, he had Patagonia fleece pullovers in five different colors, and he had a slow gait and curly, light brown hair. He smiled at everybody. A genuinely nice guy. And he was a Rockefeller—everyone at school knew that. But I had never been to his house. Lies, all lies.

"But J. Stillman Hanson's life is not the idyll it might seem," I continued. "Because although he seems to have everything in the world, there is one thing missing from that grand house, indeed from that grand life: parents. They are never around. They're always cruising on one boat or another, whether the Mediterranean or the Galapagos. Or they're skiing in Switzerland. Or they're working.

"This hadn't occurred to me until I went to visit him. I was too blind with envy to see it. But there we were, Stillman and I, talking in one of his house's ten living rooms, and I was saying, 'Man, you have it all.' And he looked around, listening as my voice echoed off the high ceiling, and said, 'What are you, crazy? You have it all. I have nothing. I was sent off to boarding school when I was barely ten years old. I never see my parents. You live at home. You have two brothers and a sister. You have your parents. You have everything.'

149

"Ladies and gentlemen of this fine house, I submit to you that the grass is, indeed, always greener on the other side. And that matters not just because of me and Stillman and our friendship. No, it matters in how we look at the world every day." *Take it to a higher level, seize the moral high ground.* "We may see people who have all sorts of consumer goods, and we instantly think that the best thing for a society would be to have more of those things for everyone, and that might lead us to some form of capitalism. But is that right? Is more stuff always what people need? Or is that just a person without lots of things seeing the other side and figuring the grass is always greener there? Maybe those people who have lots of things are miserable, and they're looking at *us*, thinking, 'I wish I had two parents at home.'"

I then talked about how countries under socialism were yearning to breathe free—the Berlin Wall had fallen just months earlier—even as capitalist societies were beset by homelessness and poverty. There was an obvious conclusion: "Ladies and gentlemen of this house, the grass is always greener on the other side. *Or so we think.* Thank you very much."

Twenty years later, I'm not too impressed with the sociology or the political economy of that speech. In fact, it's noteworthy as an example of how I could happily discard the philosophical rigor that Mr. Robison had taught me. Was I arguing that everyone in the world is equally happy but doesn't know it? Or that happiness is unattainable because envy is too powerful an emotion? It's hard to say. The ideas in the speech are a muddle.

And the anecdotes supporting the ideas were lies. Now, honesty is a tricky question in oratory. One may not invent facts to support the Strategic Defense Initiative or universal health care, but nobody thinks that every anecdote in an after-dinner speech or at a roast has to be entirely true. So may one exaggerate for effect in an impromptu speech? Absolutely—much humor depends on exaggeration. And jokes, like Rob Goffin's bit the year before about his doorbell being rung so early in the morning, can be invented; nobody puts any stake in their veracity.

But what I had said about Stillman wasn't tongue-in-cheek; I wasn't committing the misdemeanor of stretching the truth. Rather, I needed a true, straight, pathos-filled narrative to frame the moral lessons I wanted to draw at the end, and without a true one at my disposal I made one up.

And it was worse still, because I was telling lies about a boy I went to school with. Thank goodness this was the pre-Internet age, no YouTube or streaming audio or podcasts, so what happened at the debate tournament stayed at the debate tournament—Stillman never knew what I'd invented about him and his parents. I knew he would never know. But that's not the point, of course. I was using him, demeaning his family to a group of hundreds of strangers, getting laughs then trying to wring piteous tears from the (false) circumstances of his life. Pretty shameful.

It didn't even occur to me that I had done anything wrong until a month later, when Kevin pointed it out to me. We were in Madison, Connecticut, on Long Island Sound, the morning after the senior prom. I had been invited to the prom by the first girl I ever had a serious crush on, Claire Magauran, two years older than I was and way out of my league. A week after the prom, I asked her out on a second date, and I was crushed when she wasn't interested. During most of that summer I cried every night to the mixtape she had made me as a consolation prize. (I can still remember the songs I first heard on that tape: the B-52s' "Rock Lobster," Eric Clapton's "Wonderful Tonight," Depeche Mode's "Somebody.") But the night of the dance, while I still had hope, Claire and I retired with a group to Jamie Dunlop's father's beach house, where we drank beers—my third and fourth cans of beer ever—and fell asleep. The next morning, we were sitting on beach towels by the water when somehow I mentioned the England tournament to Kevin, who looked up from the sand he was flicking with a stick. "I thought that was awful," he said. I said I didn't know what he meant. "The way you used Stillman," he said. "It was terrible."

He was right, and I felt my ears burn up. I looked around to see if any of the others were listening—Claire, Jamie, Dave Leonard, whoever. They were all within fifty yards, some of them close to the water, but with the wind nobody could have heard us.

"I didn't even think of that," I said.

"I know," Kevin said, with a touch of compassion. He could tell how bad I felt. He got both sides of me: the part that had been ambitious enough to make up that story, and also the part of me that, when called on it, couldn't believe what I'd done.

I muttered something else, then turned and began to walk toward the surf. I took a long, slow twenty seconds before I was at the edge, feeling the first razor bite of the cold, early-season Connecticut water. I turned around, and now the others were looking. "Do it!" Dave Leonard shouted. He was an ornery senior, someone who alternated approval and the withholding of it, always giving me the feeling that I could impress him if only I tried harder. "You dare me?" I called back. He nodded. So I rushed in, not stopping until the water was at my nipples. I stood for a moment, feeling the icy burn, somehow thinking I deserved it for what I had done to Stillman. I wondered if I should apologize to him, then decided that since he didn't know anything, my apology would only make him feel worse. I'd have to keep it to myself. I was glad Kevin was graduating, taking with him the knowledge of what a jerk I'd been.

I walked back out of the water, taking intentionally slow steps, frozen to the bone but trying hard not to run pathetically for my towel. When I finally got to my towel and began to dry off, Dave looked at me and arched his eyebrows as if to say, "Not bad for a kid." But what he actually said, with an accuracy on more levels than he knew, was "You must have a nice case of shrink-dick."

IX

Junior year, I went abroad to debate three times: in Canada, in Scotland, and in England yet again. The late 1980s and early '90s were a good time for high school debate throughout the English-speaking world. John Robinson, Linda Martin, John Aimers, and other coaches were unifying the Canadian circuit, sponsoring several national tournaments every year. American schools were beginning to send teams to these Canadian tournaments. The Worlds tournament, which I attended twice in Reading and, my junior year, at Taunton School in England, had been started in 1988—the same year that, in Australia, another "world championships" had been founded, to coincide with Sydney's hosting the World Universities Debating Championship (which itself was a recent invention, dating to 1981). That Australian high school tournament, which became known as the World Schools Debating Championships, grew up alongside its collegiate big brother and was modeled after it: the emphasis was on debate alone, with none of the public-speaking events, like impromptu or after-dinner, that were so popular at the English event, the World Debate and Public Speaking Championships.

So by 1988 there were two high school world championships—and that's not counting the International Independent Schools Public Speaking Championships, known as "the Internationals," a tournament, first held in 1982, that was primarily Canadian but always drew some American and English teams. This last tournament had a strong focus on the public-speaking events; it was the only major tournament to offer obscure events such as radio newscast: "Each participant will be given an issue of a newspaper," the rules for radio newscast began. "After 30 minutes preparation, he must deliver, from original manuscript, a 4 minute 'top of the hour' radio news broadcast. Judging will be on the basis of the selection of news, clarity of presentation, originality, use of voice, credibility and adherence to time. The host school will provide an isolated facility for the competitors to use as a preparation room. The host school will also endeavour to provide a variety of newspapers for the different rounds, including an international and a local paper, providing always that all competitors in a given round are furnished with identical material. . . . Weather reports, sports news, interviews and editorials are acceptable, at the student's discretion and provided that they are based on the material found in the paper. No advertisements are permitted. No eye contact is expected between the competitor and the judges, since this is a radio newscast. The judges may choose to sit with their backs to the competitor."

Despite my past as an aspiring sports broadcaster, I never competed in radio newscast, which struck me in its design as a bit too artificial to be teaching a real skill. (The best radio newscast champion I ever saw, a pixieish, pouty-lipped brunette from British Columbia named Alexandra Oliver, enrolled at Yale the year after I did and is now a stand-up comedian in Los Angeles, as I discovered on YouTube one night. Maybe radio newscast did her some good.) At the Internationals, which I attended my sophomore through senior years—and which, of course, should not be confused with either Worlds—I entered parliamentary debate, extemporaneous speaking, persuasive speaking, and interpretive reading, all events that I had more or less encountered by the end of my freshman year and thus felt old and familiar to me.

Looking through old clippings, I am reminded of forgotten victories—for example, in 1989, in Boston, I was apparently the first American to win two events at the Internationals. But in my memory these tournaments are mostly a haze of English, Canadian, Scottish, and Australian accents, spoken by boys and girls in school blazers and ties, most of them sounding terrifyingly posh, a rare few of them, scholarship students from Lambeth or Glasgow, sounding less refined. These were weeks or long weekends when, already giddy to be skipping school, I was doubly giddy to be attending banquets and parties with a hundred other debaters my age from around the world. And our billets were the houses of generous parents whose children, students at the host schools, usually were eager to be our chaperones for the duration of the tournament, trying to show us some local culture, or, better yet, drag us to some local parties.

My first trip in junior year was to Victoria, British Columbia. The Internationals were at St. Michaels University School, and Loomis sent the team of Oppenheimer and McDuff. Victoria is an Anglo-phile city, and our hosts, the students of SMU (we pronounced it "smoo"), were English as could be, in school uniforms of white shirt and blue blazer, the latter adorned with a patch of the school crest. Dark V-neck sweaters factored in, too, mainly for girls, topping off their tartan skirts. Students played rugby and cricket. The headmaster, who greeted the assembled competitors on the first day of the tournament, was D. R. Penaluna—"the name is Cornish, from Corn-wall" I was later told by the only teacher at the school who had as grand a name, the debate coach J. Grenfell Featherstone. Mr. Feath-erstone was a coach of the bearded variety, a dramatic man with a voice like Stentor's, the kind of man one wasn't surprised to learn had had a small role in *Ups & Downs*, a boarding-school comedy film from the early 1980s. He was tremendously learned but quite self-effacing, a gentle-giant type whose debaters adored him.

I, in turn, adored his debaters. Out of school, these young sub-jects of the queen were not so different from my Loomis friends, although in grand English tradition they were more likely to smoke cigarettes, and they drank less surreptitiously and with considerably greater flair. Duff and I were billeted at the house of an SMU girl named Clare Mochrie, who took us out partying with her friends one night and, on another, allowed Duff to convince her to rent *A Clockwork Orange*. One never forgets the first time one sees the character tortured with the "Ludovico technique," his eyes taped open as he's forced to watch violent imagery on film—and my first time was in Clare Mochrie's den, with Duff cackling in amazement at Kubrick's genius as I thought about whether I could win the extemp speaking final for the second year in a row. The following night, Clare took us out with some of her friends, including the starlet-beautiful Sari Addington, whom incredibly I did not remember when we met again, the following fall, at a debate tournament in Winnipeg. But more on her later . . .

In Victoria, I did win extemporaneous speaking, one of the two events I'd won the year before in Boston. "Extemp," an event borrowed from the American public schools, was like impromptu for policy wonks. Instead of two minutes to prepare, we had half an hour. And instead of speaking on a random quotation or aphorism, one spoke in response to a policy question. The three topics to choose from might be, for example, "Should positive discrimination [the Canadians' term for affirmative action] be class-based instead of race-based?" "Should the United States withdraw from the United Nations?" and "Is NATO obsolete?" In a preliminary round I spoke on positive discrimination, basing nearly my entire speech on Stephen Carter's book *Reflections of an Affirmative Action Baby*, which I had read two years earlier. After the round, Geoff Buerger, the former college champion who has coached high schools everywhere from Massachusetts to Alaska, leaned across his desk and spoke to me with a stern, skeptical tone. "Mark, you know a lot, you really do," Mr. Buerger said. He was wearing a black robe, a tribute to his debating days at the University of Toronto, where that had been the tradition. "But you don't have to tell us everything you know. For example, we don't need to know that Stephen Carter is the William Nelson Cromwell Professor of Constitutional Law at Yale Law

School. It's enough just to tell us what his arguments are, and you did that. You were gilding the lily."

Don't tell us everything that you know. Here was a bit of advice I had never heard before, one that I could add to Mr. Robison's *Seize the moral high ground.* It's good to have knowledge, but it's better to know which knowledge to share. This was tact, or discretion. I am sure that judges had given me the same critique before, but this time it stuck. *Less is sometimes more* is how I remembered it. Maybe I just needed to hear it in Canada, from a man in a cape.

In February I went to Scotland, where a Scottish boy, just one year my elder, gave me my last great piece of debate advice.

In all my international debating, I had not met many Scots, but of the Scots I'd met not one was a bad debater. They were as gregarious as the Australians, as wry as the English, and as collected as the Canadians. They didn't give a fuck, of course. If they had, they would have won all the trophies, but instead they had a touch of merry nihilism about them, perhaps the legacy of three hundred years of benign possession by the English. They were sometimes late, often tipsy, occasionally offensive, and almost always indifferent to what the judges seemed to want to hear. They were the Harlem Globetrotters of debate, massively gifted hot dogs who just wanted to entertain.

The Scottish schoolmasters were no more organized or industrious than their debaters, so tournaments were rarely held in Scotland. But in February 1991 the very efficient Brian Gorman brought off my favorite tournament in all my years debating. Mr. Gorman was a pleasant, youngish man—he looked like the straight man in a comedic duo—who worked for an absurd entity called the English-Speaking Union, which is, as I understand it, the world's foremost perpetuator of unabashed Anglophilia. It has chapters all over the Commonwealth and beyond, and in many countries it is very active in promoting speech and debate. That year, Gorman marshaled the ESU's prestige to help mount the World Schools tournament; he got us television coverage and even corporate sponsorship. I still have my poster honoring the event and the insurance company that had helped bankroll it: the Britannic Assurance World Schools Debating Championships.

Mr. Gorman was of particular use to me, Shelly Pitman, and Roy Katzovicz, the three clueless, bedraggled American debaters who washed up on his bitterly cold shores. In the month prior to the tournament, nothing had gone right for the American team. First, in January, the United States began Operation Desert Storm, and as the Gulf War continued, many American schools, afraid of reprisals against Americans abroad, prohibited their teachers and students from traveling. Exeter coach Julie Hill, who was to have been our coach in Scotland, pulled out. Just losing a coach wouldn't have been so bad—it was more fun to travel unchaperoned, anyway—but then we started losing debaters. We were supposed to be a team of five, three of whom would debate in each round, allowing each debater periods of rest, but two of our five debaters quit. One of them, Louis Gerstner Jr., a St. Paul's student whose father was the chairman of IBM, was rumored to be worried that his father's prominence made him an especially tempting target for kidnappers. That fear struck me as rather narcissistic, but at first I didn't care, because Mr. Katzenbach, Gerstner's coach at St. Paul's, hinted to another American coach that Gerstner Sr. was trying to secure a private plane to fly us all to Scotland (and thwart the kidnappers). But that plan never came to fruition, Louis did not come to Scotland, and I never saw him again.

We would have done fine, of course, sans coach and sans Louis, if not for the fact that, in all the confusion, somebody forgot to tell our shrunken American contingent that the four topics for debate had been announced in advance. Shelly, Roy, and I met at Boston's Logan Airport; flew to Edinburgh in an airplane so sparsely populated (thanks to the war) that the flight attendants lingered in the aisle by our seats and had drinks with us; were collected at the other end by ruddy-faced Scots, one of whom, on seeing my L. L. Bean plaid shirt, said, "Oh look, he wore a tartan in our honor!"; and were taken to the local high school that would serve as headquarters for the tournament. There we met Stephen Magee, the coach that Mr. Gorman had arranged for us. And then Stephen, a sixth-former who had been one-third of the Scottish team that had won the tournament the year before in Canada, said to me, Shelly, and Roy, "So, are you feeling prepared?"

When Stephen discovered that we had no idea what he was talking about, he ran a hand through his reddish, tousled hair, adjusted his glasses, and smiled a devilish grin, as if he'd just been given three new babes to corrupt. "That doesn't matter at all!" he said. Each of the topics, he explained, would be debated twice, so that each team could debate both sides of the motion. In the first round, for example, we had to oppose the topic "This House believes that one man's terrorist is another man's freedom fighter," but in the second round we'd argue, against a different team, in favor of the motion—which meant, Stephen explained, that if we just took very good notes on what our opponents said in the first round, we could steal all their arguments and evidence for the second! And we could do the same in rounds four, six, and eight, so in alternate rounds we'd be thoroughly prepared.

Well, that was that. Having dispatched of the nettlesome problem of our underpreparation, Stephen set out to teach us the basics of parliamentary debate, as he saw them. First, he said, every speech was only as good as its peroration. I had never heard that word before, and after he'd said it twice, with his rolling Scottish r's, I still couldn't make out what he was saying. So I asked him to spell it for me, and then I got the word, but I still had no idea what it meant. "It's the end of a speech," he said, "the part where you *rrr*eally *wrrrr*ap up and sell it to the judge." The r's were flying. "You want to save the last minute for perorating. For example, if you're the proposition"—what Commonwealth debaters sometimes called the government, or affirmative, side—"then with a minute to go you want to begin laying out all your reasons that you have proven your case. Boil it down to two or three reasons, something that the judge or the audience can understand. And then somehow build to the crescendo of 'I beg to propose!' That's how you end: 'Mr. Chairman, members of this House, I beg to propose!'"

So Magee's first rule was "Perorate well." His second and final rule was the one I came to treasure, the one I wished I'd learned years before, the one that belonged on the short list with *Don't try so hard to pull at the heart-strings, Seize the moral high ground*, and *Don't tell us everything that you know.* The rule was counterintuitive, it was absurd, and it was quite simple. "You have to insult somebody," Stephen said, "and people love it if you insult your own team. *Always make fun of your own team.*" It was this strategy, he explained, that had won him and his partners the tournament the year before: "The team joke was that Martin was a Marxist, I was stupid, and Jeremy was interested in money. So when I spoke, I insulted Martin's communist ideals, when he spoke he talked about what a crass materialist Jeremy was, and when either of them spoke they talked about how stupid I was. That was basically it. So, if you can, you might be well advised to figure out what your biggest weaknesses are, and then just ridicule the shit out of each other in front of the judges."

It was pure genius. All orators know to have a little fun at their own expense, but when you're speaking solo, self-deprecation is such a cliché that it has limited returns. The CEO laughing about how bad he is with money? The retired pro quarterback talking about how he's really a big klutz? *Come on*, people think. But when you're debating on a team, you can be team-deprecating instead of self-deprecating. The moment Stephen laid out this rule, I kicked myself for all the rounds in which I'd neglected to insult Duff, Lynda, or Kevin.

Still, I wasn't sure that I could mock Shelly or Roy. I'd met Shelly, a Milton Academy senior, once before, but Roy, who attended a small day school in Rhode Island, wasn't a regular on our circuit, and we'd met for the first time at Logan Airport. And while I liked both of them, I worried that I'd be uncomfortable insulting either one for the judges' benefit. They were older than I was, for one thing; they already knew where they'd be going to college, which made them seem deserving of respect. And there was more. Shelly was just so darned nice. She had long brown hair and looked like an Ingalls sister from *Little House on the Prairie*. She knit absentmindedly as she talked, and her favorite topic was how much she loved her brother. The next September, she would be matriculating at Gordon College, a small Christian school in Massachusetts. How could I say a bad word about her?

If Shelly was too nice to make fun of, Roy was too intimidating. He practically blew confidence in bursts from his nostrils. He would be going to the University of Pennsylvania, where "maybe" he'd major in business—the implication being "If I feel like it, I will." His parents were Israeli, and he liked translating into English his favorite Hebrew insult: "Your mother farts dust." Roy might have been arrogant, but he was charismatic. By the end of the tournament, "Your mother farts dust" had become a catchphrase among all the debaters, and on my tournament poster, covered with the autographs of my fellow debaters and now hanging framed beside the desk at which I am writing, the words of George Williamson, a Scottish debater, are still legible: "Mark, does your mother fart dust?" (Some of the other comments left by signatories: "Dear Mark, Thank God you're not like Roy." "Marc, you cunt." "Mark, Watch your testicles, because my teeth are ready.")

Quickly, though, the team developed an easy rapport. We were an odd trio, but we debated well, and we managed to put Stephen's advice into practice: Shelly's goody-goody religiosity, Roy's immigrant status, and my wisenheimer nerdiness were all fair game. Competing against (better-prepared) teams from Australia, Belgium, Bermuda, Canada, England, Kenya, New Zealand, Pakistan, Scotland, and Wales, we self-mocking Americans won about half our rounds. Even better, we had fun, and so did our opponents. There was no tournament, in all my years, at which the debaters placed so high a premium on making every round enjoyable. It was as if a unanimous, unspoken agreement dictated that just this once no competitor would take himself seriously. Other teams seemed to have gotten Stephen's memo, and insults flew. If one was debating against the Bermuda team, then their arguments were so weak as to "have disappeared into a Bermuda Triangle of ignorance." Against the English, stern mockery of the monarchy was required, preferably including sexual innuendo about the queen. The Canadians were the fifty-first American state or, alternately, a pimp-slapped little colony that didn't have the guts to take Queen Elizabeth off its currency.

How to account for this most agreeable collective action, this weeklong pact to practice frivolity in debate? It may have been the small size of the tournament, with scarcely more than fifty debaters. Bused around Scotland to compete in different cities, trotted out in our ties and blazers to assure our ESU benefactors that, yes, we were having a wonderful time, a spirit of camaraderie arose almost instantly. The preliminary rounds began on February 4, and by the 6th we were a merry band of debaters, full of in-jokes and, of course, flirtations: I took a very prurient and sadly unrequited interest in Catherine Smith, a Scot with enormous breasts whose father became leader of the Labour Party a year later.

The tournament directors had the good judgment to build into the schedule plenty of nondebating time. During the off afternoons I wandered Edinburgh, stopping into used bookstores and second-hand clothing stores. In one of them I bought a magnificent three-button, single-vent tweed jacket, surely made bespoke for some wealthy man; when I got home I asked Juanita Martinez, a good friend of my mother's and an accomplished dressmaker, to refurbish it with new wood buttons and a full satin lining, and to this day it's my favorite article of clothing. As I played the flâneur, I would often stop on the street and just listen to Scots talk; with their long vowels, distinct r's, and the hint of a chuckle beneath every phrase, their speech was like ambrosia for the ears. One afternoon, the officials of the English-Speaking Union took us for tea at Edinburgh Castle, high above the city on Edinburgh Rock. The Scottish debaters were unimpressed, but the rest of us were awed—awed to be young and faced with a new kind of opulence, and doubly awed as only the colonized can be, with that special admiration that all English speakers have, in spite of ourselves, for the ancient traditions and artifacts of the Motherland.

As Roy, Shelly, and I muddled through our team rounds, we also competed in the individual competition running concurrently. It was nothing more than a sideshow, really, meant to fill the time between rounds, as team results were tabulated. For the individual event, we were broken off from our countrymen and randomly assigned to teams of six; each team was then matched against another team for a round that included twelve debaters, each of whom was to give just one speech. There was no pretense of coordinating efforts with one's teammates: although the topics were distributed on the first day of the tournament, there was no prep time set aside in the schedule, so our job was to give the best speech we could and then sit back and hope everyone else faltered. Besides the topic "This House believes that all you need is love," all I remember from the sole preliminary round is that the opposing team included the wonderfully named Joost van der Spek, a tall Dutchman with a blond crew cut that looked like the tip of a cigarette: if one tapped his head, I thought, his hair might fall off like ash. I placed high enough in that round to advance to the semifinals, in which the teams were reduced to three speakers per side, debating the topic "This House would follow the law rather than its own conscience."

On February 9, 1991, the last day of the championship, when the finalists for both the team and individual competitions were announced, we were not surprised that the American team had not made the cut. But when my name was announced—last, as I recall— as one of the six individual finalists, I felt a shivery elation. I was a junior in high school, I'd won many trophies, but at this tournament, where I had no reputation to precede me, and where my under-staffed, underprepared American team had become known mainly for teaching foreigners profane Israeli oaths, I didn't think I stood a chance. When my name was called, Shelly and Roy and Stephen, our coach, jumped out of their seats and gathered around me, slapping my back, ruffling my hair, and hollering for joy. Their excitement surprised me—ultracool Roy, quiet, ever-knitting Shelly, and defending champion Stephen, all happy for *me*—and I resolved to win this one, for myself and for them.

The final round was held at six-thirty in the Merchants' Hall on Hanover Street, a large, domed room, paneled and pillared, the walls adorned by chandelier-lit portraits of the Edinburgh Merchant Company's founders and benefactors. The hall is surely smaller than I remember it, but that night, with BBC cameras set up to record, with microphone wires taped to the floor, and with the debaters and coaches outnumbered by older Scottish dignitaries, it felt like a chamber of Parliament. The individual championship would go first, and the topic was "This House believes that the environmental lobby has gone too far." I was the first proposition speaker.

I don't remember much about that round of debate. I remember that I heeded Stephen's advice and insulted my teammates, not the ones on the dais with me but my fellow Americans, in the audience. I charged my countrymen with the crime of being lily-livered animal-coddlers. I made derisive reference to the Endangered Species Act, the spotted owl, the bison, the polar bear. I spoke of hemp shoes and hippies' general unwillingness to shower. I apologized to the world for having exported environmental activism. I got a big laugh after one of our opponents—I believe it was the British Columbian debater Gibran "Gib" van Ert—rose on a point of information, a question that interrupts the speaker with a request that he clarify something he is saying. "I gather that this is a humorous stereotype," Gib said, "but can the gentleman from the United States point us to any *actual* Americans who behave this way? Do they have names, or are they just figments of his imagination, useful in a debate round?" At that, I ran to the first row of the audience, found Roy Katzovicz, who by this time was virtually the tournament mascot, and yanked him to his feet. "Here is such an American!" I cried, and the room erupted.

After my Katzovicz moment, I returned to the lectern and for an instant was terrified, unsure how to use my remaining minute. I had just wrung a big laugh from the audience, but I was to be followed by a Canadian and then a New Zealander, and New Zealanders were truly funny. If all I had was my sight gag with Roy, I would not win this round. Then, as I was beginning to feel engulfed by panic, I remembered Mr. Robison's trusty advice: *Seize the moral high ground.* It took me another second to figure out what exactly the moral high ground against environmentalism was, but then I grasped an idea, felt a renewed sense of mastery, and charged ahead:

"Mr. Speaker, ladies and gentlemen of the House, it's all well and good to have a laugh at the environmentalists' expense—and we've had a few good laughs. But there is a more important point here, one that should not get lost in all the merriment. When environmentalism is pushed too far, it costs people jobs. Now, some would say that the loss of jobs is a necessary price to pay for the salvation of the planet. And perhaps they're right. But what about the loss of a way of life? What about traditional native populations who have hunted the whale for millennia, only to learn that their way of life offends the sensibilities of today's greens? What about hunters in Africa who all of a sudden find themselves described as 'poachers,' even though they're just doing what their people have always done?

"I am sure, Mr. Speaker, that the members of the opposition have rebuttals to my charges, just as we have rebuttals to their rebuttals. We on the proposition side are not arguing against environmentalism. No, sir, we are arguing for common sense. This common sense, Mr. Speaker, is common to all men and women of decency, this common sense prescribes moderation instead of a destructive zealotry, and this common sense, Mr. Speaker, is what we beg to propose!"

I don't remember anybody else's speech that night. My memory picks up again at the dinner and awards ceremony later that evening, at the George Hotel. The invitation specified "Lounge or Highland Dress," which was only fitting, as we were treated to a Burns Supper, which remains the weirdest thing I have ever seen. The Burns

Supper is a Scottish tradition dating to the death of Robert Burns, the Scottish national poet, in 1796. Every January 25, Burns's birthday, there are Burns Suppers throughout Scotland and the Scottish diaspora—wherever men wish to break out their kilts, get wrecked on single malts, speak of William Wallace, and insult the English. As the supper begins—indeed, as ours began in 1991, on a very frosty night in an Edinburgh banquet hall, a week or so after Burns's actual birthday—a bagpiper enters the room playing a ceremonial air. He is followed by other dignitaries, one of whom is the chef, carrying on a tray the beautifully dressed haggis, the traditional Scottish dish consisting of a sheep's innards boiled in the sheep's stomach. When the music has died down and the haggis has been laid on the head table, the host, who by this point has been drunk for hours, recites Burns's poem "Address to a Haggis," a poem that, if not as well-known as the poet's "Auld Lang Syne," has a far more brilliant premise, being essentially an ode to stuffed, boiled sheep offal. The first two stanzas are:

> Fair fa' your honest, sonsie face,
> Great chieftain o' the puddin-race!
> Aboon them a' ye tak your place,
> Painch, tripe, or thairm:
> Weel are ye wordy o' a grace
> As lang's my arm.

> The groaning trencher there ye fill,
> Your hurdies like a distant hill,
> Your pin wad help to mend a mill
> In time o' need,
> While thro' your pores the dews distil
> Like amber bead.

I understood the poem then no better than I do now, but I remember that after it was read the master of ceremonies took a knife from a scabbard and sliced open the stomach before him. As little giblets spilled over the scarred metal serving plate, the audience, filled with very Scottish types who seemed to have been imported for the occasion, leapt to its feet in applause, the men's kilts and ladies' scarves a blur of plaid. Then everyone, we teenagers included, began to drink Scotch whiskey.

After dinner, the judges' verdicts were announced. I don't remember hearing my name called, only the excitement of my teammates and, especially, our coach Stephen, all of them yelling, "You did it! You won!" I remember rising to collect my first-place prize, a beautiful sanded hardwood gavel and block. When the program ended, all the debaters and coaches adjourned to the hotel bar and stayed for hours, safe against the heavy snow falling outside. I remember that when at last I found a taxicab to drive me back to my host family's house, the driver would not turn up their street, fearful that his car would get stuck in the snowdrifts. He deposited me by the side of the main road, and I took my satchel with its gavel inside and went gingerly through the snow. I must have gone slowly, given the weather, but in my memory I am skipping.

X

Before Sari Addington, the second girl and only debater whom I ever kissed, my romantic history had been rather thin. After Sari Addington, I nearly left debate forever.

Sari and I met at a debate tournament in Winnipeg in October of my senior year. My history with girls up to that point had consisted mostly of unrequited crushes, including Claire Magauran and Karina Bozzuto, whom I had taken to the Snowball dance my sophomore year; Karina went on to date an absurdly good-looking public school Israeli immigrant *sabra* dude named Nimrod Weiselfish. (I wasn't sure that my memory served me correctly—could his name really have been Nimrod Weiselfish?—so I went and asked Google and, yes, there was Nimrod, in bright, colorful photos, surfing a big wave in Hong Kong. Today, apparently, he surfs in exotic locales, has an MBA from MIT, and is the subject of this priceless post in a fantasy-football forum: "I went to college with a guy named Nimrod Weiselfish. That kid slayed more 'tang than anyone I've ever met. Dude was straight out of an Abercrombie catalog.") Junior year I did kiss a girl for the first time. Her name was Amy Singer, and we made out on Jordan Oland's parents' bed after watching *The Shining* on TV. Jordan's parents were out of town, and Lynda, whom he was dating at the time, had the idea of setting me and Amy up, and she

168

figured inviting us over to watch a movie in a bedroom was a sure-fire plan; Jordan and Lynda disappeared right after the movie ended, leaving me and Amy alone. After that, Amy and I dated, sort of, for two weeks. That was in March of junior year.

So when I met Sari the following October, I didn't have much experience. I figured my luck wouldn't change anytime soon, and I had already written off women for my senior year, consoling myself with some version of Slater's classic line in *Dazed and Confused* (a movie that was still two years away): "It's quality, not quantity, and wait till I get to *college*, man."

That Zen-like indifference to scoring chicks went double at debate tournaments. Unlike Duff, who was in Winnipeg with me, I hadn't gone there looking to hook up. Debate was a serious thing, and I was in it to win it. Plus, I had lately developed a crush on a classmate named Nina Smith; the crush had been nascent as early as freshman year, but because of her superior looks and social standing it had always seemed particularly hopeless. Late in junior year, however, we had become friends, and I began to allow myself to hope for more, and now in Canada I felt loyal to the thought of her, back home in Connecticut. So despite the fact that I was standing in line for my registration packet at Balmoral Hall—Manitoba's premier girls' school—girls were not on my mind.

But you couldn't miss Sari. I noticed her first as she walked down a hallway with her sidekick, Kirsten Benzon. They were two of the three competitors from St. Michaels University School in Victoria, British Columbia, the school where we had competed the year before. I didn't remember these two girls in particular, but I recognized their school uniform: their plaid skirts and the crests on their blue blazers. Sari and Kirsten were about the same height, and both had light hair, but Kirsten was fair while Sari had dark skin—she looked deeply tanned, although it was October and she lived in Canada. I was later to find out that her coloring came from her mother, who was Sri Lankan, but at the time I could only think that Sari and Kirsten looked like a pair of mix-and-match girls' school nymphettes—the light one and the dark one—plucked from a lewd music video (that video would get made a couple of years later: "Crazy," by Aerosmith, starring Liv Tyler and Alicia Silverstone as the jailbait). They walked the hall as if they owned it.

During lunch that first day, Duff and I, finding courage in numbers, walked over to their table and introduced ourselves. They looked at each other, looked back at us, then kicked out a couple of empty chairs and told us to sit down. All I could think was: *auspicious*.

From the beginning, Sari and Kirsten were in charge. They decided that Sari would hang with me and Kirsten would get Duff. And they decided that we would be the cool foursome at the tournament. Based on what little I could piece together about their lives back home in Victoria, Sari was the popular girl—the athlete, the social-ite—while Kirsten was dreamier, more bohemian. Sari played field hockey, Kirsten smoked pot. But in the little mini-society of high school overachievers who came together for four days that October, they assumed the birthright of pretty girls everywhere, which is to be the adjudicators of cool. And by acting as if it were so, they made it so. We four found each other between rounds, grabbed coffee in the cafeteria, sat on the steps in front of the school pulling our coats tight against the cold, and looked out on the other hundred young orators with a mix of condescension and compassion: How sad were they not to be us?

Having never been popular like this before, I was surprised to dis-cover that popular kids actually don't have that many friends. To maintain an aura of exclusivity, they have to limit their circle. At most debate tournaments I was gregarious, trying to catch up with old friends and meet as many of the newbies as I could. Here, in Winnipeg, I felt disconnected from the crowd, not at the center of things. Being a senior, I was bound to feel a little alienated anyway; my eyes were fixed on the future—my early application to Harvard was sitting on my desk at home—and I didn't care so much any-more who the superstar freshmen and sophomores were. But being pulled along in Sari's wake exacerbated the sense of estrangement. I decided I could live with that. With her, I felt like the social superstar of the event: I was a senior, I already had a reputation as someone who might win the tournament, and I was sure that other boys were jealous that I was hanging out with someone so hot.

Once I got used to the idea, being the center of attention did not feel lonesome; the really exciting thing about being popular is that even if you have very few peers, you don't care. When you're unpopular, you're constantly making a study of other people, making a taxonomy of other cliques, trying to understand how this group of friends fits in with that one. Uncool kids so often grow up to be interesting people in part because they are the scholars who map the genome of popularity. Popular people, by contrast, are blissful idiots. They don't care about other cliques—why would they? I was startled in college when my friend Rob Haskell, who had debated for Roxbury Latin and had been at the Winnipeg tournament, told me that he'd thought of me and Sari as the boring people. "I hung out with the interesting people there," he said. It took me a moment to make sense of that; at age twenty, I still figured that in Winnipeg my small crowd had been the only one that mattered. But Rob was gay and arty, and he had found the whole idea of Sari tiresome, he told me. His respect for me had barely survived my friendship with her.

The dark flip side of popularity is its precariousness. With Sari, I did feel privileged, like some Chosen One, but I also worried that I might be dropped at any moment. She controlled my good fortune, was the arbiter of my fate. There was a rumor floating around the tournament that during her vacations from school Sari worked as a model—"a *Ralph Lauren model*," one awed Canadian whispered to me. She was the kind of girl who caused boys to ride their bikes into trees. What could such a girl want with me? When would she notice some taller, hunkier debater she was meant to be with?

But I guess the taller, hunkier debater wasn't there, because by early Sunday morning, a very long two days after we'd met, I began to get signals that Sari might be interested in more than a wholesome friendship. It seemed possible that she might like me as much as I liked her.

"We've met before, you know," she said, as we ate bagels and drank coffee before rounds on Sunday. Debaters almost always skipped breakfast, preferring an extra half hour of sleep, but Duff and I and the girls had agreed to meet early.

We'd met before? I thought she was making a metaphysical claim, like maybe we'd met in a past life. That seemed kind of heavy, and also strangely erotic. My next thought was *How far did things go in our past life?*

"When did we meet?" I asked.

"Last year, when you came out to SMU for the Internationals," she said. Okay, so not a past life. Disappointing. "The night Clare Mochrie took you and Duff out to that diner, and then to the party—I was in the car with you guys."

"How is that possible?" I asked. It didn't seem possible that I had met this girl and not remembered.

"You guys were busy paying attention to some other girl."

"Nooo! I would totally have ignored any other girl for you."

"Sadly, you didn't."

Later that day, after lunch, the four of us huddled to make plans. Sari and I had each made two of that afternoon's final rounds. I was excited—I could win extemp for the third year in a row—but she didn't seem to care. I was beginning to understand her a little better: she was smart and talented and ambitious, and if SMU was sending a team somewhere, she wanted to be on it—but she didn't have to win. She liked to be noticed, but she could be noticed just by sitting in the back row, watching others, looking fabulous. All she needed was to be at the debate tournament, or playing in the field hockey match, or cast in the school play; she could win, or not, because in a more important sense she was always the star. That was a prerogative of being cool.

Sari, Kirsten, and Duff agreed that they would cheer me on at the extemporaneous-speaking final, then we would watch Sari's finals, and later we would sit together for dinner and the presentation of trophies. And then we would figure out what came next.

Whatever we decided, we were definitely ditching our billets. Duff and I had been placed with the family of a local anesthesiologist. He was a soft-talking man, almost hard to hear, which struck us as hilarious—he'd found the perfect occupation, putting people to sleep for a living. He and his wife were empty-nesters, their daughters long ago graduated from Balmoral Hall, and they were happy to have kids in the house again. I said to Duff, "We have to tell them we're not coming home after dinner." Duff agreed and said he would call them.

After the trophies had been awarded—I'd won extemp for the third time, unprecedented at the Internationals—Sari and Kirsten disappeared for fifteen minutes with some fellow Canadians. Duff and I thought they might have ditched us, but then they reappeared, smiling proudly. They had our plans all set. "We're going with some guys to this bar," Sari said, nodding her head in the direction of some tall guys I didn't know. "We'll hang out there for a while, and then we'll take it from there, okay?"

This got me worried—who were these "guys"? Duff and I definitely did not want other guys around tonight. Our plans did not involve other guys.

We needn't have worried. We ended up at a bar and grill in downtown Winnipeg with some Canadian debaters whom the girls knew from the circuit, but they weren't any kind of threat. Sari sat down right next to me and ordered our beers; the drinking age in Manitoba was eighteen, but, as everywhere, for pretty girls it was flexible. The waiter, who was peppy and wore suspenders (Canada having imported T.G.I. Friday's style of manufactured fun), brought a round of lager for everyone, and we toasted the tournament, toasted Sari's final rounds, toasted my win in extemp speaking and fourth place in parliamentary debate—I thought to myself how little it seemed to matter—toasted a night on the town, toasted adults not being anywhere in sight, toasted . . . being young and drunk on a cold night in the middle of nowhere.

As the drinks went down the hatch, we heard the first thwips of freezing rain on the roof above. By the time we got outside two hours later, the sidewalks were iced over. The Canadian boys faded away, hopped cabs to who knows where. Sari clutched my arm as we walked away from the restaurant. The light of the streetlamps bounced off the frozen, glassy roads, drops of melted water fell from my eyelashes, and through the blurry haze I tried to mark the curbs right in front of us.

"Where are we going?" I asked. She held my left arm tight. I wasn't dressed warmly enough, just a blazer, shirt, and T-shirt, and I felt my teeth starting to chatter. I tried to hold them steady, afraid that shivering was unmanly.

"There's a park down this street. Let's go there." Of course she knew where a park was. She knew everything.

Duff and Kirsten walked behind us. After a mile, we got to the park and found ourselves on a path through quiet woods. *Maybe we should leave a trail of bread crumbs*, I thought, but I didn't say it. I didn't know what to say. I kept my head down, glancing up only to look at the side of Sari's face, that marvelous profile—her strong chin, her right eye, her straight, long nose, her cheek with a touch of rouge. At first she was looking down, but then her eyes shot to the right, and I was caught staring. She smiled, letting me off the hook, telling me it was okay, we were thinking the same thing.

When our locked gazes became too much, I took my eyes off Sari and looked in front of us. The asphalt path stretched on, and to either side were only trees, now dripping with water that had we stopped to watch would have frozen before our eyes, becoming the tiny icicles shimmering all around us. Several steps behind, Duff and Kirsten were whispering. I could hear his soft, fast patter, then her quiet laugh in response. My jacket was nearly soaked through, my shirt was wet, and the chill in my core was getting so bad that I had either to get inside or to get very close to another person.

And then the path broke through the trees and emerged in a clearing, and I looked up, and I had my answer: a full meadow's length ahead of us there was a wood and iron bench, sitting in the far corner of a field, perfectly sized for two.

I was scared, but I was also excited, and I was cold—so with an alacrity that surprised me, I dropped my left arm, the one Sari held in its crook, and let my hand fall into hers. I laced our fingers together, and I felt warmer already, her mitten drying my bare hand. I stepped onto the grass and left the road, leading her along. I didn't look back, but I heard Duff's voice and Kirsten's laugh getting more distant as we two couples diverged.

As we crossed to the bench, the earth and ice crunching underfoot, the rain still falling and freezing, then melting and freezing again, we talked about the next day. *When does your plane leave? How early do you have to get up?* And we talked delicately about time beyond that. *Do you think you might come to that tournament in March? What have you thought about college for next year?*

At the bench, we sat down, her on my left. I felt as if I'd never kissed a girl before. I'd certainly never kissed a girl the way I wanted to, the way I was sure it should be done: confidently, with neither hesitation nor aggression, just certainty that this was what we both wanted. We were sitting close, our sides fast against each other, but still I was shaking, from the cold and from anticipation. I didn't know it then, but I would always shake when about to first kiss a girl I really liked. Biting a girl's lip became a real fear of mine, right up to the girl I would marry. Sari was the first girl to give me the shakes.

And then I did it. I looked at her, and we were kissing. I held her face in my hands, as if to keep her from pulling away. I felt her hair. I hugged her. She was real, and this was happening. When we stopped for air, we whispered to each other. For hours, we kissed and whispered.

I got so cold. My brother had been stricken with chilblains as a little boy, wearing mittens that had soaked through in the snow, and I was even more naked to the elements than that. I could have stayed all night, watched the sun rise—I wanted to—but I began to worry and said we should go home. We walked back to the main road, hand in hand, and like a miracle a taxicab appeared. Sari gave the driver her host family's address, and he took us to the castle-size house where she and Kirsten were staying. The house was dark; nobody had waited up. I got out of the cab with her, and we hugged.

"Stay in touch?" I said.

She nodded. "Stay in touch."

Then she turned and walked away. The driver idled his engine until she was inside, and when the door shut behind her we drove away.

Back at the house where I was staying, the door was unlocked. I crept slowly inside, trying not to creak any floorboards as I made my way down the stairs to the basement bedroom. Duff was still gone, his bed untouched. I looked at the clock radio on the nightstand, saw that it was just after four in the morning. The overheated cab had started to take the chill off, but it was pulling the blankets up to my ears that finished the job. My flight was at ten, so there wasn't much time to sleep. I closed my eyes and thought of Sari.

Had it stopped there, had I never seen her again, Sari would have lived on as just a memory and an ache, and I would have increased my devotion to the art of oratory, for it had brought me to her. Debate had gotten me a girl. For the rest of high school and all of college, I would have gone to every debate tournament I could, always looking for the next Sari.

But it did not end there. Back in Connecticut, back at school, everything seemed drab and colorless, just the old routine of English class, French class, economics, English elective, history elective, cross-country practice, homework. Duff felt it, too. We'd see each other at the day-student lockers and flash thin, tight-lipped smiles of exasperation, as if to say, "What the fuck are we doing back in high school?" He missed Kirsten even more than I missed Sari. That last morning in Winnipeg, he had rolled into the bed next to mine at six o'clock, with time for barely an hour of sleep before having to rise and catch a flight. I'd opened my eyes just as he was about to close his, and he'd looked at me and uttered one word: *"Amazing."*

He wanted that feeling back, and so did I. I was talking on the phone to Sari a couple of times a week, and in those days before phone cards, Skype, or cheap long distance, the November bill ran to about a hundred dollars. My mother mentioned it to me but wasn't as aggrieved as I would have expected. "Just watch the minutes," she said, letting it go at that, in an act of kindness. Sari and I wrote letters, too, and in one of them she suggested that Duff and I come visit her and Kirsten over Christmas break. We could all go skiing at Whistler Mountain, the famous resort just north of them in British Columbia. I checked with Duff, and he confirmed that he had gotten the same invitation from Kirsten. We strategized about how to sell the idea to our parents, and, more important, how to ask them for the money. We decided that it would be best if we did our research first, found the lowest plane fare, then approached them. That way, we'd look as if we knew what we were doing, and we could ask for a specific, and we hoped reasonable, amount. We began making phone calls, and after about five calls I got lucky. An agent at Carroll Travel, in downtown Springfield, told me about a promotion at Stop & Shop, our local supermarket: for a limited time, with any purchase at an area Stop & Shop, the store would give the buyer a coupon for a huge discount on domestic or Canadian travel on USAir. A five-hundred-dollar ticket would be 40 percent off.

I told Duff, and we got ourselves to Stop & Shop for our coupons. Then we went to our parents. I gave them the hard sell: my Harvard application was in the mail, my grades were good, I did my chores, so would they let me take a one-week trip to British Columbia, about half of which I had the savings to pay for and the other half of which would be my Hanukkah present?

My dad looked at my mom, and she shrugged. "Okay," my dad said.

Duff also got the parental go-ahead. We bought the tickets and notified the girls that we were coming. Sari and I were talking twice a week, sometimes more. In early December, when the letter came from Harvard, I called Sari and told her I had been accepted. "Are you going?" she asked. "Well, I won't decide until I hear from Yale in April," I said. "What about you?" "I'm seriously thinking about university in the States," she said. (As a Canadian, Sari always said "university," not "college," and I found this adorable.) "You should come on a college visit," I said. "Yeah, I'm definitely talking with my parents about that," she said. We talked about my visit at the end of December, and I made a tentative joke about where her parents would want me to sleep. She laughed and said that was not for them to worry about.

We were exchanging two or three letters every week. I don't remember what I wrote, but I still have her letters. They are sweet and hopeful, at times frank and enticing: "I think we have something very special together, and I hope it lasts for a LONG time," she wrote on October 31. "Not meaning to scare you, with the sniffling words of a lovestruck teenager—but hey, I can't help it." A week later: "Sometimes I wish I could just see you—while you're at school, or at home—through some hidden video camera so I could glimpse into your life—but technology has not quite advanced so far—I'll have to settle for the phone." In that same letter: "I want to know more about you—the small details that people share—tell me about your favorite color, your fantasies, your most embarrassing moment (I have quite a few tales to tell!)." Days after that: "Don't worry about us not having our own room. I'm sure we can work something out—I've overcome more difficult obstacles before!"

Duff and I flew from Hartford the day after Christmas, stopping in Minneapolis, then Seattle, en route to Vancouver. Duff was a bubble of energy on the planes, couldn't stop talking about all the fun we were going to have; he had his usual uncomplicated, cocksure demeanor. I didn't have as much to say. My usual loquaciousness— the loquaciousness that, in a sense, had made this trip possible—was tempered by a queasy mix of anticipation and fear. We were seventeen years old, off on a three-thousand-mile voyage to see girls with whom we had spent only a few hours alone. Two days after arriving in Victoria, we would leave for a ski trip with them, and we'd be staying in a ski hostel with no parents within a hundred miles. Was this an errand of young love or a booty call? It was both. Which did I want it to be? Was I ready for this?

As it turned out, I had nothing to worry about. All decisions would be made for me. We arrived in Victoria at the end of a long day of travel, and the girls—lovely, flirty, nervous—greeted us at the gate. Duff and Kirsten were holding hands by the time we left baggage claim; Sari and I were a little more circumspect. They had brought separate cars, and as we left the garage, with Duff and Kirsten driving to her place for the night, and me and Sari headed to the Addingtons', we planned to meet later for dinner.

Sari's house was small, but in an extraordinary neighborhood, the last strip of civilization before the Strait of Juan de Fuca: one could see the water from her backyard. In the United States, such a prime piece of land would have been clotted with monstrous, overbuilt houses, but this was Canada—there were perfect lawns, nice cars in driveways, no sign of disorder, and no ostentation.

Inside, nobody was home. "My parents must be out," she said. I carried my suitcase as she led me through the house, giving me a tour. I was getting antsy. I felt the shakes again, the chatter in the teeth, the nervousness that would only go away when we finally kissed. What I wanted beyond that, I wasn't sure, but I had to have the kiss. At last we arrived at the end of a short hallway, and she turned to face me, standing between two doors. "This is my bedroom," she said, nodding to her left, and then, nodding to her right, "this one is yours." I put my suitcase down at the entrance to my bedroom.

"So your parents aren't here?"

"No. They won't be back for a while, I think."

I leaned in to kiss her. And just as I was about to close my eyes, just at the point when our lips would have touched, she pulled away.

"I don't think so," she said.

I was very confused.

"I've been thinking," she said. "I think maybe we shouldn't, you know, do anything on this trip. Not fool around."

"Why not?" I was trying very hard not to sound annoyed. No sex I could understand. But no kissing? Had I flown three thousand miles not to be kissed? I could have stayed home for that. I wasn't even a good skier.

"It's just that we don't know if we'll ever see each other again after this," she said, "and I don't want things to get too serious."

"Would it get too serious for us just to kiss?"

"I just don't know if it would be right."

"Why didn't you tell me this before I came?"

"I wasn't sure how I felt."

I didn't know what to say. I knew I did not want to be the guy who berated a girl for not putting out. I was horny, but mostly I was just hurt. I liked her, a lot.

"But I love you!"

Had I just said that? I hadn't planned to say it. But now that it was out there, I was pretty sure I meant it. But it sounded so desperate! I knew how it must have seemed to her: that I was using the L-word to get down her pants. Which was sort of true, but not really, not given the way I felt about her.

I was very confused.

"I'm tired," I said. "Do you mind if I take a nap?"

"Okay. But give me a hug first." And then she pulled me to her and gave me a warm, tight hug that made me love her even more, and miss her, and also really hate her.

That night we met Duff, Kirsten, and a group of their Victoria friends for dinner. The fact that they'd invited others to dinner, on the very night Duff and I had arrived, brought my anger to the surface. After we had ordered our food, I asked to be excused and went outside. I tried to be brusque about it, with a cold edge to my voice, so that Sari would know how I was feeling. I wanted to punish her for this. She didn't follow me right out, which made me angrier, but after five minutes she stepped out of the restaurant to find me pacing on the sidewalk. I could see her breath in the cold when she spoke.

"What's wrong?" she asked.

"I think you know what's wrong."

"That I won't fool around with you? Is that what it is?" She didn't sound as compassionate as I would have wanted. She sounded accusatory.

"That's part of it. But it's also what fooling around represents. Closeness. That you care about me. That my being here means something to you." *My* being here? My overly correct way of talking sounded out of place, even to me, in what was shaping up as an argument.

"So you need sex to feel all those things?"

"Not even sex. It's not all about sex, you know. Just closeness."

Now she took a step toward me. We were staring each other down. Through the windows, we could see people eating inside the restaurant, looking warm and toasty and happy. I wanted to be one of them.

She turned away—there was that gorgeous profile again—and stared into the distance, as if there were answers out there.

When she faced me again, she had settled on a decision. "Okay," she said, "if we need to hook up for you to have a good time this week, we can."

I looked at her, trying to figure out if she meant it. Was this kindness? Was it guilt? Pity? Desire?

I thought about what kind of girl would make such an offer, and what kind of boy would accept.

"That's not what I want," I said.

I walked back inside, joined Duff and Kirsten and the others, ate my dinner. The next day the four of us went to a museum in Victoria, and the day after that Sari's father drove us all to Whistler. Mr. Addington stayed that first day to ski with us, and late in the afternoon he and I shared a chairlift ride up the mountain. He was all chipper and in good spirits—happy, I think, that his daughter had found a fine chap like me. He had no way of knowing that for two days Sari and I had hardly spoken.

For the next three days, Sari and I exchanged perfunctory comments and occasionally attempted polite, formal conversation. We tried not to sit next to one another at the hostel's communal breakfast table. During the day, on the slopes or at the ski lodge, if one of us accidentally brushed against the other, we both recoiled. Waiting in line for the chairlift, we would rearrange ourselves, so that I took all my trips up with Duff or Kirsten. Of course, Sari was still as beautiful as ever. She would catch me staring at her—on the way up the mountain, from my chairlift seat to hers; in line at the lodge cafeteria for lunch—and we would both look quickly away, and it was hard to say which of us was more ashamed. It was hell.

Meanwhile, Duff and Kirsten were laughing, sharing inside jokes, shooting knowing looks, sneaking kisses on the slopes. They were in love. McDuff—what a motherfucker. Everything went his way.

We spent New Year's Eve at a party in the ski condo of one of Sari's high school friends, and I got drunk on wine coolers and made a miserable attempt to hit on a girl in a pink sweater. The next night, the last of our ill-starred vacation, we hitched a ride from the base of the mountain back to the hostel in a Jeep with a bunch of ski bums; INXS's *Live Baby Live* was blasting from their speakers, and I closed my eyes and pretended to sleep and listened to "Mystify": "Some silken moment/Goes on forever/And we're leaving broken hearts behind"—and I sang along in my head. Slowly, as Michael Hutchence and I sang our plaintive duet, I began, almost in spite of myself, to feel a little better. A misery as severe and total as mine could not last forever; it had to lift. And when it did, it began to seem a little bit absurd. Here I was, seventeen years old, way up in the Canadian north with a girl I had kissed once for a few wonderful hours. And here she was, next to me on the back bench of this van, sleeping. Her face was slack, the face of a dead-tired girl. At that moment, she wasn't the perfect, untouchable Sari, and she looked so, so young, and that touched something in me. I felt a twinge of compassion. She didn't know what she was doing. Neither did I. *Leaving broken hearts behind . . . mystify me.*

I missed my brothers and my baby sister, all home in Springfield, probably eating ice cream and watching television. I wanted to get back to them—and to school, to *Gypsy* rehearsals, to AP English class, to my unrequited crush on Nina.

The song ended, and there was silence in the Jeep as we descended the roads into Whistler Village. Outside, it was just black with patches of white caught in the moonshine. Life wasn't too bad, I thought. The week would end. We'd get back to our corner of New England, where all was life-sized and manageable. The hurt and the anger would dissipate. I knew that. But at that moment I couldn't help thinking: "Oh yeah, one more thing: *Fuck debate.*"

When school started up again in January 1992, I carried with me, like extra books in my backpack, the exceedingly long, painful, awkward week that I'd just spent in British Columbia. It was never spoken of: when friends asked me how our visit with the "debater girls" had gone, I just said "Fine" and quickly changed the subject. But I felt different. Just as meeting Sari had given me new worlds, losing her—and so abruptly, so violently—had aged me. Young love had come and gone a bit too quickly.

There was more. Duff and I never recovered. He knew that I didn't want to talk about any of it, and he maintained a compassionate silence. But that week, which had been so splendid for him, so catastrophic for me, revealed the thinness of our friendship. Girls and debate had been our two great topics, and avoiding them left us with little to say to one another. We managed to talk, but it was pathetically obvious what we weren't talking about.

I don't know that any of our friends picked up on a change. Duff and I still had a jocular banter that we could perform for a crowd. One day that February, we got into a wonderfully silly argument about the virtues of *Beverly Hills, 90210*, a new TV show that I had seen two or three times and heartily endorsed. Duff had not yet seen Brandon and Dylan, Kelly and Brenda, only read about them in the magazines, and he was mocking me for my newfound passion, which marked me, he said, as inexcusably lowbrow and possibly gay.

I countered that only someone with obvious intellectual insecurities accuses another of being a lowbrow, and he responded by asking how soon could he expect me to grow sideburns like the men on my new favorite show? By the time the argument was well under way, with the quips flying, we were seated with our trays at a circular eight-person table, and six of our female friends (many of whom were already converts to *90210*) had joined us and were listening with amusement. Before Duff and I wound down our argument, with his promise to watch two consecutive episodes and my promise to grow ridiculous sideburns if he didn't become a fan, other classmates had crowded around the table, forming an audience two concentric circles deep.

The public *90210* spat is one of my favorite memories of high school: two friends passing an enjoyable fifteen minutes, entertaining themselves and an appreciative audience of peers, debating. When it was over, Heather Hunt, whom I sometimes gave a lift to school in my parents' minivan, walked with me to the conveyor belt where we deposited our dirty dishes. "That was great," she said. "You guys are hilarious."

While we continued to have lunch together, giving good debate in the dining hall, every time there was the prospect of a few hours alone with our friendship, one of us pulled back. I'd suggest we hit a party together, but Duff would beg off; after March vacation, he asked if I wanted to get a pass out of spring team sports by taking squash lessons with him at the Hartford Racquet Club, and after initially saying yes I changed my mind and said no. My stated reason was that I wanted a final season with the track team, but in truth I was just avoiding time alone with Duff.

In the waning months of our senior year, we did debate together at a few more tournaments, but I had lost heart, in the friendship and in debate. Duff was there when I lost the Lincoln-Douglas tournament at Kingswood-Oxford in April, turning in a smug, inadequate performance in the final round against Khalif Ford, a very gifted senior from Deerfield who had the enraging habit of obsequiously calling me "Sir" during cross-examination. I had beaten Khalif at several tournaments, but this time I deserved to lose. Duff and I tightened our games when we partnered for our last high school tournament, at Deerfield in the first week of May, and for a bit of whimsy we wore long khaki shorts with our blazers and ties—a move we would not have dared to make a year earlier. It was not quite a screw-you to the league—and we weren't the first to essay shorts—but it was a don't-mind-if-we-do, a statement that our horizons were broader, now, than the Debating Association of New England Independent Schools.

It was what Sari had done to me, what British Columbia had done to me, and what the setting sun of high school proclaimed with its dimming rays: *It just doesn't matter*. College acceptances were coming, and the school year had entered the lame-duck interlude: even the most academically minded, those who had held off senioritis until the last college letter was received, were in free-fall. For me and my friends, there was not much energy left for studying or sports or extracurriculars.

It didn't help our focus that, all of a sudden, my day-student friends and I all seemed to have found love. Seth Lobis and Amy Singer had started dating in January, and over the course of that spring they were joined in couplehood by Monique Martineau and Ron Chowdhury, Jen Murray and Tony Riccio, Lynda Duna and Cary Devorsetz, and—best of all—me and Nina Smith.

Yes, Nina had come around, on March 17 to be precise. For this, I could thank Sari. Returning from British Columbia, I desperately needed to focus on another girl. Before, the problem had been that although I liked Nina, a lot, I had never felt any reciprocation. And since she was a close friend, I wasn't sure I could handle the awkwardness of being rejected by her; we had all the same friends, and I couldn't avoid her. But here was the good news: by so thoroughly shell-shocking me over Christmas break, by giving me the nihilistic sense of *it just doesn't matter* that follows a grievous loss, Sari had put me in a state of mind not to care. *Hell yeah*, I thought, *I'll call Nina, tell her how I feel, get rejected, and not give a damn.*

Even so, I needed a month to gather my courage. But finally, on a cold February night, I took my parents' phone, the one in their bedroom with the extra-long cord, shut myself in the bathroom as best I could (the cord prevented me from closing the door fully or locking it), and dialed her number. She answered.

"Nina?" I said.

"Mark?"

"Yeah, it's me."

"Hey. What's up?"

"So the thing is," I said, taking a deep breath, "I really like you. And not just in the friend way, but really like you. I have wanted to tell you that for a long time, and then I decided the way to do it was just to ask you out, but we have always gone out so much just as friends, that when we did go out, you didn't get it, you know? How do you ask someone out on a date who you've always gone on dates with? When I asked you to a movie, how were you supposed to know I wasn't just asking you to a movie? So I guess I just have to tell you. So I am telling you."

I carried on that way for five minutes, pausing every minute or so to see if she had anything to say, which she didn't. When I finally finished, I felt a sense of exhilaration that overwhelmed any embarrassment. I felt like a man.

She didn't say anything for about ten seconds, then, at last, her answer came: "Okay, I *really* need to think about this. See you tomorrow?"

"Okay, sure," I said. "See you in school." And I hung up.

Tomorrow came, I saw her in school, and she didn't say anything, not that day or the next. But the day after that, she asked if I wanted to take a walk, and when we were on the back side of the mile-long loop around campus, walking the paved road and looking out across the soccer fields, to the far side where the woods interceded just before the Connecticut River, she said, "So, I've thought a lot about this, and I like you, I really do, but I just don't think I like you that way. I'm sorry."

And then I did something the wisdom of which continues to surprise me. I said, "Okay, thanks for your honesty. If you change your mind, let me know."

How did I know that playing it cool was the wise thing to do? I certainly had never played anything cool before. Later that day, I thought to myself: *Maybe I've learned something from Dylan—of 90210, that is*. I also found that I had written myself a pretty useful narrative, one that was dignified, which felt like the next-best thing to triumphant: *I had the balls to tell her how I felt. I got shot down, but I did it like a man. All things considered, that's not so bad.*

The next day, our friendship was better than ever. Having already lost, I had nothing to lose, and she had a newfound respect for me. She hadn't known I had it in me. We now had an easy rapport in place of the old one-sided object worship. We talked on the phone more. I told her the story of Sari and British Columbia, and the fact that Nina found it hilarious helped me laugh about it.

On March 15, during our spring vacation, she called me and said, "Do you want to go out to dinner?" Sure, I said. Spring break had been boring so far, and it would be a relief to see somebody other than my parents and siblings. Two days later she drove up to my house in Springfield. We drove downtown in my car and tried to go to Tilly's, an Irish pub and restaurant, but couldn't get past the St. Patrick's Day crowd spilling out the door. We settled for Spaghetti Freddie's instead.

As the dinner rolls arrived, Nina told me that she had something she wanted to discuss, something important. "You know what you said a couple months ago?" she asked. "About us dating? Well, I've been reconsidering . . ."

Now debate *really* didn't matter.

After Christmas break I had missed the tournament where I could have qualified for a fourth trip to England. Now, in the spring, there wasn't much debate action left, but I didn't really care. I'd debate when I got to college, I figured. Until then, there was so much to do, in that remnant sliver of spring and in the summer ahead.

March through August—it became more than I had even known to wish for: walks with Nina on sparsely traveled trails in the Connecticut woods, kayaking with her in Long Island Sound, parking in the Plymouth Voyager. And time with other friends: a road trip with Seth, Amy, Nina, and Heather Moran to Sanibel Island, Florida, leaving the day after graduation; a camping trip, organized by Jen Murray, to the top of Bear Mountain later in June; group excursions to the movies (I remember *Far and Away*, with Tom Cruise and Nicole Kidman, at the Showcase Cinemas in East Hartford, preceded by a stop at Friendly's for ice cream); and a rock pilgrimage with my classmate Adam Larrabee to Stowe, Vermont, where Phish—not yet the post–Jerry Garcia head favorites they soon became—was opening for Santana. On the Stowe trip, Adam and I met up with Greg Navage, a guitarist who had graduated from Loomis two years ahead of us and now attended Middlebury College, not far from where the concert was. The night before the show we camped out in the grass field behind the Middlebury president's house; we were awakened at six in the morning by a woman who I assume was the president's wife. The next day, the day of the show, we swam in Otter Creek, hung out with Phish-heads from all over, and ended up crashing at some off-campus house a bunch of Middlebury students had vacated for the summer. I fell asleep to the sound of Adam teaching Greg jazz chords on the six-string, and I awoke to a dawnish silence, broken by the intermittent sound of Adam turning pages on the porch. "What are you reading?" I asked, when I found him sitting in a deck chair, sipping coffee. "*The Old Man and the Sea*," he said. It was that kind of summer.

In that long March-to-August haze, as pleasant and time-warped as any extended drug trip—even if the only drugs consumed were the odd vodka shot at a party and some Otter Creek ales after the Phish show—I thought of debate and oratory exactly four times: at the last two tournaments I attended; when I was chosen to give the class oration; and on Class Night.

I found out about the class oration in early May, on the day I decided where to go to college. The first week of May, I got my acceptance letter to Yale. Now I didn't know what to do. I visited Harvard and then Yale, and I loved them both. I visited Yale a second time, liked it less than the first time, and decided to go to Harvard. To confirm that decision, I visited Harvard again. Thinking I might major in history, I decided to sit in on Stanley Hoffmann's European history class. Minutes before his lecture was to begin, as his teaching assistants were writing notes to their discussion sections on the chalkboard, the girl sitting next to me, whose corkscrewed black hair was held in a pile on her head by a chopstick, poked me in the arm.

"Hey, are you a pre-frosh?" She spoke more loudly than necessary.

"Uh, yes."

"Where else are you thinking of going?"

"Yale," I said.

"Oh my *God*, do *not* go there!" She was now shouting, and people in the row in front of us turned to look. As a visiting high schooler, I wanted to be as invisible as possible.

"Why not?" I asked.

"I used to go there, and *I didn't have any friends*! But *here*, at Harvard, I am *so popular*!"

And that was how I decided to go to Yale.

I bid Harvard farewell from the cockpit of the Plymouth minivan at about three in the afternoon. I was directing one of the plays in Loomis's annual spring one-act festival, and we had a rehearsal that night, so I drove the hundred miles back to campus without stopping. I parked in the circular driveway of Founders Hall and got out of the car. I heard a shout from across the circle—"Mark!"—and saw Beth Rackow, our yearbook editor and class president.

"Hey Beth," I said, walking over to her. "What's up?"

"You were elected class speaker today!" Beth always spoke with exclamation points.

"I was?" I hadn't even known there was such a post, let alone an election for it.

"Yeah, at the class meeting, third period! You were one of the only people nominated. You got a majority on the first ballot! Everyone was saying it obviously should be you."

If you had asked me to give the odds that I would win any class-wide position, I would have said close to nil. I had my group of friends, which had grown to include those friends of Nina's whom I hadn't already known well. All told, I'd say I rolled about twenty deep in the Loomis Chaffee Class of 1992. And in our class of about two hundred, I knew the rest well enough to say hi. But I was definitely a day student and a brain, one of the guys Jamie Drew refers to, in Rich Cohen's beautiful memoir, *Lake Effect*, as "the Speed Walkers, who, with their minds fixed on college, did everything extremely fast." The boys and girls with class-wide cool were boarders and jocks—guys like Schuyler "Sky" Fauver and Brett Fahlgren, tall guys with lean, hairless physiques, fine, floppy hair, and that special prep school speech, laconic and unhurried, the natural precursor to their parents' lockjaw. And they hung with girls like Katie Dobson and Carly Foord-Kelcey, both so beautiful that metaphors still fail me.

According to Beth, it wasn't my close friends who had nominated me and spoken on my behalf. Rather, it was classmates who knew that what they were to lacrosse or field hockey, I was to debate. They were just giving me my due, inspired by that late-senior-year comity, when the graduating class papers over and conveniently forgets all that has divided them for four years and just decides, *Hey, our class rules.* It felt good.

Two weeks later, on Class Night, I won the senior English prize, which was not something I deserved. I shared the prize with Seth Lobis, one of my best friends, my road trip partner on our planned trip to Sanibel Island. In addition to having serious, deep-cut knowledge of classic rock, and a strong affinity for Boston sports, Seth was something of a lit-crit prodigy. He was the kind of boy who read Harold Bloom in high school—if you can call that a kind of boy, rather than just a unique specimen. We ended up doing a lot of school together—he and I would both go to Yale for college and graduate school—but I'd accepted in that first class together, Mrs. Archibald's AP English class, that I wasn't the scholar of books that he was. His papers were longer and better; his in-class comments shrewder; his allusions broader and more apt. Why, then, did I share the English prize with him?

"I think it was, in part, a way to honor your debating." So said Mr. Robison, who, although not a member of the English faculty, seemed to have some intelligence on the matter. That made sense. With no debate award to give me, I was given a piece of the English prize for my contribution to spoken English. But was that fair? That's not what the prize was for. It was for scholarship, and I was not much of an English scholar.

"Bullshit." So said Adam Larrabee, the campus rock-and-roller, blue-eyed poet, and master poon hound. "Speaking is your art, just like guitar is my art. Art is art. End of fucking story." At seventeen Adam already seemed legendary. He was beautiful and heroic. He didn't drive, swore he'd never vote, and was madly in love with the only girl in school he couldn't get but wore her rejection like a proud scar. I would have followed him off a cliff, and he would have painted the cliff paisley on the way down. I always took it as an act of generosity that Adam forgave me for being a debater. To hear him validate my passion this way, even compare it to his own love affair with his ax—it made me feel for a moment as I had two weeks before, when Beth told me I was going to be class speaker: like a big man on campus. Not big like Sky and Brett, and not big like Adam and the other members of his band, Bye and Bye, which played on the Quad every fall and spring and induced the hot boarder girls to do the Deadhead dervish dance right in front of the stage. But big anyway.

Given the two central purposes of competitive debate and oratory, to win trophies and to become a sharper thinker, it's a little ironic that at the end of high school what gladdened me most about my sport were the small, lapping tides of affection from classmates.

Aside from my fellow debaters, only perhaps a dozen friends, who had come out to watch the final round at one of our home tournaments, had ever seen me debate. (My mom had never seen me debate, nor had my girlfriend.) They just had a sense that my avocation counted, and that in some way I'd done them proud.

In the weeks before commencement, which was to be June 5, I worked every day on my speech. At least a week ahead of time I had to show a copy to Dr. Ratté, our headmaster. John Ratté, who earlier in his career had been a church historian at Amherst College, and who always wore expertly tied bow ties, was himself a wonderful orator: funny, confident, memorable. He valued oratory in others, too, and it was not unusual for him to invite a famous preacher to address the assembled school. The former Yale chaplain William Sloane Coffin came to speak once, as did the Reverend Samuel DeWitt Proctor, the pastor emeritus of Abyssinian Baptist Church in Harlem. Given Dr. Ratté's premium on good oratory, I was worried that I would not impress him. The day after I handed a copy of my speech to his secretary, he found me loitering with friends in Founders Hall, in the foyer near his office. As he approached me, I was worried.

"Oppy," he said, moving in so close that I could see his lips behind his full beard, "it's a great speech. You do two things well that I always try to do with my speeches. First, it's short. Second, you make good use of other people's writing—you steal good stuff. Nice job." Then, Speed Walker that he was, he turned on his heels and whisked himself away.

On commencement day, I wore a bow tie. That was the one sartorial excess I permitted myself. On this day all Loomis boys, from the class comedian to the football quarterback, fell in line, dressing as we'd been told: in ties and jackets with white carnations in our lapels. The girls, of course, wore white dresses. I have the class picture in front of me now, a beautiful color panoramic print that captures the whole class on bleachers but bends the brick dormitory halls behind us. It's easy to spot the other touches of whimsy. There's

Dan Minior with his mullet of blond hair, so very un-prep-school. Sophomore year, he ran for class president and gave his speech in a full-body Gumby costume. Martha Dodge wears a straw boater. Julie Lahman's dress has a placket with buttons on the front, like a boy's dress shirt, and her top button is buttoned, for a Molly Ringwald, *Pretty in Pink* effect. Suzie Lashgari's dress slips a little bit off the shoulders. Katrina van Deusen's dress is all the way off the shoulders. There is a small bow-tie clique, including Seth Lobis, now an English professor, as we all predicted; Jonathan Kiefer, now a gypsy writer, like me; and Tony Riccio, who was dead three years later, mysteriously thrown from a tall building during a study trip to Moscow.

Mostly, though, it's a spectrum of white boys and girls in white shirts, white flowers, and white dresses, many looking happy, even overjoyed, others pained, one girl with her eyes squeezed tightly shut, as if against the world to come.

Despite Dr. Ratté's kind words, the speech I gave that day was pretty undistinguished, full of clichés and simplistic allusions. I began with a fictional story about being on a college visit a couple of months earlier: "When I visited, I asked my host, who had gone to Andover, 'Tell me, Winthorp, would you say that your college is a diverse place, or is it pretty much all Andover students?' 'Oh, it's very diverse,' he answered. 'Why, there's an Exeter kid across the hall, and a Choate graduate downstairs, and upstairs there's even a couple of girls from Hotchkiss . . .'" It was a decent beginning, and the "Tell me, Winthorp" bit got a laugh. I drew a parallel from that story to the Loomis experience, which I argued was pretty similar: "Our favorite movie is *Dead Poets Society*, our favorite book, *The Catcher in the Rye*. I think we should be classified as our own racial group. On college applications, where it asked us to identify ourselves, perhaps our choices should have read: 'Caucasian,' 'Black,' 'Hispanic,' 'Asian,' 'Native American,' and 'Northeastern Preppy.'" (A smaller laugh.)

However, I continued, our lives of great privilege should not be understood to mean that we are somehow alien to the rest of the world. "Loomis Chaffee is not 'diverse' in the word's popular sense," I assured my classmates, our parents, and our friends, "but Loomis Chaffee students learn about life the same way that most of the teenagers from public school, from parochial school, or without a school do: by fighting with our parents, by crying to our friends about our failures, and by sharing with our friends the joys of life.

"Of course, let's not forget to enjoy life. In the words of the essayist Edward Abbey, 'Be a half-assed crusader, a part-time fanatic. Don't worry too much about the fate of the world. Saving the world is only a hobby. Get out there and enjoy the world, your girlfriend, your boyfriend, husbands, wives; climb mountains, run rivers, get drunk, do whatever you want to do while you can, before it's too late.'"

I also quoted Marian Wright Edelman, the Bible, Voltaire, and Martin Buber. All in about a thousand words. I was not the best student graduation speaker ever, but I may have been the most derivative.

Still, looking back, Dr. Ratté was right: I had made good use of other people's ideas, and the speech was short. My classmates liked it, too. In most respects, I wasn't the cream of the Class of 1992. I didn't finish first in my class, and I did not win any of the major commencement prizes, such as the memorably named Nathaniel Horton Batchelder Prize for Industry, Loyalty and Manliness. That was as it should have been. Compared to my best classmates, I was not an outstandingly gifted student, and I was not notable for my industry or my manliness. I just liked to talk.

XI

Freshman year at Yale started off better than I could have possibly imagined: my roommate never showed. I'd been assigned a three-room suite to share with Douglas McKay, from the town of St. Catharines, Ontario, and Mark Smith, of Stamford, Connecticut. The suite comprised two bedrooms off a central living room, and according to our rooming form Doug was to get the single, while Mark and I were to share bunk beds in a double. That first day in Welch Hall, Doug and I waited and waited, but Mark never came. In early evening, before we ventured forth to find the dining hall, we met Jeremy, our freshman counselor, who was living across the hall. We asked him about Mark. "Oh, I don't think he's coming," Jeremy said. "He deferred for a year." *Sweet.* Doug and I had a three-room double to ourselves. Two bedrooms and a living room. *As freshmen.*

You might not have guessed that Doug and I would work well as roommates. I was outspoken—being outspoken had got me into Yale—while he was quiet, not just in his general demeanor but in his actual voice, which was barely audible. Girls found his low volume just one of the many sexy things about him, along with his curly red hair, his effortless fashion sense, his cool spectacles, and his quietly spreading reputation as the best swimmer in Yale's freshman class. I, by contrast, was a standard-issue debater/wonk/Student Council guy, just one of hundreds in the Class of 1996. And I had a penchant for sweater vests, an affinity left over from my days as an Alex P. Keaton acolyte. The first month of school, a sophomore named Janna Wagner took one look at me in the dining hall and said, "Oh, baby, you have to lose the sweater vests." I was mortified and ashamed, but it was good advice.

Nobody had to tell Doug not to wear sweater vests, yet even so we had an immediate rapport. Things began auspiciously when, on the first Wednesday of school, it became clear, after dinner, that both of us wanted to watch *Beverly Hills, 90210*, which he called "the *Hills*." We were walking back to our massive, cavernous, three-room, no-show-roommate suite at around eight o'clock when Doug said to me, "So, do you think our TV gets any reception?" Yale dorm rooms didn't have cable TV yet, and they wouldn't until two years later, when my brother and his freshman roommate ran an illegal wire from the chapel, which for some reason was hooked up for cable TV, to their room in the basement of Farnam Hall, thus inaugurating, as far as I know, the cable-television experience for Yale undergraduates.

"I don't know," I said. "The TV's always worked before. I got it from my grandpa, and it worked at his house. But who knows with these stone walls."

"You have any idea what's on tonight?"

By now we'd made it back to Welch Hall, and we were hanging out in front. A bunch of other freshmen were milling about, and it seemed like a good place to be, somewhere we might meet new people.

"Well," I said, "there *was* this show I've been watching for a while now . . ."

Doug was already smiling.

So we fiddled with the rabbit ears, cajoling them to tune in the Fox channel from Hartford, forty miles to the north. When they wouldn't cooperate, we went to work on the TV itself, moving it left and right on the desk in our living room, propping it on books, swiveling it just a bit, a little this way and a little that, toward the windows fronting the New Haven Green. At last, at the strike of eight o'clock, success: that theme music, already in progress, and those panning shots of Rodeo Drive boutiques, those sideburns on Dylan and Brandon, those smiles on the pusses of Kelly and Brenda. By the third week of school, our suite had become *90210* central, with a steady group of ten classmates gathering every Wednesday night in the only freshman living space with a TV that could tune in West Beverly High.

For me and Doug, Wednesday nights were highlights of suite bonding; with his schedule of science classes and swimming practices, I didn't see him much during the school day. And I was soon recklessly busy with meetings of my own. At the freshman bazaar I had signed up for the Yale Political Union, the *Yale Daily News*, the Yale Democrats, and, even though I didn't play an instrument, the Yale Precision Marching Band. At the orientation meeting, the band conductor explained that those without musical talent could still be useful as appoges (pronounced *a-paazhes*), the extra marchers needed to fill out the band's elaborate formations during football game halftime shows. In the end, I decided against becoming an appoge—or a *Daily News* reporter, or a lightweight rower, or an improv comedy performer. In those first two weeks before homework piled up, and before first papers were due, the meetings were just a way to get to know my school—at each one, I met more cool, smart people whose names I would never remember. But I was saving myself: in the middle of week two, the Yale Debate Association tryouts began.

I hadn't thought much about debate over the summer. I knew Yale had won the World Universities Debating Championship in 1990, becoming the only American champion ever. I thought it would be cool to make the team. But I had enjoyed my time away. My speech at high school graduation had felt valedictory; my palate was cleansed, the last, leftover words fully gone. I had ended a six-year epoch of scholastic oratory, and I was in no hurry to begin again.

I had changed, too. The denouement of high school debate—the last, lackluster tournaments with Duff, the halfhearted performance at Kingswood-Oxford, my indifference to not making the England squad for what would have been the fourth time—had coincided with the upswing in my social life. And Nina, whom I had seen almost every day of the summer, was the first person I'd ever loved whom I hadn't picked fights with.

I'd always enjoyed arguing with my parents, my brothers, and my close friends, like Derek. I tried to keep the arguments friendly, but if they got contentious that was okay, too. I just liked the combat, and I'd have missed it if it were gone. With Nina, it was different. We didn't need antagonism to find each other exciting. In fact, from the night at Spaghetti Freddie's when we began our relationship, I felt alienated from the couples I saw around me: they all seemed to fight so much, and what was the point of that? Adam Doctoroff and Kelly McNamara, Jordan Oland and Lynda Duna, Jon Kiefer and Martha Brown—from what I could tell, they would fight, then retreat to easy relationships with their same-sex friends. I felt pretty much the opposite: as someone who argued with his friends and family, and whose favorite activity was competitive arguing on Sundays, I was grateful to have some peace with my girlfriend.

Years after Nina and I broke up, I read an essay in the *New Yorker* by Alison Rose about her friend "Francine," "so unnervingly beautiful that ugliness of all sorts falls to pieces wherever she is." I don't know that Nina's beauty received that kind of universal acclaim, but that's how I felt about her. The further I read in the essay, the more Rose seemed to be writing about my old girlfriend. Francine was "so nice there wasn't anything to do but let all the envious thoughts" her beauty might have inspired stay at bay. Rose is writing about a non-sexual friendship, but she's in love, it's fair to say, and I recognized in her love the increasingly distant memory of mine: "I'm not sure how she did it," Rose writes, but "Francine's beauty made me feel protected, calm." Yes, I thought—she understands. From the middle of March until the end of August 1992, when we left for college, I spent my between-class hallway moments, my after-school parking-lot moments, and my weekend car-borrowing moments with a girl who seemed an antidote to strife.

Whereas I was a born talker and, what's more, raised by political, sometimes fractious people, Nina was born serene and reared in a quiet household. The Smiths were not like the Oppenheimers: Nina's parents were doers, not talkers. They boated, they hiked. Nina's father almost never spoke, but he knew how to build and fix things. Eddie, the elder of Nina's two younger brothers, spoke even less, but he was an Eagle Scout. Nina didn't share the Smith men's aggressive physicality, nor their Puritan objection to wasted talk, but she was given to comments like "I'm never as happy as when I'm out on the water, sailing." That comment led, in fact, to our first fight, shortly after we began dating.

"Wait a minute," I said. "You mean you're happier when you're sailing than you are when you're with me?"

We had been dating about three months at this point. It was June, and Nina's father was preparing to return the family boat to its marina slip at Shennecossett Yacht Club, in Groton on the Connecticut coast.

"What are you talking about?" she said, pantomiming a slap upside my head. "I love you!"

"But you're happier on the water than anywhere else?"

I couldn't help myself—I had to get an answer.

"You know what I mean. I love sailing. That doesn't mean I don't love you."

"But you're happier sailing than on land with me?"

I could debate her out of this position.

"Stop it. You're being ridiculous."

"Well, which is it?"

"You or the boat?"

"Yeah, me or the boat?"

"I could never give up sailing. But I'd hope you'd go with me."

Why had I picked this fight? I was afraid—that was part of it.

She was just too beautiful and nice and popular for me. I was daring her to validate my fears. But I was also giving voice to a whole complex of insecurities that stalked me in the moments away from her, when our nights out were over, when I was back home in bed and she wasn't present to remind me that this was all real. I was the short, swarthy Jewish boy and she was the tall, tanned, blond girl who stopped traffic in a sundress. She was a natural, and I tried hard. She was popular, I was respected.

She couldn't give up sailing—but she hoped I'd go with her. We were in her bedroom, lying on top of her comforter, fully clothed. Unsatisfied by how she'd held up under my interrogation, I pulled away from her and lay, rigid, with a conspicuous inch between us. I was going to starve her out, give her a good guilt-inducing silent treatment. She would cave, tell me sailing didn't matter, I was all that mattered.

And then I had a revelation. *Mark, drop it.* I could just let it go.

"I'm sorry," I said, and rolled back on top of her for a long kiss.

We had only one more fight that summer, but it left me despondent. She and I had gone to a movie at the second-run cinema in Windsor, near our old high school, and her friend Jen had shown up while we were waiting in line for tickets. Jen was upset—Jen was often upset—and needed her best friend. Nina promised she'd just talk to Jen for a few minutes and would be inside by the time the previews were over. An hour into the movie, it was clear that Nina wasn't coming, and when the movie was over and I found her outside, I walked past her and Jen and got into my car. I turned the key and waited for her. As I drove her home, we fought, really yelling at each other. By the time we got to her house, it had started to rain, a heavy rain that finally broke a long humid spell. We sat in the car as the rain fell down. I told her she was inconsiderate and didn't care about me at all. She told me that if I couldn't respect her friendship with Jen then she didn't know me at all. I told her that if that's how she felt about things maybe we shouldn't be together. She asked me if I meant it. I told her I didn't know.

As I pulled into her driveway to turn around, and watched her walk in the rain to her front door, I knew I hadn't meant a word of it. Forty-five minutes later, when I got home, the phone rang as I opened my front door. It was past midnight, but she was calling to make sure I'd gotten home safely. "I was scared of you driving in the rain," she said. "You're not that good a driver." It was true. I loved her, I said. I didn't want to fight ever again. She promised that we wouldn't.

At the end of the summer, three days before I was to leave for Yale, I met Nina at the airport, where she was to board a plane, destined for her college in central Pennsylvania. Her parents graciously hung back and pretended not to watch as I hugged her good-bye. When she turned to walk through the metal detector, I retreated to the main hall of the terminal and, when I felt sure that her family couldn't see me, knelt to the floor and sobbed. Airport janitors and baggage handlers walked around me. They weren't seeing anything they hadn't seen before. After five minutes I stood up, dried my eyes on my shirtsleeve, and walked through the automatic sliding doors and away from the departure lounge ghost of the first girlfriend I'd ever had.

A week later, I got to college. The day of our first *90210* viewing, Doug asked me about this girl whose first letter had been waiting for me when I arrived at Yale. I told him her name and what she was like, trying not to sound too infatuated. "You guys doing the long-distance thing?" he asked. Yes, I said. Doug gave me the skeptical, slowly spreading smile I would see a million more times before we graduated. *Good luck with that* he was thinking.

But that was all right. I didn't want to fight about it. Nina had taught me that much. All was right in my world: I had a girl, I was going to visit her in early October, I had a very cool roommate, he dug *90210*. Classes were good; I was trying not to sweat a C+ on my first history paper. Debate tryouts were coming up, and I was eager to speak again. I'd make the team—but I'd be okay if I didn't.

Two weeks later, I stared at a list on a bulletin board in the Yale post office, wondering why my name wasn't on it. My short tryout speech for the debate team had been pretty good, I thought, and I'd answered all the team officers' questions smoothly. I quickly skimmed the list a second time, then went over it slowly, hoping that a more methodical read would turn up different results. No such luck. These six freshmen and one sophomore were, apparently, better debaters than I was, at least in the judgment of the upperclassmen who got to decide. I'd told myself that I would be fine if I didn't make the team, but I hadn't expected that to be a problem. It seemed there was nothing to be done, and so, feeling quite numb, I walked out of the post office and onto the Old Campus.

September is a glorious time in New England, and especially glorious on a courtyard the four sides of which are defined by tall, castellated neo-Gothic fortresses. It was a perfect, cool day, temperatures were in the mid-sixties, the leaves had not yet begun to fall, and the serenity of my surroundings helped steady my walk; I had wanted for so long to walk across a courtyard like this on a day like this, and for a moment I could pretend that my rejection was small and insignificant.

After I had walked the perimeter of the courtyard, I returned to the corner with the post office and went back inside, hoping I'd have mail. I turned the key in the box and pulled open the tiny door. There was a letter from Nina. She'd written to me every day so far. Wanting to prolong the experience of her daily letter, I folded it and put it in my back pocket, to read in my dorm room.

It was going to be okay.

When I got back to Welch, I was relieved that Doug wasn't home. I picked up the phone, drew out the long white cord, went in my bedroom, closed the door behind me, and sat on my bed with the phone in my lap. I dialed Nina's number. It was the middle of the day, but I figured there was a chance that she'd be in her room.

She was. "Hello?" she said.

"Nina?" I felt the beginnings of a tremor in my voice.

"Hey!"

She sounded so happy, and I felt bad about what I knew was coming. It didn't seem fair to ruin her mood.

"I didn't make the debate team," I said—and by the last word, I was sobbing. I told her about the list in the post office. Yes, I told her, I had checked and double-checked. No, there was nothing more I could do.

Nina was wonderful. After I had run out of things to say, she tried her best to put me back together: "I'm so sorry . . . that's so unfair . . . you're a wonderful debater . . . it'll be okay, baby, it will . . . I love you." None of it made me feel any better. In fact, hearing myself discussing my saga aloud was the opposite of cathartic: in the telling, what had happened to me sounded so lame, so un-saga-like. I was a freshman who had been a somebody in high school, and now I was in college, at a college I had chosen because I'd thought it would be fun to be with a thousand people who had all been the somebodies of their high schools. I'd gotten exactly what I'd wished for. I was such a cliché that a cliché had been invented for the likes of me: little fish in a big sea. Across the campus, I knew, other freshmen were feeling like little fish in other ways. I'd talked with one of them, a girl who hadn't made the violin section of the Yale Symphony Orchestra and now didn't know if she could ever look at her instrument again. I'd been sympathetic, reassuring her that none of it mattered, that college was a place to discover new sides of ourselves, et cetera.

I was ashamed to recall that I'd been a little exasperated with her, too—had she really thought that being all-region in high school mattered at Yale? And now here I was, squinting through tears, rocking on my bed and clutching the telephone console as if it were a baby needing to be held. Nina kept telling me it would be okay, and soon I was exhausted by her supportiveness. I loved her, I said, but I had to go, I would call later. I hung up the phone and dried my eyes, worried that Doug would stop back between classes. I wondered what I was supposed to do next.

I wish I could say that I went to my philosophy class that afternoon, talked about Plato, left, ate dinner, slept soundly that night, and awoke the next morning with a renewed conviction that debate didn't matter. I got to that place eventually, but not just yet. Instead, the next day I went to visit Mark Ryan, the dean of Jonathan Edwards College, the residential college where I'd live sophomore through senior years (Yalies are assigned college affiliations as freshmen, but don't live in their colleges until sophomore year). Dean Mark had impressed us all the first week at a freshman barbecue by knowing what our main activities in high school had been. "You're a swimmer, right?" he'd said to Doug, then turned to me, looked at my name tag, and said, "And Mark Oppenheimer—debater, yes?" So he knew that I was supposed to make the debate team; maybe he could do something about it.

"Mark!" he said, gesturing to the chair in front of his desk. "What can I do for you?"

I sat down and looked at Dean Mark. He had bright blue eyes and a trim, elegant beard; he looked like a kindly, deeply concerned psychoanalyst. He could feel my pain.

"Well," I said, trying to sound rational, "you know that I debated a lot in high school." Dean Mark nodded. "And I was very excited to debate for Yale. In fact, it's one of the reasons I came to Yale, because—I don't know if you know—Yale has a history of having a very good team. But I tried out for the team, and I didn't make it."

"I'm so sorry," Dean Mark said, in a genuine voice that I was grateful to hear but which embarrassed me slightly. I looked away, first at the books on his shelves and then at his wainscoted walls. "Do you have any idea why?" he asked.

This was a question to which I had given a lot of thought, and I had arrived at a theory. The team president that year was a senior named Adam Rothman, who had been a debater at Milton Academy, one of the teams in my high school league. Maybe, just *maybe*, I had defeated Adam four years earlier, when I was a high school freshman and he was a senior, in a bruising round of debate that I had long forgotten but that had poisoned him against me. And now maybe he was exacting his revenge.

But I couldn't prove that theory, and in any event leveling such charges against the team president was not going to get me on the team. So I offered Dean Ryan my second-best explanation, Theory B: "I think it may be that they don't understand the league I come from," I said. "The tournaments I won and the championships I attended were in the prep school circuit, and I noticed that a lot of the people they took were public schoolers. At least the couple I know already." I knew that to be true of one, Jerry Vildostegui, a legendary debater from Miami Beach, so saying "a couple" didn't seem like such a stretch. "I just think maybe they didn't really understand my application to be on the team."

As I was speaking, I wasn't *totally* aware that I was full of shit, but I sort of half knew it. I knew, for example, that Adam Rothman had himself been a prep schooler—my main theory of why I hadn't made the team was predicated on his having been at Milton Academy—but as that thought tried to swim to the surface I kept pushing it back underwater, telling myself that his fellow team officers were probably public-school policy debaters. The only possible reconciliation of the two theories was that Rothman hated me from our prep school days, his fellow officers misunderstood me because I'd been a prep schooler, and they had all colluded to keep me off the team, each having his or her own, malign reason for perpetrating this injustice. *That* was a nifty theory!

Truly, though, I was just in a lot of pain; although by the end of high school I had suffered from a bit of debate fatigue, and in theory wasn't so committed to debating in college, I still couldn't believe that the team didn't want me. Debate was still my identity; it was what had gotten me into college. If I was going to leave debate, it had to be on my terms. Because if I wasn't good at debate, I wasn't sure what I was good at, or why Yale would want me. I thought maybe Dean Mark could help. Where I was from—prep school—deans were very powerful. Maybe he could get me on the team and make the hurting stop.

He couldn't, of course. He shook my hand and saw me to his office door, promising to look into it. I bumped into him at least once a week for the next four years, but we never again spoke of debate. He'd given me what I needed, fifteen minutes of compassion, and trusted that I would soon heal myself. And it was true, I did feel better in time. But I was still terribly moved when, my senior year, at one of the last debate team parties before graduation, a freshman girl, obviously drunk—and cute, with a long ponytail that stood perkily up from the top of her head then fell down her back—tapped me on the shoulder and said, *"Mark Oppenheimer, is it true that when you didn't make the team freshman year your dean wrote a letter trying to get you on the team?"*

As I was about to deny it, I thought of Dean Mark, and how concerned he'd seemed, and what a mensch he was. That sounded like something he would do. But if he'd done that, and everyone knew it except me, how was it that I hadn't been mocked mercilessly for the past three years? Debaters aren't shy about ridiculing their teammates, not just during debate rounds (as the Scots did), but in the dining hall, at the bar, in the van on the way to tournaments. The only way that I would have been spared constant, brutal teasing would be if—I guess it was possible—my teammates, the ones who had welcomed me to the team sophomore year and thereafter tolerated my indolence and lack of total commitment to the sport, had been too kind to bring it up.

"Yes," I told the girl with the antigravity ponytail. "Yes, I went crying to my dean and he wrote a letter. Man, freshman year—that was a long time ago."

She smiled triumphantly and gave one fast nod, as if gloating after winning a bet. Then she turned and ran back toward a gaggle of freshman girls, leaving me to contemplate how much, once upon a time, I had cared.

Between my rejection as a freshman and my ability to laugh about it as a senior, a lot had happened. Time and the hectic, invigorating jumble of college life, in which every day contains a week's worth of activity, had healed my debater's ego, just as Dean Mark had surely predicted. In fact, the very next Saturday night I had impressed a bunch of Doug's swimmer friends by taking a ten-second swig from a bottle of Stolichnaya. "Doug, your rommate's crazy," Topher Nichols had said in amazement. Sunday morning in the dining hall, Doug and I had had a competition to see who could eat more "Eli's Breakfast Sandwiches," as the menu on the bulletin board called egg-bacon-and-cheese sandwiches. Doug had seven, but I was proud to finish six, especially with the vodka still jackhammering my temples. On Sunday night, I had stayed up until three in the morning talking with a suite of three very cool, very odd girls, including an Exeter alumna who swore that she could give herself cunnilingus.

College was awesome.

For the first time I could remember, I had free time. Classes met three times a week for about an hour; even with lots of reading and a short paper due every Friday, I still had to fill about twenty waking hours every week. I read books for pleasure, such as *Linden Hills*, by Gloria Naylor, whose *The Women of Brewster Place* I had read in high school after seeing the TV miniseries version. I decided it would be cool to start an undergraduate book review, and I wrote to Naylor to ask if she would serve on our advisory board. She wrote back a polite note, declining. John Hersey and Camille Paglia also declined. I dropped the idea and started going for long runs out Whitney Avenue, past where the graduate students lived in three-family houses, into quiet neighborhoods with driveways and swing sets. The swing sets—and the minivans, and the children my sister's age—made me homesick, so one Saturday in late October I took an Amtrak train to Springfield to surprise my parents. From the train station I took a taxi cab to Pineywoods Avenue, and when I went inside, my parents, instead of being overjoyed, looked worried. "Is everything okay at school?" my father asked. Over the course of the next six hours, during which time I had lunch, took a nap, and walked around my old neighborhood, where I recognized nobody, I realized that yes, everything was okay. That night I took a train back to New Haven.

For me and Nina, the fall continued to go well. We talked and exchanged letters every day. I called so often that I got to know the voices of her roommate Heather and her new best friend Sarah, who was always in their room. I was such a fact of life in their world at Dickinson College that after I didn't make the debate team I received a condolence card from Heather and Sarah. In mid-October I visited Dickinson, borrowing a big, gas-guzzling sedan from Scott Pike, the only freshman I knew with wheels, and driving five hours from New Haven to the heart of Pennsylvania's Amish country. Pike's car radio was broken, and in the silence I contemplated how good it would feel to hold my girlfriend again.

That weekend was the first time since our postgraduation trip to Florida that we'd been together for more than twelve hours. And even though there'd been no parents chaperoning in Florida, we'd been in a small condominium with three other friends. This was something new, different, and altogether amazing. This was college, and we could do what we pleased. We could even share a bed, and when you're eighteen and haven't seen each other for six weeks you don't care that the bed is a cramped twin extra-long. I arrived on Friday, and my leaving on Sunday afternoon was unbearable. Hadn't I just been through this, in late August, leaving her? Now I had to do it again?

But when we next saw each other, when Nina visited Yale in early November, things didn't seem right. The connection was strained; we were out of sync, like telephone callers in different countries unable to master the time lag. I took her to the college production of *West Side Story*, and in the dark University Theater I turned in my seat to stare at her, wondering how I actually felt. After she returned to Dickinson, I started writing her less frequently. I was letting go of the relationship, and that made me sad, but I couldn't seem to reverse things. A red-haired vixen in my freshman literature class followed me home from a party one night; when we got to my room in Welch Hall, I explained to her that I had a girlfriend, and she leaned over and whispered in my ear, "Long distance never works." I wasn't attracted to her, but as she turned and left, I worried that she was right—that some other, more appealing girl would eventually come between me and Nina. Or maybe just time and distance would do us in.

When Nina and I saw each other over Thanksgiving, the connection seemed strong again—we watched movies, partied with friends, got naked in our parents' houses after they'd gone to bed—and I decided I'd be *crazy* to break up with her. But when I got back to Yale I realized what had happened: Thanksgiving had been an aberration. On our old turf, we knew how to be boyfriend and girlfriend, but we weren't going to survive college. I knew what I had to do. I called her one night during my final exams—for some reason, the date December 18 sticks in my mind—and told her what I was thinking, that it had to end. She cried, but I didn't. In order to make such a call, to hurt the person I'd loved more than I'd loved anybody, I'd had to justify it. Before calling her, I'd made a mental list of all her flaws, all the reasons that I could do so much better and that she, in fact, was culpable in the whole mess, holding me back and keeping me from fully enjoying college. So when she broke down in tears, I was numb, tired, and eager to get off the phone.

After it was over, I went into the living room. Doug looked up from his chemistry homework. He'd heard the whole thing, I could tell. "Are you all right?" he asked. "I guess," I said.

Of course, I didn't enjoy my new freedom; I hated it. What had I done? For weeks after Christmas break I lay awake on my bed and listened to two CDs over and over again: *Automatic for the People*, by R.E.M., and *Gordon*, by the Barenaked Ladies, a Canadian band that Doug had introduced me to. The official song of this breakup, the one that still throws me back to the winter of 1993, was the Barenaked Ladies' "Enid": "It took me a year to believe it was over/ and it took me two more to get over the loss./I took a beating when you wrote me those letters/and every time I remembered the taste of your lip gloss." Powerful stuff, when I was eighteen. Powerful still.

At first, being alone made me miss debate again. I developed a powerful longing to go back to senior year of high school, when I had two faithful security blankets, debate and Nina. I was tyrannized by nostalgia, and it didn't help that Nina and I still exchanged occasional letters and spoke on the phone about once a week. Even though the breakup had been my decision, she was clearly healing faster than I was, and my neediness was, I think, starting to become annoying. When she finally kissed another boy, she made sure to casually slip that fact into one of our conversations. Painfully, I took the hint. We both needed to move on. And then, toward the end of February, as the frequency of our phone calls gradually diminished, as more time elapsed since I had seen her face, I began to feel better. As I did, my attachment to all things high school, the people and the activities and everything that made up the old me, began to lessen. Who I could become began to interest me more than who I had been.

I discovered that not being a debater was in fact the liberation that toward the end of high school I'd suspected it might be. Finding myself without Nina or debate—being generally unencumbered by the past—was sad, but it could also be exhilarating. I had so much to learn about who the rest of me, the nondebating me, was.

Aside from the kids in my dorm and Doug's teammates, the first crowd I got to know well were the actors. I was cast in three plays that spring. I played the drunk Mexican in Tennessee Williams's *Summer and Smoke*, several small roles in *Henry IV, Part I*, and Alan's father in *Equus*. The *Equus* production is still one of my most exciting memories from college, not because I was any good but because my cast mates really were. Several of them were headed for careers in theater. One was Blake Lindsley, who popped up after graduation with small parts in *Swingers* (she was the cigar-smoking girl) and *Starship Troopers* (the profile of her left breast is visible in the shower scene). In the starring role of Alan, Adam Stein was astonishing: fully nude, sobbing, magically convincing as an adolescent boy even though he was a college senior with thinning hair.

One Saturday at midnight, after a late performance, the whole *Equus* cast went together to the Neutron Bomb, a dance being held in the dining hall of one of the residential colleges. Just as we got there, the deejay queued up Nirvana's "Smells Like Teen Spirit," and we all went crazy. Kurt Cobain was still alive, I was whipping my head all over, moshing unself-consciously, and a cute, cool actress named Juliette McGarry—who a month earlier had humiliated me in rehearsal by saying, "That sweater vest is *perfect* for the dad's part," not realizing that I was actually wearing the sweater vest as me, not as a character—was hopping up and down right next to me in a tight circle of thespians. Once, she crashed into me, intentionally. Juliette McGarry and Blake Lindsley and Adam Stein—they all seemed fragile and weird, artistic and deep. Did I fit in here? It didn't seem impossible.

After spring break I started dating Katie, a member of the women's ice hockey team. We got drunk together at a party in the off-campus house where four of Yale's top swimmers lived. One of them had mysteriously dropped out of school the previous week, and I went through his closet and looked at all the philosophy books he had left behind: Hume, Kant, Bertrand Russell. Stuff that, as a debater, it had come in handy to pretend I'd read. Katie had a boyfriend back home, a former drug addict whom she'd met working at Au Bon Pain the summer after high school, so our relationship was just a fling, destined to end soon. In early May, after our last exam, a classmate and I threw a big party in his dorm. We bought bottles of beer and fifths of liquor at Zachary's, a wino shop just far enough into a shady neighborhood that the proprietor didn't card students. By 10 P.M. I was drunk. At eleven o'clock Margaret, a short, darling girl with thick black hair and sloping eyes, cried out, "Oh shit, I forgot to take my birth control pill!" At midnight I put the Red Hot Chili Peppers on the CD player. I started spinning around, then the room started spinning, and the last thing I remembered before vomiting on the landing outside the door to the suite was Clare Connors, a blond Hawaiian *haole* whom we all secretly loved, shouting along with me the lyric "Give it away, give it away, give it away, give it away now!"

The next morning, I threw all my notebooks and tests in a big trash can by Phelps Gate. Summer was here. Katie and I hugged good-bye. She was going home to Boston, and I had a job answering phones at Loomis for May and June. For those two months I saw Nina occasionally, usually in a group with the others: Monique and Beth, Tony and Lynda. It was a pleasant time, with no expectations and no letdowns. In July I went to New York, where I volunteered at the American Civil Liberties Union and at night wandered the streets around Union Square. In August, I spent all my money on a trip to Switzerland, where I wandered the country by myself. On my last night there, at the Geneva hostel, I met a girl with the improbable name Saasha Celestial-One. She told me that her parents had invented both her first and last names and that she had recently been expelled from Andover (I didn't ask why). We sneaked onto a boat in the Lake Geneva harbor and kissed in the hull for an hour. The next morning, on the plane back to JFK, I felt proud that I had a mildly adventurous story to tell everyone at college. That seemed a fine capstone to the summer. I was ready to get back to school.

I didn't intend to join the debate team the next fall—*fuck them*, I'd decided—but it happened anyway. I already knew four of the six sophomores on the team. Jonathan Cohen I knew from high school debate; Jerry Vildostegui and I had been in several classes together as freshmen; Jed Shugerman had, like me, joined the Yale Political Union; and Elisa Korentayer had played my daughter in the Tennessee Williams play. I liked them all, so when Jerry asked me, in September, "Are you going to try out for debate again?" it didn't sound like such a terrible idea. "They made a mistake last year," he said. "I'm sure you'll make it this year."

"I don't know," I said. "I don't really have the time." That was a lie. I was just afraid of getting hurt again.

"Don't be ridiculous," Jerry said. "We really want you on the team."

"We?"

"Jon Cohen, me, Elisa. You have to try out."

They all wanted me? This was really flattering. I would try out.

This year, when I went to Yale Station to look at the final list, I saw my name. I wasn't elated, or even particularly smug. I was actually more nervous than anything—by the middle of the previous spring, it had become pretty easy to think that debate was behind me; like the dead parrot in the Monty Python skit, the debating me was no longer—I was a former debater, an ex-debater. What would it mean to be a debater once again?

In fact, I quickly discovered that "APDA," the American Parliamentary Debate Association—the league comprising Yale, most of the other Ivy League schools, Stanford, Amherst, Swarthmore, Smith, Fordham, New York University, and a couple dozen others—was not for me. It had *parliamentary* in its name, but it was nothing like the debate I'd known in high school. APDA debate seemed like the worst Olympic sport imaginable, both stupid *and* corrupt: synchronized diving scored by the East German judges.

I only attended three tournaments my sophomore year, but that was enough to see this new sport for what it was. For starters, the tournaments began on Fridays at about noon and ended after dinner on Saturday nights, meaning that competitors were gone from their home schools for two full days, missing the campus social scene on Fridays and Saturdays. In effect, to be a serious debater on the APDA circuit meant that all of one's friends were on the APDA circuit. The people you drank with on Fridays, hooked up with at after-parties on Saturdays? Fellow debaters. The league thus attracted people who felt more comfortable around debaters than around their classmates back on campus. For many debaters, the APDA social scene was a godsend, but for me it was a real turnoff.

One could be casual about debate, attending only a tournament every other month or so, keeping one's distance from the incestuous scene, but that didn't help one's point totals. Because the APDA judges were—and, as one who cares about the integrity of competitive debate, this still amazes me—other debaters. In high school, our judges had been either parents, who might show slight home-team favoritism but were basically pretty honorable, or our coaches, who had an incentive to be fair: if your coach was suspected of always tilting against a particular rival school, that school's coach could exact revenge when he judged you. But on the college circuit, one judged at one's own tournament: the judges at the Princeton tournament were Princeton debaters, the judges at the NYU tournament were NYU debaters. Which meant, of course, that a debater could find herself being judged by the skeevy boy who'd thrown up on her at the after-party of last week's tournament. Or by the girl she'd vanquished in an intense final round a month earlier.

It got worse still. Because the format was supposed to be parliamentary, and parliamentary debate is supposed to be impromptu, the topic for each round was announced only half an hour before the round began. But that did not mean that debaters began formulating their arguments only half an hour before the round. Rather, APDA debaters came prepared with "cases" that they planned to "run" regardless of what the announced topics were.

Here's how it worked. On the van ride to, say, the Fordham tournament, my teammates would be tossing around various cases—"Supreme Court justices should not have lifetime tenure," "The Ivy League should begin offering athletic scholarships," "In a two-party system, the most honorable thing to do is abstain from voting," and so forth. A good case was one that allowed for humor and intellectual play, was somewhat surprising or counterintuitive, and was not too "tight," or obviously correct (a case like "Three-strikes sentencing laws should be repealed" came dangerously close to being too tight, because there are so many good arguments in favor and, it's generally agreed, practically no good arguments against). Debaters tried to arrive at a tournament with three cases ready to go, which meant having thought through the good arguments in favor of them and anticipated the most likely arguments against them. Out of five rounds, your team wouldn't be the government, which proposes the case, more than three times, so three cases was all you needed. A very strong team, one whose members could reasonably expect to "break" to the "out rounds"—that is to say, make it to the quarterfinals or beyond—had to have more cases prepared, to use as needed.

The student directing the tournament, usually the president of the host team, would stand up at the front of the auditorium and announce the topic. Then one or two hundred debaters would huddle up with their teammates, the government speakers scrambling to match the topic with one of the cases they had prepared—that's what the half hour of prep time was used for. Let's say the nominal topic was "This House believes in pacifism," and the cases you and your partner had prepared in the van that morning were the ones I listed above, about the Supreme Court, sports in the Ivy League, and abstaining from voting. "Which of these is the closest to pacifism?" you'd ask your partner, as you sat cross-legged in the hallway outside the classroom where your round would start twenty-five minutes later.

"I don't know," she says. "Maybe the one about the Supreme Court? We could argue that lifetime tenure raises the stakes over each court nomination, leading to unnecessary conflict, which is antithetical to pacifism?"

"Maybe," you reply. "But the Ivy League one works, too. The Ivy League is so bad at sports, football especially, so if you want to reduce the amount of really violent tackles in the world, just get more athletes, and more of your best athletes, to Ivy League schools, where they'll play like pansies for four years and never make it to the NFL."

"I like it, I like it. But we could also run the abstaining-from-voting case. We say that the current system is just mindless, bloody warfare, and it's the job of any concerned citizen to opt out. To not opt out is to endorse the system. Plus, this is the system that has given us Vietnam, the invasion of Grenada, the invasion of Panama—basically, the American political system, both parties, causes death. So refusing to participate is actually the thing one should do. Hence, an endorsement of pacifism?"

After some brief discussion, an APDA team about to debate as the government, or affirmative, settles on which case offers the most winning way to "squirrel," or twist, the topic. A decision is made, some final notes are jotted down, and the team goes into the classroom and writes their team name—"Yale B," "Swarthmore A," "Columbia C"—on the board. Soon, a debater from the host school enters, sits down, writes down the debaters' names and schools on his ballot, and begins the round: "I call this house to order," he says, "and call upon the prime minister to deliver his opening speech."

Then the prime minister, the first government speaker, begins by squirreling the topic:

"Mr. Speaker, I thank you, my honorable opponents, and my colleague on the government side. The topic we have before us today is 'This House believes in pacifism.' When we on the government side consider this topic, we are, of course, led to think about the United States, one of the main purveyors of war in the world. Wherever there's a war, it seems, the United States is in it. This has been the case whether a Democrat is president or a Republican is president. Consider Vietnam, the most ignominious of American wars. It was begun by Kennedy, then continued by Johnson, and then it took Nixon way too many years to pull out of it. It was a bipartisan failure, Mr. Speaker.

"Thus, one has to ask, is participating in American two-party democracy, and thus giving aid and comfort to Democrats or Republicans, participating in war? The obvious answer is yes. And because we support pacifism, and want to end the United States–perpetrated bloodshed, we the government reinterpret this resolution to mean that in our current two-party system in the United States, one should abstain from voting in national elections.

"We have three arguments in favor of this resolution. . . ."

From there, the debate continues in parliamentary fashion, the government and opposition speakers taking turns, but with the actual resolution about pacifism completely ignored until the rebuttals. Then, after an hour of debate about voting, each debater concludes his rebuttal speech by saying, bizarrely, "And that is why, Mr. Speaker, we believe that this House should believe in [or, if on the opposition, reject] pacifism"—as if that is what they've been arguing about all along.

This blatant fiction was not winked at, or politely tolerated, but actively encouraged. It was assumed on the APDA circuit that good debaters prepared cases in advance; any debater who actually argued the announced topic would reveal himself to be a naïf, a tyro, or an idiot.

Why, then, did APDA persist in having stated resolutions? I never knew. I suppose it was a genial nod to the idea that this was parliamentary debate. And insofar as the fast-talking policy style was generally avoided, no exhaustive research was required, and terms like "the government" and "Mr. Speaker" were used, then it was parliamentary debate, I suppose. But in a league filled with former policy or Lincoln-Douglas debaters, the idea of going entirely by one's wits was too frightening. So the league had evolved an ugly hybrid: the pretense of being impromptu coupled with the reality of preparation—but not genuine, careful, thoughtful preparation, just hungover rap sessions in the van, which generated clever cases, vaguely supported by invented or exaggerated facts and statistics. It was parliamentary debate without the whimsy, policy debate without the integrity.

So I rarely debated during college. The team required that, in order to remain on the roster, one had to debate at least once a term, and I never debated more than that, except for the fall of my sophomore year, when I debated twice. I remember partners more than I remember specific rounds. My first partner was Nancy Jacobson, at the Harvard tournament in the fall of sophomore year. A freshman from the New York suburbs, Nancy seemed full of purpose, certain to work hard, get into law school, and land a good Jewish husband (she did all three). That spring I debated at the MIT tournament with Jay Readey, a six-foot-seven ex-rower with deep Christian convictions and a wicked, subversive wit. Late in the day on Saturday, as the judges were tabulating scores, the MIT tournament featured an impromptu-speaking competition, as a sideshow to pass the time. Jay and I both entered, and on the blackboard where the contestants had to write their names he wrote, "No my name ain't 'baby,' it's Jay—Mr. Readey if you're nasty," surely the best Janet Jackson allusion ever made by a white crew dude from the Cleveland suburbs. Junior year I debated at the University of Pennsylvania with Elisa Korentayer, an Israeli-American who invited the whole team to spend Friday night at her parents' house in the Philly suburbs; her mother showed us a portfolio of head shots from Elisa's abortive career as a child model. At the tournament on Saturday, I persuaded Elisa that we should squirrel one of our topics into the case, "Resolved: Circumcision should be made illegal." She was convinced we could never win that case, but we did. We made it to the quarterfinals of the Penn tournament, then promptly lost. It was my most successful showing at an APDA tournament.

Not debating much, I had the extracurricular schedule of the consummate dilettante. I continued to act in plays, and the most hilarious moment of my four years at Yale came during a performance of *Hedda Gabler* in the Silliman Dramatic Attic, a small theater space in one of the dormitories. I was sitting upstage, pantomiming conversation with Michael Bakkensen. He was playing Judge Brack, and I was Tesman, Hedda's feckless husband, and we were supposed to be speaking to one another intensely but inaudibly, as the audience was paying attention to Hedda, Lovborg, and Mrs. Elvsted downstage. Michael wanted to make me laugh, to make me crack onstage, and it so happened he had good material, since he was currently having a carnal affair with one of the actresses downstage. "You see her?" he would whisper, leaning toward me with his Judge Brack bearing intact. "She swallowed my cum right before call. Ten minutes before we began putting on our makeup, my cock was deep down her throat. And I easily have eight, nine inches when hard. She took it all. Sure, she may have gagged some, but she knew what her job was. She kept at it, yes she did. And she swallowed it. And that means that as she speaks, right downstage, playing her part, speaking her lines, she is digesting my semen." I nodded, biting my tongue so hard that it nearly bled. Bakkensen was crude, but he was funny.

I loved the actors. They always said and did things I wouldn't.

There were drugs at theater parties, and muffled sex behind closed bedroom doors. Although I acted, I wasn't an actor, not at heart. I wasn't a politico either, even though I was a member of the Yale Political Union. I did become president of Yale Democrats my junior year, but when a seat opened up to represent Ward 1 on the New Haven Board of Aldermen, the seat that was always held by a Yalie, I wasn't interested, and my co-president ran and won. Junior year, Doug and I edited *Temptations*, the Jonathan Edwards College newsletter. I dated, although every relationship seemed to end after precisely two months.

I was perfectly happy being a halfhearted debater, a fallible, occasional weekend warrior. I didn't like all my teammates equally, but as a group the Yale '96 debaters were a more agreeable crowd than any other I could lay claim to. I never fully committed to debate, never put in the hours, but there was no group at Yale with whom I felt more at ease. These were the wisenheimers, the kids who as children had never known when to shut up, and around each other we didn't have to. Jerry Vildostegui, who as a senior became our team president, had the kind of promiscuous intelligence that has always left me awed. A major star on the high school debate circuit, when Jerry got to Yale he considered being a math major before rejecting that for philosophy, and he spoke fluent Spanish, the gift of his Cuban-American parents back home in Miami. Jerry had a much older brother, Luis, whom he idolized, and parents who had been so excited by their late-in-life second son that they had named him after the patron saint of childbirth, San Gerardo. Jerry had the infectious, unself-conscious cheer of an adored younger son, and he liked taking out his driver's license to show what he'd looked like as a tan sixteen-year-old who could go to the beach every afternoon. "You see how happy I looked?" he would ask, and, looking at his photo, we could see exactly what he meant.

Jed Shugerman, from Bethesda, Maryland, was the kind of guy I'd expected more of at Yale: bookish, political, Reform Jewish, liberal, suburban. Weren't there a million of these guys coming out of

Brookline, Shaker Heights, Scarsdale? Jed was very smart yet disarmingly simple: he was the kind of guy who always wore a baseball cap, and who always had hat-head when he took it off. Jed was the kind of friend I'd needed more of in junior high. Jonathan Cohen was from Halifax, Nova Scotia, and we'd met at two tournaments in high school. He eagerly gave hugs and was an enthusiastic booster of everybody he liked—tell a mildly funny joke, and Jonathan would laugh uncontrollably, but totally sincerely. Like Jerry, Jonathan majored in philosophy.

There was Elisa Korentayer, the Philadelphian, today a singer-songwriter with a more Hollywood last name; Gary Stewart, a Jamaican American who in high school had debated for Bronx Science, the elite high school in New York City; Krista McGruder, a libertarian sorority girl from Missouri with a libidinous penchant for athletes; Farzana Kanji, an Ismaili Muslim from New Mexico; and Andy Wilmar—half Korean, half something Nordic, and all Californian—whose slow surfer drawl made him unusually pleasant to listen to.

The team met every other Tuesday night at 10 P.M. in the Berkeley College Swiss Room, an ornate private dining room. The team president would read the latest tournament results, ask who was attending which future tournaments with which partners, and occasionally preside over a "pub round," just for practice. Our rounds were judged by our team coaches, Andre Dua and the marvelously named Leif Wellington Haase. I got along well with Leif, a Canadian graduate student who believed in old-fashioned parliamentary debate virtues and scorned the professionalism and unctuousness of so many American debaters; and although I sometimes suspected that Andre was a pathological liar, I liked him—his dubious tales of having partied with models and been consulted by politicians in his native Australia were admirable for their shameless unlikelihood. After Andre or Leif delivered his verdict, we would go to Naples, a pizza joint highly regarded by students for its willingness to card only the student who paid for the pitcher of beer. At Naples, conversation would run from John Rawls, about whom somebody was always writing a paper, to the politics of GESO, the nascent graduate student union, which as callow undergraduates we were all disposed to loathe, to the imagined sexual predilections of any debaters who weren't around the table that night. Rawls, organized labor, sex— they all got the full midrashic treatment over pitchers of beer, our arguments going down byways to which the footnotes had footnotes. These were the friends I'd been missing all my life, the people whose best debating happened on their off hours.

It was my fondness for this gang that drew me to my last international debate tournament. The World Universities Debating Championship was to be held during Christmas vacation at University College Cork, in Ireland. The university Worlds was a more prestigious tourna- ment than all the "world" or "international" championships that I had attended in high school, because it truly was a unified belt: there was only one English-speaking university Worlds. But as Yalies we tended to take Worlds less seriously than, say, the Harvard or Princeton tour- nament, primarily because it seemed awfully hard to win. Only two American teams had ever won Worlds—Yale in 1990 and Harvard in 1993—and many of our best debaters had fared miserably. Many judges in foreign countries had an anti-American bias, to be sure, but the bigger problem was that after years of APDA debating, even the best American speakers often couldn't switch to a more truly parlia- mentary style, in which clever squirreling was no substitute for wit, charm, and bombast.

Whether or not my parliamentary knives had gone rusty, it was unlikely I'd get to Cork. Yale could send only three two-person teams, and, having debated less frequently in college than all of the other seniors, I lacked seniority. Jerry and Jon, who had been the most successful '96 debaters, were going as our A team, and the B and C teams would be some mix of Jed, Elisa, Farzana, Krista, Andy, and Gary—and possibly even Jeff Kulkarni, who had joined the team our junior year and was notable for being the only member of the Yale Debate Association also to hold membership in Delta Kappa

Epsilon, "Deke," the most beery, boorish, and proudly troglodytic of Yale's few fraternities. (Deke pledge week required of all its "butt-holes," or pledges, that they live together in one dorm room and not shower for the entire seven days.) As it turned out, several of the debaters ahead of me in the queue had other plans for Christmas break. After Gary, Krista, Farzana, and Jeff all took a pass, I was offered a spot in the six-person delegation, as Jed's partner.

I met up with the other Yale debaters at JFK airport on December 26, 1995. The Harvard and Princeton delegations were there, too, along with debaters from several other APDA schools. Every school was allowed three two-person teams, but not every school was bringing that many; it tended to be the teams richest in talent, and money, who sent the full complement of six. The other Yale debaters had all been much more active on the circuit, and they each recognized a dozen or so debaters from other schools, but I knew only three. There was David Lat, a hilariously outrageous Harvard debater, short with naturally spiky hair, who had graduated from New York's Regis High School, the free, highly selective school for Catholic boys that graduated many of the best Ivy League debaters from my era. Years later, Lat would become briefly famous after he revealed to *New Yorker* writer Jeffrey Toobin that he was the anonymous author of Underneath Their Robes, a dishy legal blog; Lat then resigned from his job at the U.S. attorney's office and soon became an editor of Wonkette, the even more scurrilous D.C. gossip website. Lat's partner for Worlds was Eric Save, a dashing, well-tailored fellow whose full name, he told us over drinks in Ireland, was Eric Save de Beau-recueil, which seemed oddly fitting, a perfect objective correlative to Eric's self-aware pomposity. The only other non-Yale debater I knew on that flight to Ireland was my old Andover nemesis Doug Kern, who, it was reassuring to discover, had not changed at all: he had the same pleasant, Orville Redenbacher, Midwestern nerdiness; same intense, intelligent gaze; same jumpy way of constantly looking around, as if wondering when the reinforcements were going to arrive.

I don't remember much of the flight. There was free alcohol on Aer Lingus, and I remember, quite foggily, being drunk but unable to sleep. I've always been adrenaline-racked on intercontinental flights, excited by the sense of being neither here nor there, all the old commitments thousands of miles behind me, a foreign land lying ahead. Having so many fellow collegians on one flight, all of us bound for a week of debate—it reminded me of high school. Nobody stayed in his seat except Jed, who had spilled his third Guinness on his pants and had a large dark spot on his crotch; the rest of us patrolled the aisles, switching seats, looking for familiar faces, and when I didn't find many I just introduced myself to people who looked debaterly.

By the time we landed the next morning in Ireland, we were exhausted. The bus that was supposed to meet us at the Shannon airport was not there when we arrived, so all the debaters, with our whiskey breath, with smudged makeup on the girls and 6 A.M. shadows on the boys, settled into a small coffee shop in the terminal. Before the Irish economic boom, the "Irish tiger," the airport had that Second World seediness—dirty carpets, cigarette smoke deep in the fabric of everything. We ordered coffee and waited, too tired to talk, just craving hot showers. Finally, two women about our age sashayed in, and we knew before they opened their mouths that they were from University College Cork and were here to pick us up. They seemed like one of those inseparable duos I find so annoying—they probably described themselves chirpily as "best girlfriends" or "partners in crime"—and they led with their breasts. As they rounded us up and brought us to the bus outside, one of the debaters asked about their skimpy clothes. "How do you get by wearing so little in the cold?" he said. One glanced over her shoulder with a come-hither look, exhaled a coil of cigarette smoke, and said, "We don't just get by, we get on!" I had no idea what that meant, but it sounded dirty, and I was totally grossed out.

The bus left all the American debaters at Jury's hotel, a Holiday Inn–style place in the center of Cork. There were no debate rounds until the next day, so we could have gone to sleep, but we decided to fight through our fatigue and stay awake until nighttime, hoping to lick jet lag. The six of us from Yale went looking for some food and ended up at a small pub near the hotel, where we ordered plowman's lunches and, in the spirit of the trip, pints of Murphy's Irish Stout. All of us, that is, except Jed, who somewhere over the Atlantic Ocean had lost his voice entirely; he ordered a tea with honey. The barmaid who brought our drinks nodded to a table across the room and said, "Drinks are on them."

Our benefactors, whom we beckoned to join us, were four debaters from the University of Alaska. We had never met them before, but they had heard us speaking, recognized that we were fellow Americans abroad, and reached out in friendship. It was a generous move, and I wish I could say that we were delighted to make their acquaintance. But we were very tired, and they were deeply, unsettlingly weird.

The Alaskan debater I remember best was named Mark. He was about thirty years old, wore thick glasses, had a very *Eight Is Enough* bowl cut of brown hair, had served in the Marines, and was putting himself through school by selling Amway products on the side. "A lot of people think Amway is some sort of cult," he said, as I drank the beer he'd paid for. "But that's not it at all. It's just that it's all about loyalty, just the way the military is. And I'll tell you, they appreciate the military. They play the fight song of each branch of the armed services at every Amway convention. They recite the Pledge of Allegiance. Amway honors its veterans. That means a lot to me. And I'll tell you something else: Amway is the only place I have seen the kind of loyalty I saw in the Marines. Your upline, the man who brought you in, is one hundred percent loyal to you, because he only makes money if his downlines make money. He wants me to succeed. He would do anything for me to succeed. How many of us can say that about our bosses? Can you say that about your boss?"

I could not.

"And I am a sponsor, the upline, for three other guys who are my downlines, and I am intensely, totally loyal to them. Their success is my success, and it's my sponsor's success. So all up and down the chain, there is loyalty. You see what I mean?

"Look, I'm a veteran. I'm a university student. I'm a Jew. I'm an Amway entrepreneur. I'm a debater. That's who I am. And it's really a pleasure to meet you guys."

Jed's voice returned just in time, and we debated eleven times over the next five days: nine preliminary rounds, then octofinals and quarterfinals. As usual, I hardly remember anything from the debates, but I remember the people. Say this about debaters: they aren't shy. I suppose some people take up debate as a cure for shyness, but they don't end up at world championships. The tournament at Cork was an international summit of loud, memorable, even outrageous personalities. Besides Mark the Jewish Amway-selling ex-Marine, there was Mike the aggressively flirtatious gay debater from Brown; he had about him a nihilistic, party-boy chic that I associated with Charles Wainwright, my tormentor from junior high school, although Mike was actually a pretty sweet guy—his act was more of a joke that he trusted everyone would get. There was Viola, the Chinese-American debater from the University of La Verne, in Southern California, who wore bright red lipstick and stiletto heels and enjoyed hugging male debaters she had just met. She was like some oratory sex kitten sent by the devil to taunt hard-up debater boys. Stephen Magee, the great Scottish debater who had coached me to victory in Edinburgh five years earlier, was in Cork, debating for the University of Edinburgh. There were a pair of prissy-seeming girls from Fairfield University, the Jesuit school in Connecticut, one of whom got very drunk and very uninhibited at the big bash on New Year's Eve; two earnest, clean-cut boys from Willamette University, in Oregon; and a pair of very white debaters from Stellenbosch University, in South Africa. The Stellenbosch debaters could be recognized by their rugby shirts bearing a springbok, the mascot of South Africa's national team, which was then the reigning world champion. Tall, erect, muscular, with hair so blond it was almost white, the South

African debaters looked like my idea of Nazis, and when Jed and I debated them they seemed awfully angry, but it was wacky and exciting to face nerds from Oregon in one round and towering Afrikaaners in the next. Even more than the high school tournaments, which had drawn from many countries but mainly from private schools, the World Universities Debating Championship was a big jumble of all kinds of people: Ivy Leaguers, public university kids, part-time students from commuter colleges, Catholic schoolers.

The topics were generally based on current events—nuclear deterrence, the Middle East peace process, that sort of thing. The other Yale debaters and I had crammed on the flight over, skimming several months' worth of *Newsweek* and the *Economist*. From all that reading what I'd remembered best was one article about Aung San Suu Kyi, the Burmese human rights activist who had won the 1991 Nobel Peace Prize—I mentioned her in at least three rounds, hoping to show that even though we were American, Jed and I were not hopelessly parochial. We benefited from the soft bigotry of low expectations; for an American male merely to mention a Burmese woman was to score big points with European judges. She proved especially handy in a round against the South Africans. The topic was women's rights—"This House believes in feminism," or something like that. Jed and I were the opposition, arguing against feminism, and I remember trying to argue that women can change the world without identifying as Western-style feminists. "Take someone like Aung San Suu Kyi," I said, to vigorous nodding from the judges. "Is she a 'feminist'? I don't know, but she certainly has changed the world." The South Africans clearly had never heard of her, and you could almost see their hearts beating angrily beneath their springbok insignias.

My memory of Worlds is especially fragmented, I think because the usual rules of pairing and seeding were completely upended in Cork. Debate tournaments are run quite oddly to begin with. From round to round, debaters never know if they're "up" or "down"—whether they've been winning or losing. Unlike at chess, gymnastics, or tennis tournaments, results aren't posted after each round, so until the preliminary rounds have ended and the playoff pairings are announced, the best any debater can do is try to "back-tab," or guess at one's results based on the strength of one's opponents. If your third-round opponents are pretty terrific, then it stands to reason they were 2–0 before the round, which means that you and your partner were also 2–0, since at big college tournaments they match teams with like records. But at Worlds, this whole system was hopelessly complicated by the fact that every round had *four* teams, two on each side. Thus, in the round against Stellenbosch, Jed and I were one opposition team, joined by a team from, say, Oxford; Stellenbosch would have been joined on the government by Melbourne, Cambridge, McGill, or whomever.

Every round plays back in my mind as a confused jumble of accents, blazers, and school ties, with the competitors standing and sitting in rapid succession, and the judges scribbling furiously as they tried to sort out and rank eight debaters crowded into a small classroom. And of course we had vexed relationships with the other teams debating our side, since we were simultaneously with them and against them. In a round about, say, international environmental treaties, Jed and I might be arguing the same side as the two debaters known as Cape Town C, but we still wanted to be ranked more highly than the Cape Towners; it profited us nothing to persuade the judges that we were right if they nonetheless concluded that Cape Town C was the best team in the round while Yale B was fourth-best.

This tension led to the phenomenon known as "knifing," in which the second team on a given side stabbed their colleagues in the back, arguing the same position but for different, and sometimes incompatible, reasons: "Honored Judge, we are delighted to be joined in the government by the gentlemen from Cape Town, who made so fine a case for allying with China to reduce acid rain. We, however, would like to talk about a different kind of treaty, one more appropriate to alliances with capitalist countries, like South Korea or Taiwan . . ." As far as I can remember, Jed and I left our knives in their sheaths. Knifing was considered poor form, guaranteed to displease and irritate the judges and reduce speaker points all around. One should only knife the other team, the thinking went, if they had argued something obnoxiously stupid, opening a line of argument you couldn't reasonably be expected to defend.

As Americans, we were totally at sea in this four-teams-in-a-room style, and we certainly knew less about international affairs than the Europeans, most of whom seemed to have had summer internships at the EU headquarters in Brussels. Debating in a new style, with unposted results and against daunting competition, I felt during the preliminary rounds an icky, unpleasant sense that I was being slowly masticated by a debate machine whose enormity I could neither see nor comprehend.

I was surprised, then, on New Year's Eve, just after midnight, in the ballroom of Jury's hotel, when the tournament director announced that we had made the play-offs. The official tournament sponsor was Murphy's Irish Stout, and the stout flowed that night more freely than it had all week; I was drinking like someone who did not expect to debate the next morning. So although I heard an Irish voice yell— the organizers couldn't find a microphone—"Yale B, Mark Oppenheimer and Jed Shugerman," I remember the words as if through earmuffs. What I remember better was Doug Kern sitting in a corner by the bar, his knees pulled up to his chest, his face down in his hands. "What's wrong?" I said. "They didn't call our names," he said, his voice full of woe. "Princeton didn't break." Yale, Harvard, and Brown had broken to play-offs, he said. Not Princeton. Looking at Doug, I felt triumphant, then ashamed—I was clinging to an old, silly high school rivalry, and it was clear how badly he'd wanted to win this.

Around us, Scottish men were dancing jubilant high-steps in their kilts. Young men and women who had found weeklong tournament romances were kissing the passionate, abandoned kisses of people who soon would never see each other again. Our Yale teammates crowded around me and Jed, giving us hugs and congratulatory back-slaps. We weren't supposed to be the ones to make the playoffs—

Jerry and Jonathan, Yale A, had been the favorites—but the school's hopes were now with us.

Worlds broke to octofinals, which meant that thirty-two teams had a shot at winning. No record from the tournament survives at the University College Cork archives (I asked, and the people there assured me that "filing was certainly not UCC's strong point back in 1996"), but based on my memory and an old newspaper clip, I believe that for that first play-off round Jed and I were assigned to oppose the topic "This House rejects big government." Jed, whose *Economist* reading on the airplane had been more fruitful than mine, suggested that we take the former Yugoslavia as our main example; the Dayton Accord had just been signed, on December 14, and its federalist framework would, the world hoped, at last bring peace to Bosnia. I followed Jed's lead, and the judges, impressed as ever that Americans would know anything about foreign affairs, chose Yale B as one of the two teams to progress to the next round.

There was a bit of intrigue in the hours before our quarterfinal round, in which we were to face Western Ontario and two Australian schools, Macquarie and New South Wales. All the competitors were packed onto buses and driven to an amphitheater at a nearby technical college, where our round was to be taped for Irish TV. But on the bus things got weird fast, as a whispered rumor traveled from row to row that Western Ontario had already learned the topic, which was supposed to be revealed only on arrival at the studio. Was the rumor true? We had no idea, and it likely wouldn't have mattered. This was parliamentary debate in the age before iPhones and Black-Berrys, so knowing a topic fifteen minutes before everyone else conferred no real advantage. But when, on arriving at our destination, the topic was finally announced—"This House would rebuild the Berlin Wall"—Jed and I were nervous, feeling hobbled out of the gate.

That nervousness led, we later realized, to our first big mistake of the tournament, one that would prove costly. Concerned that Western Ontario, with their extra advantage in prep time, would already have developed arguments against the obvious government cases, we decided to "squirrel" the topic—*ever so slightly*. Again, squirreling is the practice of twisting the resolution to make it different and more congenial, something that debaters in our league did in nearly every round. I'd always viewed squirreling as a bastardization of the art of debate; non-American debaters felt the same way, and when judging American teams they were ever watchful for this peculiar tic, ready to shave off points. It was probably unwise, then, for me and Jed to take any liberties at all with the topic, even as gently as we did: "When we say that this House would rebuild the Berlin Wall," Jed said, seconds into his speech, "we mean the Berlin Wall in its metaphorical, cultural sense, as the wall that used to keep American culture at bay. The old communist bloc was a place of oppression, to be sure, but it was also a place where native cultures— German, Russian, Polish, and so forth—could flower without bumping into a McDonald's on every corner. Now, however, American crudeness, and even American tourists, in all our slovenly, disgusting, obese omnipresence, are destroying what's left of the singular European cultures. Last night, my American compatriots and I went to a local cinema, here in Cork, to see a movie. And what did we see? *The American President*, starring Michael Douglas and Annette Bening. And it wasn't very good at all. Where were all the Irish movies? We Americans are turning the world into our soiled playground, and we must be stopped! Ladies and gentlemen of this House, let us rebuild the Berlin Wall!"

It didn't seem to us like a terrible case of squirreling. After all, the resolution couldn't have been meant literally, right? What good argument was there for erecting another real wall to oppress Berliners? Perhaps it would have been safer to argue for a return to communism, precisely the kind of counterintuitive mischief that debaters love and that the resolution, in hindsight, seemed to invite. But if there was one rule I knew to be true of debate, it was Stephen Magee's old saw that the best humor is at one's own expense, and Jed's idea for turning the topic against Americans seemed splendid;

the squirreling that would be required seemed *de minimis* and worth the risk.

At least I had good fun with it. "We are the worst, most base, most despicable culture in the West," I argued in my speech. "New Kids on the Block! McDonald's!" The crowd groaned. *"General Hospital!"* Louder groans. *"Ronald Reagan!"* Heckles, boos, jeers. "Ladies and gentlemen of this fine house, it is abundantly clear that the fall of the Berlin Wall has been a disaster for those who once were behind the Iron Curtain. While they have gained their freedom, too often it is the freedom to watch bad American television while eating bad American food and wearing ugly, polyester American clothes. We the government would not, of course, wish anyone back into the manacles of communism. But with a judicious system of protective tariffs, the countries of Eastern Europe—indeed, all countries who suffer the scourge of too many American imports—could have some breathing room in which their native traditions might thrive."

The first opposition team to speak was from Western Ontario: Ken Hunt and David Orr. Their argument consisted mainly of a ringing endorsement of Ireland, a land that according to me and Jed had been profaned by American culture. "We argued that Ireland had one of the world's most successful cultures, they just weren't movie makers," Ken told me years later, when I asked him what he remembered of our round. "And we spouted some ridiculous blather about Marshall McLuhan, yadda, yadda, yadda."

When it was over, the two opposition teams, including Western Ontario, advanced to the semifinals, and Yale B, the last American team left in the 1996 World Universities Debating Championship, was eliminated. After the semifinal break was announced, our fellow American debaters—not just the Yalies, but debaters from Harvard, Princeton, La Verne, Willamette, Fordham—told me and Jed that they were shocked, that it was unfair, that Americans couldn't get a fair shake. One Fordham debater was particularly incensed on our behalf: "You guys were raped!" he said, running up to us after the announcement. *"Anally* raped!"

In fact, Cork has gone down in Worlds lore as a mysterious and possibly corrupt chapter in the history of international debate. According to the Wikipedia entry for the tournament, which is as official a record as exists, "There were a number of problems at this championships which combined to give a bad perception of the organizing committee and the championships as a whole. The tab system was missing several results or had results entered incorrectly, resulting in a Princeton team losing out on a break position. Official results were never released. . . ." A Princeton team lost out? Maybe Doug Kern should have prevailed after all.

The truth is, Jed and I may have been anally raped. Or we may have squirreled a bit too far, trying to get a nut that was beyond our grasp. Or maybe we were just not that funny. But how could I complain? We'd been the top American team, and as quarterfinalists we'd received a shard of brown pottery that, when fit together with the other quarterfinalists' shards, apparently makes some sort of traditional Irish beer mug. I'd had a vacation in Ireland, filled with pints of Murphy's Irish Stout and eleven rounds of sanctioned, supervised arguing. I'd been pleased to see that I still had it, more or less. I wasn't the best in the world, even in the English-speaking world, but I'd ended my debate career to the sounds of laughter, applause, and the indignant cries of fellow Americans, leaping to our defense. That was more than enough.

EPILOGUE

For many of us, growing up is about learning to watch the game from the sidelines. Most Little League stars don't make it to the major leagues, but they can still be spectators—watch double-headers on television, take their sons and daughters to the ballpark. The same goes for music prodigies, who as adults may find themselves happily sitting in the audience, watching other, better violinists or cellists.

Debaters are different, because their primary skill—talking—is something none of us leaves behind in childhood. Unlike playing third base or first violin, talking is a lifetime activity for everybody. And there are numerous careers in which the former high school or college debater can actually get paid to talk. Debaters who want to keep doing what they do best can become lawyers, politicians, or university lecturers. All three professions require analyzing facts and speaking in public, often adversarially. Some debaters become diplomats. One legendary Canadian debater, Michael Kives, who was on the high school circuit about five years after me, is now a Hollywood superagent. That may be the perfect job for an ex-debater, persuading and negotiating for a living.

For years, I prided myself on having left the world of debate and oratory behind. I never considered law school, never aspired to political office. I don't negotiate, sell, or persuade for a living. I became a journalist, and a journalist is like the debater's opposite. A journalist keeps his political opinions to himself, and he lets others do the talking. In my line of work, I am paid to shut up and listen.

On closer inspection, however, I realize that I too have stayed within the world of oratory—but as an observer, not a participant. I'm the grown-up musician or ballplayer, now happily watching from the box seats. It took me years to realize exactly what I had done: I'd found a job, a particular niche in journalism, in which I get paid to read, listen to, and think about speeches.

I could have seen this coming. It began my junior year of college, when I needed one more history class to round out my schedule. My criteria were simple: the class had to meet late in the morning, and in a building within easy walking distance of my dormitory. Basically, I wanted to wake up late, throw a bathrobe over my pajamas, and walk to class in five minutes. Only one class fit the bill: American Religion from 1600 to 1865, with Professor Harry S. Stout III, which met at eleven-thirty in the art gallery auditorium, mere yards from where I slept.

When I attended the first lecture, I had no idea that "Skip" Stout was the greatest living expert on the Puritan sermon and the chief editor of Jonathan Edwards's papers. I just knew that his class met at the right time and place. But I found that first lecture captivating, and as the term progressed I became convinced that this was the field for me. Everything about American religious history was fascinating, from the randy Mormons to the prudish Baptists, from the antinomian Quakers to the chaste Shakers. But of all the great lectures, the one I remember best was Stout's discussion of the religious roots of the American Revolution. "When the call came to fight, many colonists didn't know what to do," Stout said. "And when they were uncertain, they asked their preachers. In sermon after sermon, those preachers lent support to the cause of rebellion. And that gave the colonists the courage to take up arms against their king."

I have since learned that Stout's interpretation of the Revolution is not shared unanimously by his colleagues—there's a lively debate, and some scholars take the opposite view, that the Revolution was a secular affair. But as a twenty-year-old college student, especially one who had spent the past seven years in competitive oratory, it was a revelation to hear that sermons could change the course of history. And as I read more religious history, I realized how many of our country's great orators were deeply religious, in sensibility if not always in church attendance. Biblical allusions and sacred imagery permeated the speeches of Abraham Lincoln, William Jennings Bryan, and Martin Luther King. All of a sudden, I was in a world of preachers. I wrote a long paper about the late Unitarian minister James Stoll, who I discovered had been the first openly gay Protestant clergyman. I spent weeks trying, unsuccessfully, to find a copy of the 1969 sermon in which he had come out of the closet.

After I returned from the Worlds tournament in Ireland, I had a layover of just one day at my parents' house before flying to Appleton, Wisconsin, where the legendary Yale chaplain William Sloane Coffin was living and teaching for the year. He was the topic of my senior essay in the history major. I had read all his great sermons, from the 1950s, '60s, and '70s, in favor of civil rights and against the Vietnam War; I had read the books that had inspired him, books he repeatedly quoted in those sermons, like Augustine's *Confessions* and Reinhold Niebuhr's *The Children of Light and the Children of Darkness*. Now I was interviewing Coffin about the structure of his sermons and his techniques for effective preaching. (He was not modest. He quoted with approval a friend who had told him, "You're the best preacher in America except for every black Baptist preacher in America.")

It's hard to believe, but I went, in the span of three days, from a debate championship to an interview with a famous preacher yet never considered that there might be a connection—that my love of debate and oratory might have led me to study religion. Our passions choose us, but they can be awfully coy about their reasons.

After college, I worked odd jobs in publishing. For three months I was a research assistant for a freelance writer, then for six months I answered phones in the Washington office of the *New Yorker*. Meanwhile, I was applying to graduate programs in American religious history. I was admitted to Yale, and in 1997 I returned to study for a doctorate under my old professors. I finished my degree, but along the way I lost my enthusiasm for the scholarly life—too lonely and hermetic. I found my way into journalism, at first reporting about the only subject I knew well, religion. I worked as the religion reporter for the *Hartford Courant*, then began writing freelance articles for other newspapers and for magazines. I wrote about how 9/11 would affect church attendance. I wrote about Las Vegas wedding chapels. I interviewed an acting teacher in Los Angeles who had converted dozens of students to Scientology. And I heard sermon after sermon.

I don't write solely about religion anymore; with two young daughters, I try to stay close to home, and I'll write about whatever is at hand. Last year, I wrote a long article about my street and my neighbors, and I wrote a short article about raising vegetarian children. But I am still especially drawn to writing about speech—I wrote one opinion piece about teaching children good grammar—and, more generally, drawn to people who are good talkers. Some journalists prefer subjects who don't talk at all. They may write about wildlife, or architecture, or dance—they're after a different kind of beauty.

In many ways, I am a lot like the child I used to be. Growing up, there was nothing I enjoyed more than talking, and I still love talking. When asked to give a talk—a toast at a wedding, a guest sermon at a synagogue, a lecture to a religion class—I feel the old thrill. I start to prepare, then eventually give up, leave my notes in a half-ready state, allowing a certain element of surprise, certain that in the moment the words will come. Or maybe they won't—either way, it will be exciting. Just like in high school.

What's changed is that now I'm happy just to listen. If there's a good political speech on television—maybe an old one by Ronald Reagan, or a more recent one by Barack Obama—I sit rapt, thinking of all that the orator, and his speechwriter, are doing right. I hear in my mind rhetorical terms that I learned in high school, like *anaphora* and *peroration*. I find myself coaching the speaker silently, rewriting a sentence here, dropping a clause there. I tell him to stand up straight. I wonder what Mr. Robison or Stephen Magee would tell him to do differently.

I listen just as eagerly to the men and women I interview: the New Age guru who believes positive thinking cured her cancer, the Holocaust denier who for seven years lived with his Jewish lover, the Muslim cop, the Elvis impersonator at the wedding chapel. Some of them are deeply learned, others are nearly illiterate, and you never know which ones will be fun to listen to. The most educated man or woman can drone on in a soporific monotone, while a sixth-grade dropout can bring people to Jesus with his words. A little learning never hurts, and good ideas can add sparkle to conversation, but the truth—a truth I've known since I was a preliterate two-year-old who wouldn't shut up—is that good talkers aren't made, they're born.

ACKNOWLEDGMENTS

By now it should be clear how much affection I have for almost everyone in this book. A select group are the triple threats: they star in the book, helped me make sure it was accurate, and continue to be my dear friends. They are (in order of appearance in my life) Derek Slap, Nina Smith, Curt Robison, Jonathan Cohen, Jerry Vildostegui, and Jed Shugerman. I'm also grateful to my parents, brothers, and sister.

A few of the great characters in my life are missing from the book, like Jonathan Pitt, Willard Spiegelman, Alana Newhouse, the whole Westville gang (and poker-playing adjuncts), and my fellow *New Haven Review* editors.

There are only six pseudonyms in this book: "Hank," "Kelly," "Charles Wainwright," "George Peacock," "Webster McDuff," and "Sari Addington." Kelly I owe an apology. Duff and Sari I owe my thanks: they lent a touch of real glamour to my adolescence. They're superstars.

I wrote this book surrounded by terrific women: my editor, Wylie O'Sullivan, and her assistant, Sydney Tanigawa; my agent, Betsy Lerner; my daughters, Rebekah and Elisabeth; my pooch, J.J. My wife, Cyd, gave me brilliant critiques of this book in progress, and gave so much more, too.

ABOUT THE AUTHOR

Mark Oppenheimer grew up in Springfield, Massachusetts. He holds a Ph.D. in religion and is the author of two previous books—one about religion in the 1960s counterculture, the other about traveling the country attending bar and bat mitzvah ceremonies. A former world champion debater and coach, Oppenheimer writes about religion, vegetarianism, parenting, and urbanism for publications including the *New York Times Magazine, Slate, Mother Jones*, the *Forward*, and *Tablet*. He is the founding editor of the *New Haven Review*.

Learn more at markoppenheimer.com.